KEY CONCEPTS IN CULTURAL ST

CW00952235

Palgrave Key Concepts

Palgrave Key Concepts provide an accessible and comprehensive range of subject glossaries at undergraduate level. They are the ideal companion to a standard textbook, making them invaluable reading to students throughout their course of study, and especially useful as a revision aid.

Key Concepts in Accounting and Finance
Key Concepts in Business Practice
Key Concepts in Cultural Studies
Key Concepts in Drama and Performance
Key Concepts in e-Commerce
Key Concepts in Human Resource Management
Key Concepts in Information and Communication Technology
Key Concepts in International Business
Key Concepts in Language and Linguistics (*second edition*)
Key Concepts in Law
Key Concepts in Management
Key Concepts in Marketing
Key Concepts in Politics
Key Concepts in Psychology
Key Concepts in Strategic Management
Key Concepts in Tourism

Palgrave Key Concepts: Literature
General Editors: John Peck and Martin Coyle

Key Concepts in Contemporary Literature
Key Concepts in Medieval Literature
Key Concepts in Postcolonial Literature
Key Concepts in Renaissance Literature
Key Concepts in Victorian Literature
Literary Terms and Criticism (*third edition*)

Further titles are in preparation

www.palgravekeyconcepts.com

Palgrave Key Concepts
Series Standing Order
ISBN 1–4039–3210–7
(*outside North America only*)

You can receive future titles in this series as they are published by placing a standing order. Please contact your bookseller or, in case of difficulty, write to us at the address below with your name and address, the title of the series and the ISBN quoted above.

Customer Services Department, Macmillan Distribution Ltd, Houndmills, Basingstoke, Hampshire RG21 6XS, England

Key Concepts in Cultural Studies

Maja Mikula

© Maja Mikula 2008

All rights reserved. No reproduction, copy or transmission of this
publication may be made without written permission.

No paragraph of this publication may be reproduced, copied or transmitted
save with written permission or in accordance with the provisions of the
Copyright, Designs and Patents Act 1988, or under the terms of any licence
permitting limited copying issued by the Copyright Licensing Agency,
90 Tottenham Court Road, London W1T 4LP.

Any person who does any unauthorised act in relation to this publication
may be liable to criminal prosecution and civil claims for damages.

The author has asserted her right to be identified as the author of this
work in accordance with the Copyright, Designs and Patents Act 1988.

First published 2008 by
PALGRAVE MACMILLAN
Houndmills, Basingstoke, Hampshire RG21 6XS and
175 Fifth Avenue, New York, N.Y. 10010
Companies and representatives throughout the world

PALGRAVE MACMILLAN is the global academic imprint of the Palgrave
Macmillan division of St. Martin's Press, LLC and of Palgrave Macmillan Ltd.
Macmillan® is a registered trademark in the United States, United Kingdom
and other countries. Palgrave is a registered trademark in the European
Union and other countries.

ISBN-13: 978-0-230-00646-1
ISBN-10: 0-230-00646-9

This book is printed on paper suitable for recycling and made from fully
managed and sustained forest sources. Logging, pulping and manufacturing
processes are expected to conform to the environmental regulations of the
country of origin.

A catalogue record for this book is available from the British Library.

A catalog record for this book is available from the Library of Congress.

10 9 8 7 6 5 4 3 2 1
17 16 15 14 13 12 11 10 09 08

Printed in China

For Mikko, Toivo and Tata

Contents

List of Figures

Acknowledgements

My main debt of gratitude is to my home institution, the Institute for International Studies (IIS), University of Technology Sydney (UTS). I feel very fortunate to work in such a stimulating and supportive atmosphere, and grateful to Pro-Vice-Chancellor (International) at UTS, Professor David Goodman, who welcomed me there eight years ago in his capacity as the founding Director of IIS. David was succeeded in that role by Professor Stephanie Donald, whose friendly encouragement I now enjoy and treasure. My colleagues and friends Paul Allatson and Murray Pratt, read the final draft of the book and offered many valuable comments. Gloria De Vincenti, Heleanor Feltham, Milica Gavran, Elaine Jeffreys, Barbara Leigh, Yixu Lu, Jo McCormack, Sandra Margon, Lyn Shoemark, Ilaria Vanni and Marivic Wyndham have all helped me to navigate through knowledge, ideas and resources. My undergraduate and post-graduate students also read individual sections of the manuscript and provided helpful comments. In particular, I have benefited from conversations with Eka Srimulyani, whose passionate quest for knowledge has been a constant source of inspiration. I would also like to thank Ina Bosić, who was always there to brighten me up with her youthful energy and enthusiasm.

I am very grateful to my publisher Palgrave Macmillan for commissioning the volume. My thanks go in particular to Suzannah Burywood for encouraging me to get started on the project, and to Karen Griffiths for her help and advice during the last stages of the manuscript preparation.

Although physically distant, my father Mirosłav Mikula has always been a role model and a strong motivation behind my pursuits. Last but certainly not least, my love and gratitude go to my husband Toivo and son Mikko. Toivo's meticulous proofreading of several consecutive drafts of the book saved me from many potential errors. Each page I have written represents time spent away from my son Mikko. Without their understanding and patience, this book would never have been possible.

Introduction: Mapping the Terrain of Cultural Studies

> Concepts are the tools for intersubjectivity but only on the condition that they are explicit, clear, defined in such a way that everyone can take them up and use them. Every concept is part of a framework, a systematic set of distinctions – not of oppositions – that can sometimes be bracketed or even ignored, but never transgressed or contradicted without serious damage to the analysis at hand. Concepts, or those words that outsiders consider jargon, can be tremendously productive. They help articulate an understanding, convey an interpretation, check an imagination run wild, enable discussion on the basis of common terms; they help perceive absences or exclusions. Hence, a concept is not just a label that can easily be replaced by a more common word.
> (Mieke Bal, 'Crossroad Theory and Travelling Concepts', p. 5)

Like any text aiming to bring together the main tenets of a rich and complex field of inquiry, this compendium begins with several indispensable caveats.

To begin with, I would like to reflect on the essential terms of reference in the title of the book, 'concept' and 'cultural studies'. By definition, a concept is a product of abstraction and generalization. Clearly, these two activities are always predicated on exclusion, and are thus to some extent political in nature. The aim of the book is to be as inclusive as possible – culturally, politically and theoretically – without jeopardizing the coherence necessary to render the book intelligible and helpful to its readers. With its extensive and heterogeneous selection of topics, the book aims to reflect the theoretical and methodological fluidity of cultural studies, their declared anti-disciplinarity and the multiplicity of traditions across the globe.

In order to circumscribe the subject matter of this book, it is necessary to reflect briefly on the much-contested academic field of cultural studies. At a first glance, it may seem that a workable definition of culture itself would lead seamlessly to a reasonably straightforward definition of cultural studies. Yet, that is not the case, since 'studies of culture' are not entirely – or not always – synonymous with 'cultural studies', as we shall see below. For the two to be synonymous, several 'essential ingredients' – not only a particular interpretation of culture, but also a specific approach to scholarly inquiry – need to be in attendance.

It seems apposite to begin our survey of the 'essential ingredients' of cultural studies by querying the etymology and subsequent usage of the term 'culture'. The word derives from the Latin verb *colere*, which means 'to cultivate', in the sense of both farming (Lat. *cultura agri*) and tending to one's soul (Lat. *cultura animae*). The *Oxford English Dictionary* definition of culture – as both the cultivation of the soil and certain animals and the cultivation or development of the mind, faculties and manners – appropriately reflects the original semantic mismatch. One might say that, throughout much of human history, the former brand of culture has been the everyday necessity for the poor, while the latter has been the prerogative of the selected and privileged few, who had their primary needs catered for and could thus engage in tending to their spiritual wellbeing. Indeed, until recently, 'culture' was understood as 'high culture' and reserved exclusively for the social elites. A different term – 'civilization' (French *civilisation*, Spanish *civilización*, Italian *civiltà*, German *Landeskunde*) – was used to convey the set of principles, practices and their attendant material manifestations, which enable human beings to engage with society and its institutions. Within the academic arena, this meant that studies of 'culture' (that is, high culture) were mostly reserved for the departments of literature, fine arts and philosophy, while studies of 'civilization' were pursued by historians, sociologists and anthropologists.

As early as the eighteenth century, anthropology was the first discipline to adopt a broader meaning of 'culture', by conflating its then privileged meaning with that of what was commonly referred to as 'civilization'. An anthropological approach to culture – as opposed to the traditional aesthetic reading – includes all values, practices, artefacts and modes of behaviour that characterize a particular community and guarantee its continuing reproduction. Even though initially this more egalitarian and less judgemental approach was by and large applied by Western/European practitioners to the cultures of less developed and often 'exotic' societies and groups, it effectively presaged the blurring of the distinction between 'high' and 'low' culture we are witnessing today within the developed 'Western' world.

Due to the inertia of institutionalized knowledge, it took two hundred years and, in particular, the momentous social change worldwide following the Second World War, for this more inclusive understanding of culture to spill over from anthropology and affect other academic disciplines. The decisive turn occurred in post-Second-World-War Great Britain, with scholarly interventions by the forefathers of cultural studies, Raymond Williams, Richard Hoggart and Stuart Hall. In their work, these scholars promoted what was to become the implied *sine qua non* of cultural studies practice: an auspicious mix of investigative passion, academic rigour, literary sensibility and socio-political engagement. Their pioneering achievements will be examined in more detail under specific entries in this book.

Partly because of its origins within the British academia and its subsequent rapid dissemination along the Anglo-American axis, cultural studies remains open to charges of Anglocentrism and parochialism. Yet, cultural studies has been practised in many locations outside the Anglo-American spectrum. This border crossing has broadened the horizons of cultural studies research, as each strand contributed its own culturally distinctive flavour and white Anglo-American practitioners began acknowledging and deconstructing their own privileged position within the structures of domination under their scrutiny.

With its understanding of culture as a 'whole way of life' (Williams 1958), cultural studies spans a variety of traditional academic disciplines. In fact, it has been defined as not simply interdisciplinary, but 'actively and aggressively anti-disciplinary – a characteristic that more or less ensures a permanently uncomfortable relation to academic disciplines' (Grossberg, Nelson and Treichler 1992: 2).

In addition to this critical self-positioning of cultural studies outside the 'established' academic disciplines, its openly avowed political undercurrent – stemming from a fundamental disbelief in politics-free knowledge – renders it all the more incompatible with and sometimes even antagonistic towards disciplines based precisely on an objectivist worldview. Politics lie at the very foundation of the sense of self of cultural studies practitioners. They see themselves not merely as detached observers of cultural practices, but also and more importantly, as politically engaged participants in cultural change.

To be properly understood, these two attributes of cultural studies – its problematic positioning within the academic canon and its conscious political engagement – need to be further qualified. To begin with, the attributes need to be seen as the least common denominator among a widely divergent range of theoretical, methodological and political positions adopted in inquiring cultural practices 'from the point of view of their intrication with, and within, relations of power' (Bennett 1992: 23). The theoretical and methodological choices of cultural studies are not preset, but vary pragmatically and strategically according to the questions under scrutiny and the specific power relations at work in a particular context. This methodological *bricolage* may thus include semiotics, deconstruction, textual or content analysis, observation, surveys, focus groups or interviews, to name only a few of the research strategies employed by cultural studies practitioners.

Similarly, no homogeneous political programme underlies cultural studies research, other than a consistent interest in and commitment to disenfranchised or marginal populations, such as racial or ethnic minorities, underprivileged social classes, or those disempowered on the basis of gender, age, sexuality, geopolitical location or colonial legacies. Within these groups, the focus has been on oppositional subcultures, seen as capable of resisting the hegemonic modes of capitalist domination. This preoccupation positions cultural studies to the left of the political spectrum, to use the increasingly problematic political categorization, which many see as superseded. Cultural studies aims to represent a voice of conscience 'from within', probing and aspiring to dismantle mechanisms of domination.

In a conscious effort to overturn the hierarchy between 'high' or 'elite' and 'low' or 'popular' culture, cultural studies practitioners have tended to resort to the 'affirmative' strategy of privileging the latter, risking, perhaps, to reinforce the dichotomy by simply inverting it and thus unwittingly accepting its basic premises. Yet, cultural studies is not exclusively concerned with popular culture, 'though it is perhaps always, in part, about the rules of inclusion and exclusion that guide intellectual evaluations. . . . Cultural studies involves *how* and *why* such work is done, not just its content' (Grossberg, Nelson and Treichler 1992: 11). In other words, when examining texts and practices deemed to represent either 'low' or 'high' culture, cultural studies practitioners consistently shift their attention from the text itself to the broader socio-cultural context of its production, distribution and consumption, thus hoping to expose and contest the very power relationships at work in the formation of dominant canons.

About this Book

While it would be illusory to claim exhaustive coverage of all concepts that have been employed in cultural studies research, the result, I hope, will provide the reader with an invaluable guide not only to a limited number of canonical texts, but also to a range of important but far less familiar works. The choice of entries is based on the following overlapping and at times dissonant criteria:

- *Relevance across a broad spectrum of cultural texts and practices*

  A substantial number of entries cover those issues that have figured prominently in contemporary cultural analysis, such as agency, body, identity, narrative, representation, space, place and time.

- *Relevance for understanding the fundamental mechanisms and processes of contemporary social and cultural change*

  Some examples are diaspora, globalization, hybridity, Fordism and post-Fordism, globalization and postmodernism.

- *Practical value in signposting cultural studies research*

  Entries such as content analysis, conversation analysis, discourse analysis, ethnography, focus groups, grounded theory, interview, method, oral history, questionnaire and semiotic analysis are designed to help students plan and manage their research projects.

- *Comprehensive coverage of the theoretical traditions that have exerted a major influence on cultural studies research*

  These traditions include Marxism, post-Marxism, structuralism, poststructuralism, psychoanalysis, postmodernism, feminism, queer theory and postcolonial studies.

- *Coverage of the most prominent developments in cultural theory and critique beyond the dominant Anglo-American and Western-European axis*

  Examples include subaltern studies in India, Russian formalism, the Slovene Lacanian School and Latin American and (US) Latino cultural studies.

My selection of entries has also been significantly influenced by the existence of authoritative reference books in scholarly fields tangential to cultural studies, including anthropology, economics, geography, history, law, linguistics, literature studies, media and communication studies, philosophy, politics and sociology. This explains why certain entries, which have been used in cultural studies in more or less the same way as they have in these related disciplines, are either rather condensed, or omitted altogether.

Abject

The term derives from the Latin *abjectus*, meaning thrown away, and signifies something extremely unpleasant and degrading. In contemporary critical theory, it is most commonly used to refer to the condition of marginalized social groups. In the works of Julia Kristeva, the concept is applied to the ambiguous process of subject formation, which involves a rejection of something that exists within the self and attracts us and repels us at the same time. Abjection is something that undermines identity and social order. In Kristeva's words, the 'abject threatens the unity/identity of both society and the subject', by calling into question the 'boundaries upon which they are constructed' (1982: 54). In this view, it is only by confronting our abjections and recognizing the otherness in ourselves that we can become more tolerant toward others, and 'welcome them to that uncanny strangeness, which is as much theirs as it is ours' (p. 71). Kristeva calls a person who constantly engages with her or his own abjections a deject, who 'strays instead of getting his bearings' and whose space 'is never one . . . but essentially divisible, foldable, and catastrophic' (p. 8).

See also: **Alterity; Identity, identification, identity politics; Subject, subjectivity; Uncanny**

Further reading: Kristeva (1982).

Actor-network theory

Actor-network theory (ANT) is a material-semiotic methodological framework, which emerged in the sociology of science in the 1980s and was popularized, most notably, by French sociologists Bruno Latour and Michel Callon, and the British sociologist John Law. Actor-network theory challenges the technological determinism prevalent in earlier accounts of the role of technology in social change.

Rather than regard technological change as an outside factor that has the power to influence society, actor-network theory postulates that technology itself cannot be extricated from the social fabric. It defies the notion of a clear-cut distinction between social actors and the networks within which they operate, arguing that actors have agency only in so far as they are elements of relational networks. Actor-network theory attributes agency to precarious assemblages of materially and discursively heterogeneous elements, which include humans, machines, nature, ideas, organizations and social arrangements.

To account for the perpetual fluidity of identities and relations within these networks, actor-network theory borrows the concept of translation originally developed by French philosopher Michel Serres. In actor-network theory, translation is defined as 'all the negotiations, intrigues, calculations, acts of persuasion and violence thanks to which an actor or force takes, or causes to be conferred on itself, authority to speak or act on behalf of another actor or force' (Callon and Latour 1981: 279).

Actor-network theory is poststructuralist in inspiration, as it is closely related to the work of Foucault and Deleuze, and of the feminist scholar Donna Haraway. In particular, actor-networks could be interpreted as smaller-scale instances of Foucault's discourses or epistemes.

See also: **Agency; Base and superstructure; Cyborg; Determinism; Discourse; Episteme**

Further reading: Callon and Latour (1981), Latour (1987 and 2005), Law and Hassard (1999).

Aesthetics

The word 'aesthetics' (also spelled 'esthetics') denotes a 'set of principles concerned with the nature and appreciation of beauty, especially in art'; or the 'branch of philosophy which deals with questions of beauty and artistic taste' (*COED*). In the simplest terms, there are two basic approaches to the nature of beauty: the subjective approach, which posits that the sense of what is beautiful depends on the observer; and the objective view, according to which beauty resides in the observed object.

The foundations of modern philosophical aesthetics were laid by the eighteenth-century German philosopher Alexander Gottlieb Baumgarten (1714–62). Baumgarten used the term *Aesthetica* to describe the whole sphere of sensuous perception, which lies outside of the domain of the rational.

Drawing on Baumgarten's work, Immanuel Kant (1724–1804) considered aesthetics to be one of the three main types of cognitive functioning, along with moral and scientific reasoning. For Kant, aesthetics is a type of judgement that mediates between 'pure reason' or understanding, and 'practical reason' or ethics. It is both subjective (or grounded in the personal experience of pleasure) and objective, in that claims for beauty always depend on universal agreement.

Nineteenth-century aesthetic philosophy posited that experiences of beauty and the sublime generated a response of 'disinterested pleasure', which was considered to be highly moral. Consequently, arts were extolled as transcendental pursuits that were practised and appreciated for their own sake. In the late nineteenth and early twentieth centuries, the most notable philosophers interested in aesthetics were the Italian Benedetto Croce (1866–1952), American John Dewey (1859–1952), German Ernst Cassirer (1874–1945) and the British Robin George Collingwood (1889–1943).

Contrary to the idealist tradition, Marxist aesthetics regarded 'both aesthetic objects and the subjects of aesthetic judgment as being marked by the processes of their historical formation' (Bennett 1990: 123). Endeavouring to circumvent the determinism of traditional Marxism, the writers of the Frankfurt School posited that true art was characterized precisely by its ability to transcend the circumstances of its social production. More recently, Pierre Bourdieu (1984) argued that aesthetics was closely related to lifestyle and social status.

Cultural studies have been criticized as placing too much emphasis on politics and agency, and patently neglecting aesthetics. In response to this criticism, the Australian literary critic and cultural theorist Rita Felski has emphasized that cultural studies have never sought to 'destroy aesthetics, but to broaden the definition of what counted as art by taking popular culture seriously. It was always as much about form as about content, as much about pleasure as about ideology' (2004: 32).

See also: **Senses; Taste, taste culture; Value, value system**

Further reading: Bennett (1990), Bérubé (ed.) (2004), Hunter (1992), Korsmeyer (2004).

Affect, emotion, feeling

Affects, emotions and feelings are prominent topics in recent cultural theory in general and feminist epistemology and aesthetics in particular. They are considered to be central to embodiment, subject formation, politics and community building.

Although closely related, the three terms are not synonymous. In his introduction to Deleuze and Guattari's *A Thousand Plateaus* (1987 [1980]), Brian Massumi distinguishes between feelings, which are said to be personal or biographical, in that they depend on a person's previous experiences; emotions, which are social, since they represent the outward display of a feeling; and affect, understood as a pre-personal and pre-linguistic experience of intensity, through which a body becomes ready to act in specific circumstances. Affects are not conscious, and can be triggered by factors that are beyond our control. Because they are abstract and unstructured, affects are more easily transmitted from one body to another than feelings or emotions.

Baruch Spinoza (1632–1677), a seventeenth-century Dutch philosopher of Jewish-Portuguese origin, understood 'affect' as a power to act. He distinguished between two types of affects: actions, which are brought about by events that are rooted in our own nature; and passions, which are occasioned by outside causes. Spinoza argued that passions could be restrained through virtue, which he understood as the pursuit of knowledge and ideas.

The US philosopher and personality theorist Silvan Tomkins (1911–91) identified nine distinct affects, all of which are biologically conditioned. These were interest–excitement; enjoyment–joy; surprise–startle; distress–anguish; anger–rage; fear–terror; shame–humiliation; 'dissmell' (a bad smell); and disgust (a bad taste).

The notion of affect problematizes our understanding of how we consume cultural and media texts. Indeed, the consciously received message may, and often does, leave less impression on the consumer than her or his affective resonance with the source of the message. The power of many media texts is thus believed to lie in their capacity to generate affective resonance, independently of their ideological content. In *Empire*, political philosophers Michael Hardt and Antonio Negri describe the production and manipulation of affect as one of the three main types of immaterial labour, along with the industrial production, which incorporates information and communication technologies, and the immaterial labour of analytical and symbolic tasks (2000: 293).

See also: **Agency; Ideology; Phenomenology; Senses**

Further reading: Brennan (2004), Deleuze and Guattari (1987 [1980]); Hardt and Negri (2000); Tomkins (1995).

A

Agency

Agency is the capacity to originate social acts in ways that produce impact, independently of the constraints imposed by social structure. In mainstream sociology, there are three main orientations in the agency–structure debate, depending on the relative emphasis placed on agency or structure: (a) theories based on methodological individualism, which emphasize the centrality of human agency (e.g. Weber 1992 [1905]); (b) Marxist, structuralist and functionalist theories (e.g. Durkheim 1997 [1893]), which privilege structure over agency; and (c) theories that move beyond the strict dualism of the two factors, such as Giddens's structuration theory (1984) or Bourdieu's theory of practice and the habitus (1977 [1972]).

Inextricably linked with the notions of power, free will, subjectivity, identity and autonomy, agency in the cultural sphere is a central concept in the culturalist strand of cultural studies, concerned with theorizing the possibilities of radical social action.

Since their inception, cultural studies have taken a position against elitist approaches to culture by Leavisite critics and the Frankfurt School, which interpreted cultural consumption as passive and dictated by production. In the 1960s, Althusser's influential conception of interpellation tended to rule out the possibility of agency outside of dominant discursive systems. Edward Thompson's *The Making of the English Working Class* (1963), which emphasized the difference between a culture made for the working class and one made by it, was an important contribution to agency–structure considerations within cultural studies. Subsequently, the turn to Gramsci offered a subtler mediation between agency and structure through the concept of hegemony. More recently, feminist, postcolonial and postmodern theories have emphasized the varied and often contradictory positions occupied by the subject and the contingency of agency on specific circumstances.

See also: **Consumption; Critical theory; Culturalism; Feminism; Habitus and field; Hegemony; Identity, identification, identity politics; Interpellation; Leavisism; Postcolonialism, neo-colonialism; Postmodern, postmodernity, postmodernism; Power; Subject, subjectivity**

Further reading: Archer (1996 [1988]), Holland et al. (1998), Thompson (1966 [1963]).

Alienation

The term denotes a social or psychological estrangement of individuals from their environment and ultimately from themselves. This estrangement can manifest itself in a variety of ways: as a feeling of powerlessness or lack of agency due to external, often institutional constraints; as a lack of purpose in life caused by the instability of meaning in the social domain; as social exclusion or rebellion against established social norms; and finally, as a decentring and fragmentation of the self, characteristic of late capitalist society.

A

In classical Marxist theory, 'alienation' refers to workers' loss of control over the act of production and over the product of their labour. According to Karl Marx, capitalism deprives work of its intrinsic value and turns it into a commodity, thus alienating workers both from each other and from human nature itself.

In contemporary cultural studies, alienation is an important concept in analysing subcultures and minority groups. In addition to classical Marxism, several other theoretical strands are of relevance to the understanding of alienation in cultural studies research:

- Critical theory, which focuses on the alienating influences of consumerism, technology and the culture generated by the mass media.
- Existentialism, which understands alienation as a defining element of the human condition.
- Lacanian psychoanalysis, which sees alienation as constitutive of subjectivity, in both the imaginary and the symbolic domains.
- Postcolonialism, which postulates the alienation of the colonial subject from her or his pre-colonial identity.
- Postmodernism, which theorizes a fragmentation of the self in an increasingly 'depthless' world.

See also: **Agency; Capitalism; Consumption; Critical theory; Identity, identification, identity politics; Imaginary, symbolic, real; Marxism, Leninism, Western Marxism; Mass communication and mass media; Postcolonialism, neo-colonialism; Postmodern, postmodernity, postmodernism; Psychoanalysis; Subculture; Subject, subjectivity**

Further reading: Geyer and Heinz (eds) (1992).

Alterity

The complex dynamic between identity and alterity, the self and the other, is embedded in the very etymology of the word 'alterity', from Latin *alter*, *altera*, *alterum*, which means both 'one' (of two) and the 'other'. The notion of alterity, crucial to any understanding of our formation as individuals and as social beings, holds a prominent place in a wide range of approaches to epistemology, social and cultural theory and psychoanalysis. It has attained increased prominence in contemporary society, where everyday encounters with the 'other' have intensified both in physical spaces, through globalization and people mobility and in virtual environments, due to the pervasive presence of the mass media and new media technologies.

Twentieth-century theories of alterity have moved away from Hegel's dialectics of the self and the other through negation and synthesis in several different directions. On the one hand, the 'other' has been interpreted as existing in its own right, rather than being defined by its relation to the self. This view permeates Emmanuel Lévinas's philosophy of ethics and is prominent in French feminist thought. Another strand, central in poststructuralism, deconstruction and psychoanalysis, interprets otherness as a lack or absence, simultaneously integral to and different from the identity of the same. In Foucault's theory, otherness signifies exclusion from structures of power and potentially a privileged site of intellectual inquiry and political resistance. Alterity is also central to Edward Said's Orientalism, which criticizes the representations of the Oriental other in Western discourse as cultural projections in the service of self-identity affirmation. A number of postcolonial critics influenced by Said's work have focused on the self–other relationship in colonial settings, as well as on Western and colonial strategies of dealing with otherness through exoticization, reification and domestication.

See also: **Deconstruction; Globalization; Identity, identification, identity politics; Mass communication and mass media; Orientalism; Poststructuralism; Power; Psychoanalysis; Tropicalization/s, tropicopolitan**

Further reading: Bhabha (1994), Hegel (1977 [1807]).

Archaeology

As a critical and methodological concept in the humanities and social sciences, archaeology is associated with the early writings of Michel Foucault. Foucault branded his own mode of historical inquiry as archaeology, to differentiate it from both social history and philosophical hermeneutics. His primary aim was to investigate the discourses of the human sciences as systems of knowledge. Rather than asking whether these discourses were 'true' or not, he was concerned with mapping all their claims, objects and strategies in order to reveal how they operate within a specific episteme. Archaeological inquiry, in other words, begins from the ground up, at the level of seemingly insignificant local events. It is neutral, in the sense that it does not pass judgement on the truth and meaning of the discursive systems under its scrutiny.

As an epistemological tool, archaeology is complementary to the concept of genealogy, which was advanced in Foucault's later work. Archaeology is commonly taken to denote a synchronic analysis of discourses within a specific episteme, while genealogy implies their diachronic reconstruction from the perspective of present experience. Foucault himself thought of archaeology as the material and methodological framework for his analysis, and of genealogy as the ultimate goal of this type of historical inquiry. This goal, he emphasized, was to show 'how those discursive events have determined in a certain way what constitutes our present and what constitutes ourselves – either our knowledge, our practices, our type of rationality, our relationship to ourselves or to others' (Mahon 1992: 105).

In his own work, Foucault sought to reveal how certain discourses that lie at the heart of contemporary Western subjectivity, including

A

those of deviance, illness, madness and sexuality, have emerged from disconnected practices and ostensibly ordinary events.

See also: **Discourse; Episteme; Genealogy; Knowledge; Subject, subjectivity**

Further reading: Foucault (1972 [1969]).

Articulation

Two connotations of the word 'articulation' – expression and the joining together of different elements – inhere in the nature and application of the homonymous theoretical concept in cultural studies, which was elaborated by Stuart Hall in the 1970s. This duality of signification echoes the structuralist assumption that meaning does not simply reside in any particular discourse or practice, but is always contested and contingent on a specific set of circumstances.

Hall's theory of articulation is closely related to Antonio Gramsci's theory of hegemony, which interprets cultural forms and practices as relatively autonomous, related to but not entirely determined by socio-economic power configurations. Accordingly, meaning is not inscribed in individual texts and practices, but arises as a result of the active process of articulation, or production in use.

The significance of articulation theory for cultural studies is manifold. First, it denies the possibility of interpreting cultural texts as if they possessed discrete meanings. Secondly, it focuses on the conjunctures between texts, their audiences and their consuming practices as principal sites of the formation of meanings.

This anti-essentialist logic also applies to collective identities, ideology and political formations. Hall's 'politics of articulation' thus shifts the focus of analysis from the traditional notions of fixed identity towards multiple shifting articulations, which operate within and according to the logic of hegemony.

A

Althusser's more restricted application of the term, as a conjuncture between different modes of production in historically specific social formations, is helpful in analysing the processes of globalization.

See also: **Audience; Consumption; Hegemony; Structuralism; Text**

Further reading: Althusser and Balibar (1970), Hall (1996a), Laclau (1993).

Audience

The word derives from Latin *audientia*, which means 'hearing', the 'act of listening', or a 'body of listeners'. In media and cultural studies, the term conventionally refers to a group of people consuming – watching, listening to or reading – a media or cultural text. Clearly, technological development has a significant impact on media consumption. Most recently, the rapid development of new media technologies has allowed high levels of user control and interactivity, thus blurring the traditional distinction between media producers and media consumers (Lievrow and Livingstone 2002; Turkle 1995).

Ways of conceptualizing the audience are of vital interest to broadcast media producers, since audiences have a direct impact on their financial success. Audiences are also a concern of government regulatory bodies, which have a stake in controlling media consumption. In both cases, the control of the audience has been undermined by emerging media technologies.

Audience theories have differed in the degree of agency they attribute to the consumers of media texts. At one end of the spectrum, we find models that postulate a passive audience uncritically absorbing media messages. Within this strand, the Frankfurt School emphasized the role of the mass media and popular culture in generating and perpetuating capitalist ideology and thus contributing to the subordination of the working class. The second strand, which posits an active role of the audience in selecting media texts and using them to satisfy personal needs, takes impetus from what is known as the 'uses and gratifications' theory (Blumler and Katz 1974).

Stuart Hall's influential encoding/decoding paradigm (1980c), which perceives media consumption as an active process, has been widely accepted in cultural studies. Through ethnographic research of specific audience groups, it has been possible to explain how social determinants such as class (Morley 1980), gender (Ang 1985; Modleski 1984; Radway 1987), age (Buckingham 1993), family circumstance (Morley 1986) and ethnicity (Gillespie 1995) affect the decoding process. More recently, extreme versions of audience-centred research have been criticized for neglecting the power relations embedded in media production and consumption.

See also: **Agency; Bardic function; Consumption; Critical theory; Encoding/decoding, ethnography; Mass communication and mass media**

Further reading: Ang (1985), Hall (1980c), Morley (1980 and 1986), Radway (1987).

Authentic culture

Something is considered 'authentic' if its provenance cannot be disputed, and if it is demonstrably an original, and not a copy. Authentic culture, then, is a culture that can purportedly be traced back to an originary past of an ethnic group, or a group defined in relation to a particular locality. The notion of authenticity is associated with mass culture theory's idealization of the past, threatened by the emergence of mass-produced culture. Authenticity can also be interpreted as a function of identity, conceived in a popular essentialist way as a stable category. Within various identitarian discourses, authenticity becomes a measure that serves for excluding others who 'don't belong' and are considered fake or inauthentic. Many critics have acknowledged that, in a techno-logically advanced and globalized world, a definable authenticity may not be more than a nostalgic fantasy. Walter Benjamin was the first to describe how the emergence of technologies of mechanical reproduc-tion tarnished the aura of art, which had previously depended precisely on its authenticity and inaccessibility. Theories of the postmodern postulate that, in late modernity, authenticity has been transformed into a hyperreality of depthless culture, deprived of referentiality and meaning (Jameson 1991 [1984]). Globalization has challenged the notion of authenticity based on fixed identity categories. It can be argued that, paradoxically, in contemporary global society, authenticity pertains precisely to the hybridized transnational and cosmopolitan cultures. Authenticity is also increasingly becoming commodified: once a cultural resource – a travel package, a performance, an artefact – becomes iden-tified as authentic, its market value rises, and so does the demand for it.

See also: **Commodity; Critical theory; Globalization; Hyperreality; Identity, identifica-tion, identity politics; Mass culture, culture industry; Postmodern, postmodernity, postmodernism; Simulacrum**

Further reading: Cheng (2004), Jameson (1991 [1984]).

Author, authorship

Deriving from Latin *auctor*, which means 'promoter' or 'creator', the word refers to the creative originator and the main legitimizing principle of a text. Authors are not always easily identifiable in contemporary cultural and media texts, many of which are products of collective enterprise, intercultural borrowing and intertextuality. Most recently, the develop-ment of collaborative software and the widespread use of electronic reproduction have contributed to a rapid proliferation of textual agency.

Authorship is an ideological concept: a social, cultural and legal insti-tution embedded in the relationships of power in a specific social context. The idea of the author as a creative genius, autonomously producing original meaning, is a construct the origins of which are usually associated with eighteenth-century Romanticism. This view of authorship persisted in literary theory well into the twentieth century. Between the 1920s and 1960s, the New Criticism, motivated by a humanist conception of subjectivity and creativity, ascribed the meaning of a text entirely to the author's genius and intentions. Even today, this approach dominates common perceptions of authorship and is reflected in intellectual property legislation. Attributions of authorship are hegemonic in nature. They serve to add value to certain texts on the basis of aesthetic ideas such as creativity and originality, and act as market regulators for cultural commodities.

The main shortcoming of the theories focusing on authorial intention is that they tend to limit the latent multiplicity of meaning within each text, which can be triggered by the discursive practices that regulate its production, transmission and consumption.

An influential critique of authorial intentionalism was produced in the 1960s by French semiotician Roland Barthes. In a famous essay entitled 'The Death of the Author' (1977 [1968]), Barthes criticized the author-centred criticism as an epitome of capitalist ideology. He shifted the focus of analysis from the author to literary form and intertextuality. According to him, intertextual meaning is mediated by the reader, who 'holds together in a single field all the traces by which the written text is constituted' (p. 148). In Jacques Derrida's theory of deconstruction, writing always contains potentially infinite meanings that were never intended by the original author, but can be activated by different readers in different contexts (1974 [1967]).

Rather than eradicating the authorial role from literary analysis, Michel Foucault saw authorship as a cultural formation closely related to the commodification of literature (1984 [1969]). He introduced the notion of 'author-function': not the real author, but a name 'attached' to a particular discourse or set of discourses, which serves to authorize their circulation within a society.

See also: **Agency; Authentic culture; Deconstruction; Discourse; Intertextuality; New Criticism; Text**

Further reading: Barthes (1977 [1968]), Burke (1993 and 1995), Foucault (1984 [1969]).

A

Authority

Authority is a type of power that is accepted as legitimate and authorized by a system of social norms. The sociologist Max Weber distinguished three main types of authority: legal–rational authority, based on codified norms, such as laws and procedural regulations; traditional authority, which rests on un-codified beliefs in the legitimacy of ancient customs and practices; and charismatic authority, attributed to the extraordinary capacities of a leader (1968 [1925]). A fourth type of authority, based on expertise, is known as 'professional authority' (Haskell 1984).

Deriving part of its meaning from the word 'author', the term implies that creators have singular claims over the use and interpretation of their creation. In poststructuralism, the conception of the death of the author is related to an overall critique of authority. In postmodernism, authority is seen as challenged by a growing incredulity toward meta-narratives, resulting in what Habermas calls 'legitimation crisis' (1975 [1973]).

See also: **Author, authorship; Knowledge; Narrative; Poststructuralism; Postmodern, postmodernity, postmodernism**

Further reading: Habermas (1975 [1973]), Haskell (1984), Weber (1968 [1925]).

Avant-garde

'Avant-garde' is the French term for the vanguard of an army advancing into battle. From the late nineteenth century onwards, the term has been used to refer to the political, intellectual and artistic movements considered to be 'ahead of the mainstream' and thus in opposition to the dominant culture. Since the mid-twentieth century, a great deal of earlier avant-garde art and literature has been absorbed into the mainstream.

The emancipatory potential of avant-garde movements was emphasized by the Frankfurt School, as an antidote to the tyranny of contemporary popular culture, mass-produced by culture industries. Cultural studies, with their focus on popular and media culture, have largely overlooked the counter-hegemonic capacity of avant-garde movements.

Relying on a linear and irreversible conception of time, characteristic of modernist thought, avant-gardism has lost some of its appeal with the onset of the social and cultural changes associated with postmodernity. Yet, postmodern art often combines everyday objects and elements of mass-produced culture by employing such avant-garde techniques as *bricolage*, collage and juxtaposition.

See also: **Bricolage; Critical theory; Hegemony; Mass culture, culture industry; Parody, pastiche; Postmodern, postmodernity, postmodernism**

Further reading: Bürger (1984 [1974]), Murphy (1999).

Bardic function

Bardic function is a concept introduced by John Fiske and John Hartley (2003 [1978]) to explain the function of television in terms of social ritual, rather than relating it exclusively to government control and commercial monopoly, as a majority of earlier media theories had done. Like bards – the poets who sang the praises of heroes and chieftains in medieval Celtic societies – television is a vital social institution, which orally communicates messages that confirm and reinforce the world-view and values of the culture it speaks to. Bardic function thus reinforces the crucial role of the audience in setting the social and semiotic conditions for the production of meaning in media communication. According to Fiske and Hartley, television mediates between the audience it addresses and the reality it refers to, by manipulating the available linguistic resources to 'claw back' (pp. 65–6) the subject of its messages into a recognizable and consensual framework.

Further reading: Fiske and Hartley (2003 [1978]).

Base and superstructure

In Marxist theory, these terms are used to explain the relationship between the modes of production of material life (the base) and the legal, political and cultural dimensions of society (the superstructure). The architectural metaphor of a building, in which the construction of the foundation determines the structure of the upper levels, can be interpreted as implying a relationship of unidirectional causality and a primacy of economy over culture. This mechanistic causal model was used to sustain Soviet Communist policies, as ordained by Lenin, Stalin and other party functionaries. Yet, this simplistic interpretation, often labelled as 'economism' or 'economic determinism', does not adequately reflect Marx's foundational arguments or the later Marxist tradition, which has emphasized the relative autonomy of the superstructure d the reciprocal action of the superstructure on the base (see Figure 1).

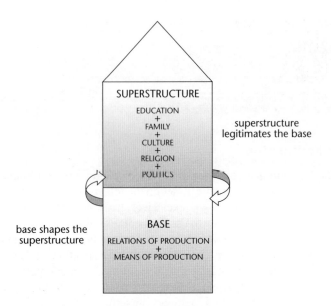

Figure 1 The base and superstructure model in traditional Marxism

Generally speaking, most versions of Western Marxism, while retaining interest in the base–superstructure dualism as a provisional plane of abstraction of limited utility, have provided more elaborate models, allowing room for individual and collective agency. Most notably, Gramsci's notion of 'historical bloc' and his concept of hegemony, which posits a dynamic unity of base and superstructure, set the framework for subsequent cultural theory. They also helped disentangle ideology from class and thus give voice to other salient social divisions, such as those based on gender, ethnicity and race, to name only a few.

Cultural historian Raymond Williams recast the base-superstructure model by critically adapting Gramsci's concept of hegemony and further elaborating the concept of the base, to include a whole range of human relationships and processes (1973). In his reading of Gramsci, Stuart Hall highlighted the centrality of superstructures in strengthening capitalism's grip (1977). Later, he emphasized that, in modern societies, the economic and the cultural dimensions were significantly entwined, since culture is material in its practices and modes of production and the material world of commodities and technologies is essentially cultural in nature (1989).

See also: **Agency; Capitalism; Class; Culture; Hegemony; Ideology; Marxism, Leninism, Western Marxism**

Further reading: Williams (1973), Hall (1977) and Hall and Jacques (1989).

Binary opposition

In structuralism, binary opposition is an analytical device that explains the generation of meaning through the principle of contrast between two mutually exclusive terms. Binarism was originally used in Saussurian linguistics, to define the meaning of one sign in relation to its 'pair' at the other side of the binary. The binary opposition between zero and one (0/1) is the foundation of digital computing.

Structuralism assumes that no single element has meaning except as an integral part of a stable set of structural connections within a system. In other words, structuralists sought to establish what something *is* by reference to what it *is not*: for example, the meaning of 'man' can be said to equal 'not woman' and the two terms together can be seen as representing a whole system, that is, the human race. Within this logic, each binary opposition also implies a value hierarchy, so that one of the terms is seen as 'positive', the other as 'negative'. Also, binaries are often interpreted as related to one another, so that, for example, masculinity becomes associated with culture, activity, reason and the public space, while femininity is seen as relating to nature, passivity, emotion and the private sphere. Ambiguous terms, which partake in both extremes of the opposition and yet don't fully belong to either of them, need to be dealt with through either repression or ritualization.

Structuralist analysis has been influential in anthropology, sociology and literary criticism: the pioneer of structuralist anthropology, Claude Lévi-Strauss, used binary oppositions such as nature/culture, raw/cooked, inedible/edible (see Figure 2) to study the kinship systems, myths and rites of different societies; Roland Barthes applied binary

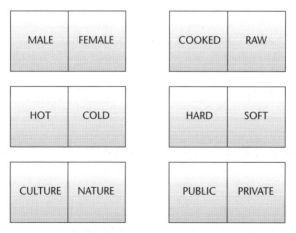

Figure 2   Binary oppositions

oppositions in his early analysis of cultural objects and social artefacts; Marxist philosopher Louis Althusser used them to analyse social phenomena in terms of the core structures of the modes of production; structuralist narratologists such as Todorov, Genette and Greimas applied them to narrative structures.

Since the late 1960s, structuralism has been criticized as ahistorical and neglectful of human agency. Poststructuralism, postcolonialism and most strands of feminism view binarism not as a supposedly universal principle, but as an ideological construct sustaining and legitimizing Western/male domination. Deconstruction seeks to destabilize binary oppositions by subverting their implicit hierarchy and leaving them in a suspended, irresoluble condition.

See also: **Deconstruction; Sign; Structuralism; Poststructuralism**

Further reading: Barthes (1984 [1957]), Genette (1980), Greimas (1987 [1970]), Lévi-Strauss (1977 [1958]), Saussure (1993 [1915]), Todorov (1977 [1971]).

Body

Traditionally devalued by Western metaphysics as impermanent and inferior to the mind, the body has become one of the most debated concepts in late twentieth-century cultural and social theory. The surfacing of the body as a key theoretical paradigm is partly related to the mounting interest in sexuality and gender, brought on by the politics of the gay and feminist movements and the advent of diseases such as AIDS, in which the corporeal, the social and the political significantly interrelate.

Contemporary poststructuralist, postcolonial and feminist theories have exposed the binary opposition between body and mind and the related oppositions between nature and culture, femininity and masculinity and the public and the private, as ideological constructs that have served to reinforce and perpetuate male and/or Western domination. Second-wave feminists in particular were concerned about the use of the body as a means of discriminating against women in patriarchy.

The body used to be understood as an aspect of nature, only marginally subject to human intervention. Since the 1970s, however, Foucault (1979 [1975]; 1980 [1976]) and numerous scholars influenced by his work have interpreted it as the ultimate site of ideological control, regulation and surveillance, simultaneously situated in and produced by discourse. Foucault maintained that, although at one time controlled by institutional coercion, in high modernity bodies became regulated via positive forms of exhortation and stimulation.

Cultural studies in particular have highlighted how consumer culture, buttressed by the mass media, has encouraged embodied subjects to

B

manage their bodies in a myriad of possible ways, through dieting, skin care, plastic surgery, decorative cosmetics, body piercing, tattooing, hair style, exercise, clothing or jewelry, to name only a few. It is through the maintenance and presentation of their bodies that individuals can express their identities, by conforming to or resisting socio-cultural norms. Another aspect of corporeality that is of interest for cultural studies is the politics of lived bodily experiences such as aging and disease, and their representations in public discourse. Furthermore, recent developments in transplant and transgender surgery, in vitro fertilization and genetic engineering have increased our control over bodies, while at the same time blurring the boundaries between bodies and machines and destabilizing the very notion of bounded corporeality.

See also: **Cyborg; Discourse; Feminism; Gender; Sexuality**

Further reading: Coupland (2003), Foucault (1979 [1975] and 1980 [1976]), Shilling (2004).

Border/lands

In geography, the word 'border' denotes the area adjacent to the boundaries that demarcate state territory (Prescott 1987). Over the last few decades, the intensified flow of people, ideas, technologies, goods and capital has challenged the notion of clearly defined national boundaries. At the same time, some boundaries – especially those between the first and the third worlds – are becoming less penetrable than ever before (Donnan and Wilson 1999).

   Symbolic and real borders also exist between ethnic groups, cultures, professions and academic disciplines, social classes or genders – in fact wherever elements of two or more distinct categories co-exist and overlap. The metaphor of the border, as a site for the production and dismantling of difference, has been used in a number of social, political and cultural theories dealing with issues of identity and belonging. The border is variably seen either as the ultimate site of domination and control, where the influence of the centre is the strongest and most obvious (an example is passport checks at state borders), or as a fertile terrain for experimentation, cultural play and resistance to dominant ideologies. Border crossing – whether by migrants, refugees, displaced persons or tourists – is always potentially a destabilizing act, which can be either empowering or disabling for the crosser.

   The word 'borderland' is often used as a synonym of 'border', but it conveys a perspective that acknowledges the centrality of the borderland itself, rather than understanding it as a function of the centre. The borderlands can be interpreted as the crucial site where a new politics

B

of identity is generated. Gloria Anzaldúa's *La Frontera/Borderlands* (1999 [1987]) is often cited as a foundational text for an understanding of the borderlands as a zone where the conceptual boundaries of class, gender and ethnicity are continually crossed and the established hegemonies challenged. For Anzaldúa, '[b]orders are set up to define the places that are safe and unsafe, to distinguish *us* from *them*. A border is a dividing line, a narrow strip along a steep edge. A borderland is a vague and undetermined place created by the emotional residue of an unnatural boundary. It is in a constant state of transition' (p. 25). Anzaldúa's conceptualization of the borderlands, however, is indebted to earlier historians of the Spanish frontier in North America and also to the pioneering ethnographic work of Américo Paredes (Allatson 2007).

See also: **Alterity; Difference; Ethnicity; Hybridity;** *Mestizaje*; **Nation, nationality, nationalism**

Further reading: Anzaldúa (1999 [1987]).

Bricolage

In French, the word *bricolage* refers to impromptu handy-work, performed by using whatever materials and methods are at hand.

In the structuralist anthropology of Lévi-Strauss, it denotes the arbitrary rearrangement and recontextualization of objects to convey new meanings (1966 [1962]). According to Lévi-Strauss, magical thought seeks to explain the nature of the universe through the process of random re-cycling of earlier experiences and myths. In his criticism of Lévi-Strauss, Derrida goes a step further, to assert that *bricolage* is in fact constitutive of all discourse: '[i]f one calls *bricolage* the necessity of borrowing one's concepts from the text of a heritage which is more or less coherent or ruined, it must be said that every discourse is *bricoleur*' (2001 [1967]: 360).

In cultural studies, the concept of *bricolage* has been employed to explain the styles of particular subcultural youth groups. For example, Skinhead style combines such seemingly disparate elements as boots, short jeans and shaved hair, because these elements articulate the group's notions of working-class vigour and masculinity. These elements, revived and borrowed from a variety of different contexts, are brought together into a new and distinctive stylistic assemblage, to articulate the group's beliefs and public identity (Hall and Jefferson: 1993 [1976]).

See also: **Deconstruction; Structuralism; Subculture**

Further reading: Derrida (2001 [1967]), Hall and Jefferson (1993 [1976]), Lévi-Strauss (1966 [1962]).

B

Capitalism

Capitalism is an economic system with far-reaching social implications, which emerged in Europe in the sixteenth and seventeenth centuries. It is characterized by the predominance of private ownership of natural resources, goods and capital. Capitalism also entails a concentration of ownership in the hands of capitalists, and exploitation of the working class in the interests of profit. The movement of capital is governed by supply and demand, profit and freedom of competition.

Throughout most of the twentieth century, a majority of capitalist countries sanctioned some form of government ownership of natural resources and capital, while socialist countries allowed a minimum level of private property. Since the 1980s, the levels of state ownership in most Western economies have decreased, while most of the countries of the former Eastern bloc have shifted to a market economy.

Early merchant capitalism, during which the emerging merchant class had mainly sought profit through the buying and selling of goods, gave way to profit making through the control of the production process during the period of industrial revolution. Marx speculated that, in advanced capitalism, big corporations would become so powerful that they would compete with nation-states in their influence over production and resources. He believed this was the last phase leading to socialist revolution (1975 [1867]).

Max Weber linked the emergence of the capitalist values of impersonality and rationality historically both to institutional change, that is, to the rise of banking and free-market economy, and to the consolidation of the Protestant values of asceticism and deferred gratification.

See also: **Class; Marxism, Leninism, Western Marxism**

Further reading: Marx (1975 [1867]), Weber (1992 [1905]).

Carnivalesque

The term is used to describe the practices and modes of behaviour associated with the popular festivities preceding the Lent period in the

Christian calendar. It probably derives from Latin *carnem* ('meat') + *levare* ('to lift', 'to remove'), referring to the tradition, during Lent, of abstinence from meat and other 'pleasures of the flesh'.

The institution of Carnival – with its grotesque elements, its temporary reversal of social hierarchies and its unrestrained celebration of excess – provided the Russian literary critic Mikhail Mikhailovich Bakhtin with a model for understanding the defiance of social order through popular culture in the work of the sixteenth-century French writer François Rabelais (Bakhtin 1968). According to Bakhtin, Carnival is never passively observed, but rather, fully experienced by everyone concerned, as there is no barrier between performers and spectators. It has a potential for cultural resistance to official hierarchies, because it engenders strong feelings of solidarity and raises awareness of the continuity of communal existence through a relentless interchange of death and renewal. Bakhtin further argued that some literary genres, most notably Menippean satire and the novel, used carnivalesque discourse to subvert the authority of official culture.

The concept has been widely used in cultural studies, to refer to the subversive potential of texts and practices in any domain of popular culture. Peter Stallybrass and Allon White in particular have interpreted it as partaking in a broader notion of symbolic inversion and transgression, which can occur in a range of different socio-cultural contexts.

Overly simplistic appropriations of the concept by some cultural studies practitioners have been criticized as a misconstruction of Bakhtin's interpretation, an exaggeration of the political power of popular culture and a form of essentialism, which identifies certain ideologies with particular forms of culture and with particular class configurations (Bennett 1986: 14–15). Lawrence Grossberg has pointed out that, rather than identifying particular manifestations of popular culture as resistant and assigning others to a cultural mainstream, where they are contained by hegemonic forces, critics should examine the movements of resistance and containment in their dialectic relationship within any popular-cultural form (1997b).

See also: **Dialogism; Heteroglossia; Popular culture, folk culture**

Further reading: Bakhtin (1968), Bennett (1986).

Celebrity

The word derives from Latin *celebritas*, which means 'fame'. A fascination with glamour and fantasy permeates today's popular culture, fostered by entertainment and media industries. Celebrity culture, once

limited to legendary and mythical creatures, royalty and exceptional individuals, today extends to many segments of society, such as film, television, publishing, music, arts, sports, politics, business and the academy.
The celebrity status does not have to be related to a person's merit, and
is indeed sometimes based purely on a set of circumstances that attracts
public attention. To quote Daniel Boorstin, the 'celebrity is a person who
is well-known for their well-knownness' (in Turner 2004: 5).

The accounts of celebrity within cultural studies emphasize its
commodification and its role in the formation of cultural identities in
contemporary society. Critics have interpreted today's preponderance of
celebrity culture as a sign of a shift in cultural taste away from authenticity, rationality, written textuality and durability towards artificiality,
sensationalism, visuality and transience (Marshall 1997, Rojek 2001).
Within this paradigm, adherence to celebrity culture is a way of compen-
sating for the loss of community attributed to contemporary society.

See also: A**authentic culture; Popular culture, folk culture; Simulacrum**

Further reading: Gamson (1994), Rojek (2001), Turner (2004).

Centre for Contemporary Cultural Studies (CCCS)

The Centre for Contemporary Cultural Studies (CCCS) at the University of
Birmingham, England (also referred to as the 'Birmingham School'), is
commonly regarded as the birthplace of British cultural studies. It was
established in 1964, as a centre for postgraduate research under the
directorship of Richard Hoggart. In 1968, Hoggart was succeeded as
Director by Stuart Hall, who remained in that position until 1979.
Cultural studies achieved departmental status in the late 1980s. The
Department was closed in 2002, to the overwhelming dismay of the
British and international cultural studies community, as a result of a low
rating in the Research Assessment Exercise (RAE) conducted in 2001.

Hoggart's book *The Uses of Literacy* (1958), Raymond Williams's *Culture
and Society* (1958) and E. P. Thompson's *The Making of the English
Working Class* (1963) are considered to be the key texts that had shaped
the intellectual agenda of the Centre in its early years. These works
shared a common interest in the socio-cultural predicament of the British
working class and in the notion of a common culture, spanning beyond
the elite canon promoted by the British education system at the time.
Over the years, the work of the Centre was influenced by a number of
theoretical strands, including Althusser's elaboration of ideology,
Gramsci's notion of hegemony, semiotics, deconstruction, hermeneutics,
psychoanalysis, feminist theory, and Foucault's theory of discourse.

C

From the outset, cultural studies were understood as an interdisciplinary project. According to Hoggart, they combined three different strands of inquiry, which he defined as historical–philosophical, sociological and literary critical (1970: 255). The Centre promoted collaborative research, with groups of six to ten researchers working on a project for three or four years. The principal focus of the Centre's research was popular mediated culture, with projects dealing with topics such as popular press, television crime drama, advertising, women's magazines and subcultural practices.

In the early 1970s, the Centre started publishing the journal titled *Working Papers in Cultural Studies* (*WPCS*) and a stencilled occasional papers series, which featured unpublished essays on a range of topics. The Women's Studies Group, established in 1974, examined female media consumption and 'women's genres' such as soap opera and fashion magazines. The resulting publication, titled *Women Take Issue* (1978), had a significant impact on feminist studies. During the late 1970s, the focus of interest was expanded beyond class- and gender-related concerns, to include issues of race and ethnicity.

Since the 1980s, cultural studies have expanded worldwide, especially in countries such as the United States, Canada, Australia and South Africa.

Further reading: Turner (2002).

Chronotope

This term, coined from Greek *chronos* (time) and *topos* (place, space), refers to the time–space configurations found in specific cultural formations. It is based on the insights about the inseparability of space and time, found in Albert Einstein's theory of relativity. The concept was introduced into literary theory by Bakhtin, who used it to explain the 'intrinsic connectedness of temporal and spatial relationships' in specific narrative genres (1981: 84).

The notion of the chronotope is relevant for cultural studies, because it underpins the contingency of cultural formations. It has gained particular currency in postcolonial and diaspora studies, concerned with the multiple constitution of cultural identity through displacement. An often-quoted example is Paul Gilroy's study of the Black Atlantic, which introduces the chronotope of the ship 'as a chance to explore the articulations between the discontinuous histories of England's ports, its interfaces with the wider world' (Gilroy 1993: 17). In Gilroy's work, the ship allows us to chart different time–space representations of the Atlantic and understand the relationship between spaces and identities, constituted through movement and contacts between different cultures.

See also: **Narrative; Space, place; Time**

Further reading: Bakhtin (1981).

Citizenship

Citizenship is a concept in sociology and political science that defines the relationship between an individual and a state or territory, mainly in terms of the rights and obligations of the citizen that this relationship entails. With its origins in the ancient Greek city-states, where it was a privilege enjoyed by the select few, it came to be regarded as a universal ideal during the French Revolution. Despite its proclaimed universalism, modern citizenship has consistently made certain groups strangers and outsiders, most commonly along lines of gender, sexuality, race and ethnicity.

The rights stemming from the relationship between modern states and their citizens typically include civil rights (free movement and speech, the rule of law), political rights (voting, running for electoral office) and socio-economic rights (welfare, health care, unemployment insurance). The precise extent, content and application of such rights differ from one state to another. Citizenship obligations are equally varied across the globe, and at their very minimum include tax payment and the observance of the law.

The very foundations of modern state citizenship have been challenged by critics and activists representing a range of disenfranchised segments of society. Among these, women's rights activists and feminists have criticized the social philosophy underlying citizenship from the perspective of gender; gay and lesbian activists and queer theorists have extended the debate to questions of sexuality; and postcolonial critics have examined its meaning in relation to colonial legacies. In addition to these three fields of inquiry, the concept is of vital interest to diaspora studies, race and ethnic studies, indigenous studies, immigration studies, urban studies and environmental studies.

Modern citizenship arose out of the nation-state. However, the stable identities associated with the nation-state model have been increasingly challenged by the global flows of people, capital, commodities, information and ideas associated with globalization. The new identities, based on displacement and dispersion, preclude commitment to a single nation-state and thus problematize the meaning of citizenship in contemporary society. Concepts such as 'transnational citizenship', 'global citizenship', 'differential citizenship', 'indigenous citizenship' and 'sexual citizenship', to name only a few, reflect the changing nature of citizenship in contemporary society.

Within cultural studies, we can distinguish two main orientations engaging with issues of citizenship. The first strand, deriving from literary studies, has been interested in teaching forms of engagement with public life through textual analysis of newspaper articles, films, television and other texts that influence people's identities in an era characterized by a growing democratization of public life. The underlying assumption of this effort is that citizenship is shaped as much by engagement with media and everyday life as in formal dealings with the state apparatus.

The second strand, influenced by Michel Foucault's concept of governmentality, has focused on cultural policy as a process of citizen-formation. Studies of cultural policy have been fundamentally concerned with the forms of governance that work between public institutions and private individuals, at both national and international levels, shaping civic allegiances and patterns of participation. Within this strand, Toby Miller (1993, 1998) attempted to show how different discourses circulating in the media triggered a sense of 'ethical incompleteness' in the audience. The spectators' desire to address and resolve this incompleteness, in order to achieve 'full citizenship', constitutes what has become known, after Foucault, as the 'government of the self'.

See also: **Cultural citizenship; Diaspora; Globalization; Governmentality; Ideology; Nation, nationality, nationalism**

Further reading: Hall and Held (1989), Marshall (1950), Meredyth (2001), Miller (1993 and 1998).

Class

As one of the fundamental categories of social stratification, class signifies a collectivity sharing the same social, economic, or occupational standing. Class divisions are commonly conceived in hierarchical terms, with higher classes enjoying more privilege and a greater prestige and authority. In Western societies, the hierarchy has conventionally involved the upper or leisured class, the middle class or bourgeoisie, and the lower or working class.

The theoretical tradition of class analysis originates from the work of Karl Marx and Max Weber, focusing on nineteenth-century industrial capitalism. Marx defines class in terms of the ownership of capital and the means of production. In Marxian terms, the society of industrial capitalism is divided into two principal classes: the propertied capitalist class, and the property-less working class, or proletariat. Class is envisioned as a substantial social force, capable of changing society.

Weber describes class as dependent on 'objective' market interests that influence 'life-chances', or access to cultural and economic resources. Market capacity is achieved not only through capital, but also through skill and education. The four main classes within Weber's framework are: the propertied class; the intellectual, administrative and managerial class; the petty-bourgeois class of shopkeepers and small businessmen; and the working class.

The validity of class analysis has been disputed by critics from different disciplinary perspectives. Other categories of stratification, such as gender, sexuality, ethnicity and race, have been put forward as more instrumental than class in determining life-chances. Also, the conventional correlation between class, cultural values and political inclinations has been debunked as no longer applicable in contemporary society.

Rather than positing class, defined in economic terms, as a foundational social category, post-Marxist theorists such as Ernesto Laclau and Chantal Mouffe (1985) focused on the social as open and constituted within multiple discourses. This model was adopted by Stuart Hall in his study of Thatcherism (1983), and has since gained wide currency in cultural studies. According to Hall, Thatcherism appealed to the 'popular elements in the traditional philosophies and practical ideologies of the dominated classes', because these elements 'have no intrinsic, necessary or fixed class meaning' and can therefore be re-articulated, so as 'to construct the people into a populist political subject: with, not against, the power bloc' (1983: 30). Class remains an important concept within cultural studies, as a fundamental category of difference that intersects with other categories, such as gender, sexuality, race or ethnicity, to produce historically contingent socio-cultural formations (Grossberg 1997a).

See also: **Capitalism; Marxism, Leninism, Western Marxism; Thatcherism**

Further reading: Grossberg (1997a), Laclau and Mouffe (1985), Marx (1975 [1867]), Weber (1968 [1925]).

Code

Codes are signifying systems, which make communication possible. In fact, as Stuart Hall has suggested, 'there is no intelligible discourse without the operation of a code' (Hall 1980c: 131). Codes are of vital interest to disciplines such as mathematics, computer science, media and communication studies, linguistics and semiotics.

The principal and most apparent code in any society is its language. In structuralist linguistics, language is interpreted as a system of signs, governed by sets of conventions, or codes.

In semiotics, a code is a set of signs – practices, texts and objects of material culture – that conveys meanings that are intelligible within a specific cultural context. Semioticians endeavour to explain the conventions of the codes that govern the production of meanings within a particular culture. Codes can be categorized in different ways. The following classification, put together by Daniel Chandler (2002: 149–50), includes the codes that have had the widest currency in media, communication and cultural studies:

Social codes
- verbal language
- bodily codes
- commodity codes
- behavioural codes

Textual codes
- scientific codes
- aesthetic codes
- genre, rhetorical and stylistic codes
- mass media codes

Interpretative codes
- perceptual codes
- ideological codes

According to Chandler, these three types of codes correspond broadly to three kinds of knowledge needed to interpret a particular text, namely social knowledge, or knowledge of the world; textual knowledge, or knowledge of the medium and the genre; and the capacity to draw modality judgements, that is, to understand the relationship between elements of social and textual knowledge (2002: 150).

See also: **Semiology, semiotics; Sign; Structuralism**

Further reading: Chandler (2002).

Colonialism

The term derives from Latin *colonia* (a settlement of ex-soldiers in a foreign land) and signifies the political and legal control of one nation by another. By extension, it can also designate a set of beliefs and cultural values held by the colonizing nation. Typically, the colonizer holds sway over the colony through a mixture of military force, authority over internal institutions, and economic control.

The age of colonialism commenced in the fifteenth century, with the European expansion in Africa and Asia and the 'discovery' of the New World. It received a new impetus in the eighteenth century, with the early development of industrial capitalism. The nineteenth century saw the strengthening of a modern colonial order, sustained by an absolute hegemony of European colonial powers over world trade and finance. After the Second World War, the spread of anti-colonial sentiment in the colonies and the economic crises in the colonizing countries both played a role in setting off a rapid process of de-colonization.

There is a widespread view in many of the former colonies that de-colonization has not brought about significant economic or cultural independence. The new forms of dependence – economic and cultural, rather than formally political – are referred to as 'neo-colonialism'.

The most influential critic of the many facets of the colonial experience was the Martinican thinker Frantz Fanon. Colonial discourse theory, initiated by Edward Said and embraced by critics such as Homi K. Bhabha and Gayatri Chakravorty Spivak, analyses the way in which the discourse of colonialism conceals the underlying political and material aims of colonization and constructs both the colonizing and the colonized subjects.

See also: **Postcolonialism, neo-colonialism**

Further reading: Bhabha (1986, 1990 and 1994), Fanon (1963 [1961]), Said (1983), Spivak (1988b), Williams and Chrisman (1994).

Commodity

A commodity is any object, activity or quality that can be sold, or exchanged for another commodity, in a market system. A commodity culture is a culture in which people understand themselves and the world they live in first and foremost through their relationship to commodities.

Marxist theory (Marx 1975 [1867]) identifies two kinds of value that a commodity possesses: use value, or its practical utility; and exchange value, or the value – usually in terms of the number of units – of another commodity for which it is exchanged. In capitalist societies, labour itself is a commodity, which can be exchanged on the labour market. 'Commodity fetishism' is a characteristic of the capitalist system, related

to alienation. Since the producers of commodities have no social relationships outside the act of exchange, the exchanged objects substitute
for, and thus reify, the social relations themselves. According to Theodor
Adorno, the 'commodity itself in consumer society has become image,
representation, spectacle. Use value has been replaced by a packaging
and advertising' (1991: 24).

The distinction between gift-based economies and commodity-based
economies has served as a conceptual tool in differentiating between
archaic and industrial societies (Mauss 1990 [1925]). It is now widely
accepted that commodity status does not reside in the nature of the
object itself, but in the set of circumstances it partakes in. According to
Arjun Appadurai, a 'commodity situation' is one in which an object's
'exchangeability for some other thing is its socially relevant feature'
(1986: 13).

Theories of the postmodern have postulated that, in late capitalism,
commodities have become pure ideas or signs, rather than objects with
a capacity to satisfy specific needs. In other words, their use value is
entirely a social construct (Baudrillard 1988 [1907]).

See also: **Capitalism; Consumption; Fetish; Postmodern, postmodernity, postmodernism; Value, value system**

Further reading: Appadurai (1986), Frow (1997), Marx (1975 [1867]).

Common culture

The notion of common culture can be interpreted in a number of different ways. First, it can be seen as a basic set of values, attitudes, experiences and resources that is common to all members of a specific social
group. Secondly, it can refer to a common heritage attributed to or imagined by a national community. Thirdly, it can be seen as the minimum
common denominator that binds people in multicultural societies, or
across national borders. Fourthly, it can refer to the Eurocentric notion
of the commonality of Western culture, constructed through appeals to
its assumed Greek, Roman and Christian roots. Fifthly, it can be envisaged as the culture of 'common people', experienced and negotiated
through everyday life practices.

Two approaches to common culture within cultural studies deserve
more attention. Reflecting on the increasing mobility between cultures
as part of our experience of modernity, Raymond Williams emphasized
the need for a common culture as a 'position' from which communication and understanding between cultures is made possible (1970:
316–17). Culture, for Williams, is both the particular structure of experience ('the structure of feeling') that defines a specific community and the

endeavour of proposing, evaluating, and sharing new meanings and experiences within the framework of already shared meanings ('the community of process'). The crisis of contemporary culture, according to Williams, resides in the fact that such a common culture, beyond the experience of particular communities, does not exist. On a rather different note, Paul Willis (1990) pays tribute to the creativity of common culture, interpreted by him as the culture of ordinary people, which emerges through their leisure pursuits and their relationship with commodities, rather than through work experience or political affiliations.

See also: **Everyday; Structure of feeling**

Further reading: Williams (1970), Willis (1990).

Communication

Communication is a form of interaction, but exactly how this interaction occurs and what it involves is subject to different interpretations. Communication between humans may unfold by means of any of the available sensory channels – taste, touch, smell, sight, or hearing – and may involve any combination of these regimes. In contemporary society, the nature of communication has been deeply affected by the development of new communication technologies.

There are two main schools in the study of communication: the process school, sometimes also referred to as the transmission school, and the semiotics school (Fiske 1990). The process school originates from the study of telecommunication systems, conducted during the Second World War by the US scientists Claude Elwood Shannon and Warren Weaver (Shannon and Weaver 1949). This school interprets communication as the transfer of information between a source and a receiver. It sees a message as a finished entity, the content of which is determined by the sender's intention. Communication is deemed successful if the information received is the same as the information transmitted. This, however, is not always possible to achieve, because of a variety of interfering factors that can distort the intended signal. These interfering factors, which can originate variably in the source, the receiver, or the message itself, are commonly referred to as 'noise'.

The semiotics school, which is of particular relevance to cultural studies, interprets communication as the generation of meaning that occurs in the process of interaction. Meaning here is a matter of negotiation between the sender and the receiver. Semioticians study the manner in which signs are invested with meaning and constructed into codes. The lack of correspondence between the meaning encoded by the sender and that decoded by the receiver is not seen as a failure in communication, but as a reflection of the receiver's cultural experience, which affects the generation of meaning in a specific communicative context.

See also: **Audience; Semiology, semiotics; Sign; Structuralism**

Further reading: Fiske (1990), Williams (1962).

Connotation/denotation

In semantics, these two concepts serve to distinguish between the primary or literal meaning of a word (denotation), and its secondary or associative meaning (connotation). Connotation, sometimes also referred to as 'affective meaning', refers to a range of associations attached to a particular word, which depend on anyone's personal or socio-cultural experience. The denotative meaning of the word 'mother', for example, is 'female parent', while its connotative meanings may include 'affection', 'warmth', 'caring' and so forth, depending on the interpreter's specific experience.

The application of connotative meaning in certain figures of speech, such as simile or metaphor, is of particular interest to literary studies. In logic and philosophy, the term 'denotation' refers to the specific instances – objects, practices, qualities or events – to which a word can be suitably applied, while the concept of 'connotation' is interpreted as the abstract definition of the word.

See also: **Metaphor, metonymy, synecdoche; Trope**

Further reading: Chandler (2002).

Consumption

Deriving from Latin *consumere*, meaning to use up, eat or waste, 'consumption' refers variably to the act or process of ingesting food, acquiring commodities, and utilizing products and resources of material and immaterial culture. In economics, it signifies direct utilization of goods and services by the consumer in capitalist societies and is seen as closely bound to the production and exchange of commodities. Although some consumer practices can be traced back to pre-modern times, the birth of modern consumption is usually associated with the development of industrial capitalism in the eighteenth century.

The concept is of vital interest to a wide variety of academic disciplines, including anthropology, cultural studies, political science, communications, psychology and psychoanalysis, sociology, political science, art, literature and media studies, history and geography.

Today, consumption permeates all aspects of life in developed societies, and has arguably become one of the main resources for identity construction and maintenance. According to Daniel Miller (1995), it has become such a pervasive facet of modern life, that it could – and indeed should – replace kinship as the main focus of anthropological investigation. In a similar vein, theories of the postmodern have interpreted consumption as the main reason for existence in contemporary society, postulating that signs of the commodity have become more important than the commodity itself (Baudrillard 1998 [1970]).

In addition to being interpreted as a fertile terrain for the construction of identities, consumption has also been interpreted as a political act. Indeed, today's consumers can transform their purchasing preferences into political statements, for example by choosing to buy only locally grown organic produce, by boycotting certain goods on ethical or environmental grounds, or by supporting 'fair trade' to promote better employment conditions in the developing world.

Within cultural studies, the initial interest in issues of consumption was related to the study of television audiences (Morley 1980, Ang 1985). These accounts saw the consumption of media texts as an active process, rather than a passive reception of the meaning already embedded in a particular text. The original focus on the media was later expanded to include a wide range of commodities and practices of consumption. Specific subcultures have been identified with and through particular consumer objects and practices (Willis 1990). The act of shopping has been interpreted as a social activity built around social exchange. Consumer objects, as well as the spaces and places of consumption, such as corner shops, charity shops, supermarkets and shopping malls, have been examined in terms of the social relations they embody and extend.

See also: **Agency; Audience; Capitalism; Commodity**

Further reading: Douglas and Isherwood (1996), Daniel Miller (1987, 1995 and 1998).

C

Content analysis

Content analysis is a quantitative research method used in social sciences to examine the subject matter of media texts. It involves establishing the frequency of predetermined categories within a well defined textual corpus. Because it is based on a systematic analysis of statistical data, it is considered to be one of the most objective methods of media analysis. To avoid personal bias in determining the categories to be utilized in a project, the researcher needs to define them with reference to a clear theoretical and contextual framework. Also, the nature and size of sample must be relevant and representative.

Content analysis is rarely used as a stand-alone method. It is considered to be more effective when conducted in conjunction with other research methods, such as textual analysis and audience research, to explain how the chosen categories relate to other meaning latent in the text, and how their established frequency relates to audience response.

See also: **Method, methodology**

Further reading: Hansen et al. (1998).

Content industries

Content industries are involved in the development, production and distribution of content, in a range of media formats, including image, sound, text or any multimedia combination thereof. They encompass the different aspects of print publishing (magazines, newspapers, books, corporate publishing), electronic publishing (information-based websites, electronic databases, audio and video text services) and the audiovisual industries (radio, television, video and audio recordings, and film). Based on the value of intellectual property, they are also sometimes referred to as the 'copyright industries'.

See also: **Mass communication and mass media**

Convergence

'Convergence' refers to the integration of different technologies and their respective industries and markets through digital networks. The flexibility of digital technology has enabled media providers to use several parallel platforms to disseminate and manage content. Convergence has had an impact on the communications policies in a number of countries, as well as on the corporate strategies within the Information Technology (IT), telecom, media and consumer electronics industries, including several large corporate mergers during the 1980s and 1990s.

See also: **Mass communication and mass media; Network**

Conversation analysis

Conversation analysis is a research method that focuses on the social aspects of linguistic interaction. Originally a subdiscipline of sociology, it is sometimes regarded as a discipline in its own right, with a significant bearing on sociolinguistics, anthropology and social psychology. The principal aim of conversation analysis is to bring to light the structural properties of 'talk in interaction'. The analysis is always based on audio or visual recordings of specific interactions. These are then transcribed, taking note not only of the specific linguistic utterances, but also of as much extra-linguistic detail as possible, including turn-taking, overlap talking and pauses. The research is intended to be data-driven, rather than based on pre-established theoretical concepts or ideological preferences. Issues such as gender or class, for example, are only seen as relevant to an analysis if participants in the conversation have specifically invoked them. The principal task of the conversation analyst is to identify any patterns in the sequential organization of talk. Some patterns that have been of particular interest to analysts are openings and closings of conversations; adjacency pairs (e.g. compliment–compliment response; greeting–greeting); topic management and topic shift; conversational 'repairs' in the event of communication failure (e.g. requests for clarification of a particular point in a speaker's message); expressing agreement and disagreement; introducing bad news and processes of troubles-telling; and, above all, patterns of turn-taking.

In addition to examining everyday interactions between individuals, conversation analysis has also been used to study talk in various institutional contexts, including medical, juridical and educational establishments.

Conversation analysis has been of relevance to cultural studies research, because of its capacity to provide a better understanding of how certain cultural constructs (for example, identity parameters such as gender, class etc.) are put to use in everyday talk interactions.

See also: **Method, methodology**

Further reading: Hutchby and Wooffitt (1998).

Cosmopolitanism

Deriving from the Greek noun *kosmos*, meaning world, and *politês*, citizen (from *pólis*, which means city), cosmopolitanism signifies a worldview that considers all human beings as belonging, in the first instance, to a single global community. The Greek Stoics used the word to express the notion that all people were manifestations of a universal spirit, literally 'citizens of the universe', and should therefore treat each other with empathy and compassion. German philosopher Immanuel Kant (1963 [1784]) distinguished between *jus gentium*, or international right between nation-states, and *jus cosmopoliticum*, or the right of individuals regarded as citizens of a universal state of mankind.

Cosmopolitanism does not imply that all human beings are the same, but promotes respect for other cultures and a desire for peace. In contemporary political theory, the term is commonly used to denote a style of global politics based, at least partly, on what are considered universal laws and institutions. Most recently, it has been associated with the notion of 'global citizenship', which is founded upon an increasing sense of the importance of loyalties that transcend the nation-state, not only in the realm of corporate business, but also in the sphere of transnational humanitarian and activist networks. The US philosopher Martha Nussbaum (1996, 1997) has advocated the ideal of global citizenship as a goal of liberal education, emphasizing the need to educate students to be attuned to and comfortable with the multiple frames of reference existing in different cultures.

From a postcolonial perspective, European cosmopolitanism, based on the liberal idea of the 'empathetic self', is regarded as part of a broader colonizing project. A number of scholars have called for a radical rethinking of the concept from the colonial margins, which would take into account the non-oppressive and non-hierarchical multi-civilizational models from non-Western cultures.

Within cultural studies, cosmopolitanism has been interpreted as a phenomenon related to contemporary diasporic communities. The notion of 'vernacular cosmopolitanism' has been used to signal a way of knowing based on the particularity of everyday experience in the globalized world, informed by the overlapping perspectives brought together by global flows of refugees, migrants, and other subaltern groups (Bhabha 1994, 1996).

See also: **Citizenship; Colonialism; Diaspora**

Further reading: Breckenridge et al. (2002), Brennan (1997).

Creolization

The word refers to the process of linguistic or cultural transformation, which occurs as a result of contacts between different cultural or ethnic groups. The origins of the word 'Creole' can be traced back to Latin *creare*, to produce or create. In Romance languages (French *créole*, Spanish *criollo*, Portuguese *crioulo*), it was used to denote a person native to a locality, or a person raised in one's house, usually a servant. In contemporary usage, the word 'Creole' most commonly refers to the locally born descendants of French, Portuguese and Spanish settlers in the West Indies. In the US state of Louisiana, it is used to distinguish the descendants of the original French settlers from the Cajuns, who arrived there after thay had been expelled from the former French colony of Acadia (now part of Canada) in the eighteenth century.

The concept has wide currency in sociolinguistics, where it signifies the creation of new language systems when distinct linguistic communities come into contact. This typically occurred as a result of colonial expansion, most notably in the former European colonies of the Caribbean, such as Jamaica, Dominica or Haiti. The first stage of language change in these circumstances is referred to as 'pidginization'. The emerging pidgin language uses the linguistic resources of both the language of the colonized and that of the colonizer. It operates with very few words, and is not a native language to anyone. In the next stage, known as 'creolization', all aspects of language – phonology, morphology, lexis, syntax and semantics – become more elaborated. Also, the descendants of pidgin-speaking parents can become native speakers of the resulting creole language.

Along with its semantic cognates, syncretism, *métissage*, *mestizaje* and hybridity, the concept of creolization is also of great consequence to postcolonial and cultural studies, where it is seen as a force capable of subverting, inverting, and possibly even supplanting the Eurocentric ideologies of race, identity and aesthetics. Creolization here applies not only to language, but also to other areas of cultural change, such as literature, music, cuisine, and so on. Critics have called attention to the conflictual nature of creolization as the principal feature that sets it apart from hybridity, which is seen as a natural and essentially non-conflictual cultural process. Stuart Hall has emphasized the creative power of creolization in the face of the historical traumas of displacement, transportation and loss (1990a).

Moreover, creolization has been interpreted as a precursor to the postmodern aesthetic of fragmentation and instability; and as part and parcel of globalization, especially in urban areas. Declaring that '[w]e are all Caribbeans now in our urban archipelagos' and that '[p]erhaps there's no return for anyone to a native land – only field notes for its reinvention', James Clifford has posited creolization as a model of the poetics that underscores the postmodern critical practice (1988: 173).

See also: **Diaspora; Hybridity;** *Mestizaje;* **Postmodern, postmodernity, postmodernism**

Further reading: Clifford (1988), Hall (1990a).

Critical theory

Critical theory is an umbrella term for a diverse body of social and cultural criticism that sometimes have little in common, other than a

tendency to subject their own grounding notions to an ongoing evaluation, and a belief in the emancipatory potential of social critique. A
subdivision of what is sometimes called 'Western Marxism', critical
theory operates dialectically, by identifying the internal contradictions
within a system of thought, and then pushing them to the point where
something different comes into being. Deriving from the German philosophical tradition, and associated first and foremost with the Frankfurt
School of Critical Sociology and the later work of Jürgen Habermas, the
term has since been used to refer more broadly to critical approaches in
psychoanalytic theory, poststructuralism, postmodernism, feminism,
gender studies, queer theory and cultural studies.

Conceived originally as a critical response to both the nineteenth-
century positivist epistemology and the economic determinism of classical Marxism, critical theory denies the possibility of a detached and
value-free social science and endeavours to address the historical and
ideological factors that underlie cultural and social practices. Rather
than interpreting social life as primarily determined by economic relations, members of the Frankfurt School emphasized the importance of
culture and engaged in a critical study of art and the mass media. They
brought together Marxism and Freudian psychoanalysis to develop an
understanding of the individual in relation to capitalist society. They saw
their work as practical and normative, rather than descriptive, since its
ultimate aim was not to expand a body of knowledge, but to bring about
social change. Nevertheless, Frankfurt critical theory held a rather
pessimistic view of society, believing that capitalism succeeded in overcoming many of its contradictions and absorbing the working class into
the system.

The work of Jürgen Habermas does not share the pessimism of the
first generation of critical theorists. Habermas is primarily interested in
the institutional structure of democratic society and its potential to
counter the destructive effects of capitalism and the state administration. His theory of the public sphere promotes the ideal of free rational
discussion between equals, which – although currently corroded, is
nevertheless an ideal that should be pursued.

See also: **Capitalism; Marxism, Leninism, Western Marxism; Public sphere**

Further reading: Berman (1989), Habermas (1991 [1962]; Held (1980).

Cultural analysis

Cultural analysis is an emerging field of interdisciplinary inquiry which
creatively traverses a range of humanistic disciplines, including philoso-

phy, literature, visual culture, religious studies, film and media studies, and argumentation theory. It is closely related to cultural history and cultural studies, and associated primarily with the Dutch cultural critic Mieke Bal and the Amsterdam School for Cultural Analysis (ASCA). Described as the 'cultural memory in the present', it is predicated methodologically on the critic's keen awareness of her or his socio-cultural standpoint in the present moment. Practitioners of cultural analysis examine historical data from a contemporary theoretical viewpoint, and interpret them in terms of their current meanings and relevance.

See also: **Method, methodology**

Further reading: Bal (1996), Bal and Gonzales (eds) (1999).

Cultural capital

Coined by French sociologist Pierre Bourdieu, the term refers to one of the four forms of capital – economic, social, cultural and symbolic (see Figure 3) – which have an exchange value and operate as markers of distinction in stratified societies. Originally developed in the context of education in France (Bourdieu and Passeron 1977), the concept has since been applied to a wider sphere of social relations, where cultural competences serve to create and reproduce social inequality (Bourdieu 1984).

Cultural capital, or the cultural knowledge and skills people draw upon as they engage in social life, is not distributed evenly across the social spectrum. Subordinate or marginal social groups, such as the working class or immigrants, lack knowledge of what is valued and considered appropriate within the dominant culture. This inequality is handed down from one generation to another, maintained through the

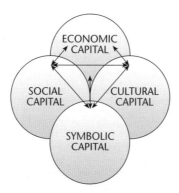

Figure 3 The four forms of capital according to Pierre Bourdieu.

education system and other social institutions. Also, the economic, social and cultural forms of capital are mutually convertible, in the sense that one form can be – and indeed often is – exchanged for another, within the broader process of social reproduction.

Bourdieu has distinguished between three principal states of cultural capital (1986):

- the 'objectified state' refers to things in somebody's possession, such as books, works of art and so on;
- the 'embodied state' refers to a person's disposition, way of thinking, or habitus;
- the 'institutionalized state' consists of the institutional acknowledgement of a person's status, for example through academic degrees and other educational qualifications.

See also: **Capitalism; Class; Cultural field; Value, value system**

Further reading: Bourdieu and Passeron (1977), Bourdieu (1984 and 1986).

Cultural citizenship

The concept of cultural citizenship was developed in the mid-1980s by a group of Mexican-American and Puerto Rican-American scholars and activists in the United States to highlight the generation of new rights by ethnic minorities' social movements. The Latino Cultural Studies Working Group regards cultural citizenship as a 'broad range of activities of everyday life through which Latinos and other groups claim space in society, define their communities and claim rights. It involves the right to retain difference, while also attaining membership in society. It also involves self-definition, affirmation and empowerment' (Flores 1997: 262).

The regulatory aspects of cultural citizenship have been of central concern in the work of cultural theorist Aihwa Ong, who has defined it as a 'dual process of self-making and being made within webs of power linked to the nation-state and civil society' (Ong 1996: 738).

John Hartley interprets cultural citizenship in terms of 'rights to identity', understood as 'membership of an actual or virtual community based not on nation but on, for example, ethnicity, gender, sexual orientation, region, age, etc.' (1999: 208). According to Hartley, mass media – notably television – have played a major role in making the emergence of this form of citizenship possible.

See also: **Citizenship; Identity, identification, identity politics; Nation, nationality, nationalism**

Further reading: Flores (1997), Hartley (1999), Ong (1996).

Cultural dominant

The term was used by Fredric Jameson to explain the continuity and discontinuity between the modern and the postmodern, by allowing a cotemporaneous presence of the features of both. The logic of cultural dominants is based on a dialectical view of history, which rejects the possibility of a clear-cut temporal rupture between different cultural formations. According to Jameson, radical 'breaks between periods do not generally involve complete changes of content, but rather the restructuration of a certain number of elements already given: features that in an earlier period or system were subordinate now become dominant' (1983: 125). This cultural dynamic has been explained by Raymond Williams in terms of the co-existence, in any given moment, of dominant, residual and emergent forms of cultural production (1980).

See also: **Dominant, residual, emergent; Modernity, modernization, modernism; Postmodern, postmodernity, postmodernism**

Further reading: Jameson (1991 [1984]).

Cultural flow

An important concept in contemporary social anthropology, flow underscores the fluidity of cultural interaction on the global scale. According to Swedish theorist Ulf Hannerz, the twentieth century marked a turning point in world cultural history, when humankind finally had to 'bid farewell to that world which could with some credibility be seen as a cultural mosaic, of separate pieces with hard, well-defined edges'. Because of the increasing intensity of cultural exchange, the world is 'becoming one not only in political and economic terms, as in the climactic period of colonialism, but in terms of its cultural construction as well; a global ecumene of persistent cultural interaction and exchange' (1991: 107).

See also: **Scape**

Further reading: Hannerz (1991).

Cultural policy

The etymology of the word 'policy', from Greek *pólis* (city), points to its semantic affinity to politics in a more general sense. Cultural policy is indeed inherently political and involves the regulation of cultural initiatives and resources, most commonly through government funding and administration of the arts sphere. According to Jim McGuigan, cultural policy is about the 'clash of ideas, institutional struggles and power relations in the production and circulation of symbolic meanings' and should not be understood as 'an ostensibly apolitical set of practical operations that are merely administered and policed by government officials' (1996: 1–2).

The increased interest in issues of cultural policy since the 1980s has led to the creation of a number of institutions dedicated to policy-related research, in countries such as Japan, Denmark, Australia, Britain and the United States (Milner and Browitt 2002: 211).

In the late 1980s and 1990s, an initiative to shift the focus of cultural studies from textual analysis to cultural policy came from a group of academics associated with the Key Centre for Cultural and Media Policy Studies at Griffith University in Queensland, Australia. The group was led by Tony Bennett, and included scholars such as Colin Mercer, Ian Hunter and Stuart Cunningham. The members have largely concurred in rejecting the neo-Gramscian strand of cultural critique as too concerned with textual analysis and thus overlooking the institutional conditions at work in the cultural field. Inspired primarily by Foucault's notion of governmentality, Bennett has interpreted culture as a 'historically specific set of institutionally embedded relations of government, in which forms of thought and conduct of extended populations are targeted for transformation' (1992a: 26). He has argued that the appropriate function of cultural studies should be to train 'cultural technicians', committed to 'modifying the functioning of culture by means of technical adjustments to its governmental deployment' (1992b: 406).

The cultural policy approach has had a considerable impact worldwide, most notably in Australia itself. However, a number of critics have questioned its viability, arguing that 'knowledge that is produced solely for official use and funded accordingly rarely questions the fundamental aims and objectives of the client organization' (McGuigan 1996: 14). Moreover, cultural policy studies have been criticized for adopting a 'top-down' rather than a 'bottom-up' approach to culture; for interpreting governmentality almost exclusively in terms of state regulation; and for constructing an untenable dichotomy between policy analysis and cultural critique (McGuigan 1996, Morris 1992, O'Regan 1992).

See also: **Discourse; Governmentality**

Further reading: Bennett (1992a), McGuigan (1996).

Culturalism

'Culturalism' refers to a humanist and literary tradition of speculation about the relationship between culture and society, which can be traced back to the eighteenth century and had its major proponents in Germany and Britain. Culturalism has had a significant impact on the early development of British cultural studies. The term itself is of recent coinage, and is mostly used to distinguish between the 'culturalist' and 'structuralist' approaches in cultural studies in the 1970s and 1980s.

In tracing the genealogy of cultural studies, critics have seen its constitution as a disciplinary formation in the confrontation between a version of humanist Marxism, also referred to as culturalism, and the anti-humanism of Althusser's structuralism. The critics commonly associated with the culturalist approach in cultural studies are Edward P. Thompson, Richard Hoggart and Raymond Williams. They rejected the economic reductionism of classical Marxism, arguing for the centrality of the human actor and experience. While acknowledging the significance and relative autonomy of the cultural realm, Althusser questioned the relevance of the subject and experience for historical inquiry. In the mid-1970s, culturalists opposed the poststructuralist versions of Althusserianism, which often integrated Foucault's theories of power, Derrida's deconstruction and Lacanian psychoanalysis. Culturalists argued that such positions could not theorize resistance, since they reduced agency to the pre-established repetition of textual or libidinal processes. *Mutatis mutandis*, poststructuralists contended that culturalists' persistent humanism and their essentialist view of class identities made it impossible to theorize the production of subjectivity as an effect of ideology.

The resolution of this impasse came through elaborations of Gramsci's concept of hegemony. Stuart Hall (1980b) interpreted hegemony as a structure of ideology, which shapes subjectivities in ways that limit the possibilities of counter-hegemonic action. With time, he assimilated this view of hegemony to a developing structuralist and poststructuralist theory.

See also: **Hegemony; Ideology; Marxism, Leninism, Western Marxism; Post-structuralism; Structuralism**

Further reading: Milner (1994), Turner (2002).

Culture

Culture is 'one of the two or three most complicated words in the English language' (Williams 1976: 87). It derives from the Latin verb *colere*, which means 'to cultivate', in the sense both of farming (Latin *cultura agri*) and of cultivation of the mind (Latin *cultura animae*) (see Figure 4). Until recently, 'culture' was understood as 'high culture' and reserved exclusively for the social elites. A different term – 'civilization' – was used to convey the set of principles, practices and their attendant mate-

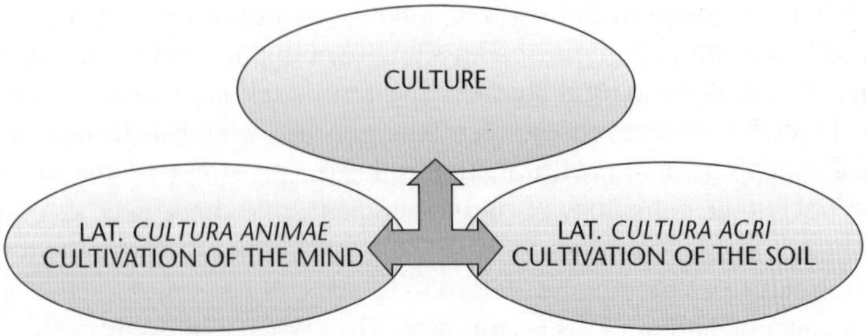

Figure 4 The etymology of the word 'culture'

rial manifestations, which enable human beings to engage with society and its institutions.

Raymond Williams (1976) traced the contemporary meaning of 'culture' to the Enlightenment period, emphasizing that our understanding of culture has evolved over time, in response to the processes of modernization. Culture initially signified skilled human activities through which nature was controlled, as is evident from compound nouns such as agriculture, horticulture, viticulture or apiculture. Encounters between Europeans and other cultures through exploration and colonial expansion allowed the term 'culture' to be applied to specific groups of people, as in 'Caribbean culture' or 'primitive culture'. Enlightenment ushered in the idea that human nature can be cultivated through civilizing processes, and 'culture' was used to refer to the activities aimed at such cultivation of the spirit, such as fine art, music, poetry, literature and dance. Culture thus became a signal of refinement and status. Williams' definition of culture as a 'signifying system' through which a social order is 'communicated, reproduced, experienced and explored' integrates the anthropological/ sociological sense of the term and the meaning of culture as 'artistic and intellectual activities' (1976: 13).

See also: **Mass culture, culture industry; Material culture; Popular culture, folk culture; Value, value system**

Further reading: Williams (1976 and 1989).

Culture jamming

The term was coined by San Francisco band Negativland in 1984, to refer to billboard alteration, and other forms of media sabotage that seek to assert the right of the audience to actively engage with and subvert hegemonic texts. It has since been adopted and used by other media activists in relation to a range of practices aimed at challenging the objectionable corporate practices and the commercial exploitation of public spaces. This form of activism is also sometimes referred to as 'guerrilla art' or 'citizens' art'. According to Canadian author and activist Naomi Klein, 'the most sophisticated culture jams are not stand alone ad parodies but interceptions – counter messages that hack into a corporation's own method of communication to send a message starkly at odds with the one that was intended' (2000: 281). Jammers increasingly utilize cyberspace to bolster their activism and develop and share their culture-jamming images.

See also: **Cyberspace; DIY culture; Hegemony; Parody, pastiche**

Further reading: Branwyn (1997).

Cyberspace

The prefix 'cyber', in words such as cyberspace, cybernetics, cyber-democracy, cyber-culture, cyber-café or cyber-sex, derives from Greek *kubernetes*, meaning steersman, and is thus etymologically related to the verb 'to govern', which has the same origin. The word 'cyberspace' was coined by a Canadian science fiction writer, William Gibson, best known for his 1984 novel entitled *Neuromancer*. In Gibson's fiction, 'cyberspace' refers to the space that computer hackers enter by connecting their minds into a computer network.

The word has since come into common usage, denoting the interconnected non-physical sites created by computer networks, the communities of users that inhabit them, and the hardware and software that make them possible. Cyberspace environments include websites, local community networks, bulletin boards, multi-user domains (MUDs), chat groups, Internet Relay Chat (IRC) channels, e-mail discussion groups and so on.

Since the mid-1980s, critics have variously questioned or praised the potential of cyberspace to foster participatory democracy, destabilize the exclusionary mechanisms of identity politics, and promote the production of new kinds of identities and subjectivities.

See also: **Democracy; Identity, identification, identity politics; Network; Virtual, virtual community, virtual reality**

Further reading: Ludlow (ed.) (1996), Rheingold (1993), Turkle (1995).

C

Cyborg

The word, which derives from 'cybernetic' and 'organism', signifies a blend between human and machine, the organic and the artificial/technological. A continuing presence in science fiction, cyborgs are also present in real life, in such forms as cyberspace, pacemakers or artificial limbs, or wherever the boundaries between the body and the machine are difficult to pin down. The US feminist Donna Haraway used the cyborg metaphor in her 1984 essay 'A Manifesto for Cyborgs'. The hybridity of the cyborg, for Haraway, has the potential to disrupt the essentialized dichotomy between nature and culture and, by extension, a whole range of other oppressive patriarchal dualisms, and 'refashion our thinking about the theoretical construction of the body as both a material entity and a discursive process' (Balsamo 1996: 11).

See also: **Body; Hybridity**

Further reading: Balsamo (1996), Halberstam and Livingston (1995), Haraway (1990 [1984]).

C

Dd

Deconstruction

The concept of deconstruction was elaborated in the late 1960s by the French poststructuralist philosopher Jacques Derrida, as a powerful critique of the major Western philosophical and metaphysical traditions. The word itself is meant to signify the practice of breaking down and then reassembling the constitutive parts of a larger entity. The aim of deconstruction is to expose and subvert the processes of construction of binary oppositions within texts and philosophical systems, and ultimately to demonstrate how language is utilized to maintain oppression and inequality. According to Belgian-born US deconstructionist literary critic Paul de Man (1979), literary texts differ from other kinds of writing, because they overtly play with the instability of meaning through their use of figurative language. In addition to philosophy and literary theory, deconstruction has had a significant impact on a range of other fields of knowledge, including art, architecture, linguistics, sociology, anthropology, feminism and postcolonial studies.

Deconstructionist critics work on the premise that all texts have an assumed ontological centre, and that they are all based on dichotomies, in which the first element is considered to be 'truer' than its binary counterpart. Deconstructionists further believe that all binaries can be overturned, because of their inherent 'undecidability', or the existence of elements that fit neither component of the binary. They endeavour to narrow down the multiple meanings of a text until they uncover its central binary, and then to demonstrate that this central binary does not fully determine the meaning of the text. Rather, texts are governed by an endless deferment of meaning, or *différance*. The aim of deconstruction then is to look for and expose the manifold disjunctions and gaps that contradict the assumed central meaning. The meanings that are left out or silenced in a particular text are referred to as 'aporias'. Deconstruction thus reverses the official meanings of a text in favour of its multiple alternative or subversive readings.

See also: **Binary opposition;** *Différance*; **Poststructuralism**

Further reading: Culler (1982), de Man (1979), Derrida (1981).

Democracy

Deriving from Greek *demos*, meaning people, and *krátos*, meaning strength, might or authority, the term refers to a system of government in which power is said to reside in the people, who can rule either directly, or through freely elected representatives. Ancient Athens had a system of direct democracy, in which eligible males were appointed to public offices by allotment, and decisions were made in meetings of the assembly, which all citizens were supposed to attend. Direct democracy, however, is only efficient in small-scale communities such as the city-state, and is not easily achieved in the modern nation-state with millions of citizens. By and large, modern states rely on a system of representative or liberal democracy, in which leaders are elected by popular vote and held accountable by their electorates. Universal suffrage and competitive political parties are thus considered to be the fundamental requirements for the functioning of a democratic system, with constitutional referenda often providing the principal way in which direct democracy is practised. The number of world democracies has significantly increased since the downfall of authoritarian regimes in Eastern Europe, sub-Saharan Africa and Latin America. Most recently, the nature of democracy has been affected by globalization and by the new ways of political interaction made possible by computer-mediated communication.

See also: **Citizenship; Globalization**

Further reading: Williams (1989).

Desire

In Jacques Lacan's psychoanalytic theory, desire is the fundamental drive that underpins human reality, and is equated with human life itself. Desire, according to Lacan, is set into motion by a longing for wholeness, which can never be fully satisfied. It is maintained by an endless displacement from object to object: as soon as an object of desire is acquired, desire moves on to a new object, in a perpetual quest to achieve the unattainable *jouissance*. The initial state of being, characterized by a mythical union between the child and the mother, or *'jouissance* of being', has to be sacrificed in compliance with the symbolic 'law of the father'. The resulting lack, or absence of *jouissance*, is thus constitutive of human existence. Arising as a consequence of the imposition of the symbolic order, desire is always socially conditioned. The law itself has a dual function: it both prohibits *jouissance* and nurtures the human desire to recapture the original state of fullness.

D

Deleuze and Guattari interpreted the psychoanalytic theory of desire as symptomatic of Western modernity, which assumes an imagined centre to the system of signification. In the case of psychoanalysis, this imagined centre is identified with the symbolic figure of the father. The postmodern interpretation of desire offered by Deleuze and Guattari is built around the concept of assemblage (French *agencement*). Desire, in this view, is both productive and produced as a consequence of a specific social assemblage, and animated by an endless interplay of creative transformation and stabilization, or, in their language, deterritorialization and reterritorialization.

See also: **Deterritorialization/reterritorialization; Identity, identification, identity politics; *Jouissance*; Psychoanalysis**

Further reading: Deleuze and Guattari (1987 [1980]), Lacan (1996 [1958–9]).

Determinism

Deriving from Old French *déterminer*, meaning 'to fix', 'determinism' refers to the philosophical doctrine that assumes that occurrences and conditions are always fully determined by a cause, or a set of circumstances that preceded them. Deterministic theories deny the autonomy or free will of the human subject. Traditional Marxist theories are often criticized for their economic determinism, which explains society in terms of the economic structure or relations of production. Other deterministic theories variously postulate that historical events and circumstances are dependent on antecedent economic, political and social conditions ('historical determinism'); that social change is brought about by technological progress ('technological determinism'); or that social phenomena exist as a reflection of biological or genetic features ('biological determinism'). Psychoanalytic theory, which contends that the development of a child's psyche is largely determined by the child's biological sex, has been severely criticized by feminists for its biological determinism (see Buhle 1998). The notion of determinism thus extends our understanding of agency beyond its human dimension.

D

Raymond Williams argued that Marxist accounts of determination misconstrued Marx's own theory of base and superstructure. According to Williams, determination should not be interpreted as involving a relationship of causality, but rather as a complex and dynamic process of 'setting limits and exerting pressures'. Society, he argued, should not be seen as the 'dead husk', which 'limits social and individual fulfilment. It is always also a constitutive process with very powerful pressures which are both expressed in political, economic, and cultural formations, and . . . . are internalized and become "individual wills"' (1977: 87).

See also: **Actor-network theory; Agency; Historicism, New Historicism; Marxism, Leninism, Western Marxism; Psychoanalysis**

Further reading: Archer (1996 [1988]), Williams (1977).

Deterritorialization/reterritorialization

Deterritorialization, or destabilization of links between culture and territory, is an important concept in diaspora and globalization studies. As individuals and groups move across the globe, they are simultaneously deterritorialized, or uprooted from one territory, and reterritorialized in another. This does not happen as a simple unilateral process of assimilation, but as a result of complex social re-articulation. The notion of territorialization, as the social process of mapping identity onto space, challenges the essentialism of national identity theories.

The concepts of deterritorialization and reterritorialization have been extensively theorized by French philosophers Gilles Deleuze and Félix Guattari. A territory, they argued, is created through deterritorialization, whereby milieu components are separated and made more autonomous, and reterritorialization, through which those components attain fresh meanings within the new territory. Deterritorialization, for Deleuze and Guattari, epitomizes the liberating feeling of disconnection, and foregrounds a delight in interstitial subjectivity. It represents the lines of flight that simultaneously make the existence of a territory possible, and destabilize its fixed character. It is always relative, because it 'has reterritorialization as its flipside or complement. An organism that is deterritorialized in relation to the exterior necessarily reterritorializes in its internal milieus' (1987 [1980]: 54).

See also: **Diaspora; Globalization; Hybridity; Identity, identification, identity politics**

Further reading: Deleuze and Guattari (1987 [1980]).

D

Diachronic/synchronic

These words both derive from the Greek noun *chronos*, meaning time, in combination with prefixes, dia- (from Greek *dia*, meaning through or over) and syn- (from Greek *sún-*, meaning together or alike) respectively. In structuralist linguistics, 'diachronic' refers to the study of the historical development of a language, while 'synchronic' signifies the study of a language, as it exists at any particular point in time. The two concepts are now more widely used to distinguish between the analysis of change and the analysis of static conditions in social sciences and other disciplines.

See also: **Différance**; **Structuralism**

Further reading: Saussure (1983 [1915].)

Dialect

The word derives from Greek *dialectos*, meaning a way of speaking. It refers to a distinctive form of a language that is used in a specific region, or by a particular social group. A dialect is sufficiently distinct in the use of idioms, vocabulary, grammar and pronunciation patterns (accents) to be considered a discrete linguistic form, yet not so different as to be classified as a separate language. It consists of any number of individual varieties of language use, called idiolects, which are regarded as having a common core. In practice, the distinction between what is a language and what is a dialect is always primarily a matter of politics, or, to quote the well-known dictum, a language is a dialect with an army and a navy. Dialects can be imagined as existing in a continuum, in which neighbouring dialects are mutually intelligible, but those that are far apart can diverge to the point of mutual incomprehensibility. Dialects that relate to social class, profession, age and gender are called sociolects. In major cities, it is possible to identify local dialect areas, for example London's East End. In recent times, increasing people mobility, mass education and the mass media have corroded the integrity of regional and social dialects.

See also: **Language**

Further reading: Crowley (1996).

Dialectic

The term derives from Greek *dialektike* (*techne*), meaning (the art) of debating. Dialectic was practised in Athens as early as the fifth century BCE, as a method of logical reasoning about abstract issues. In Plato's *Republic*, it represents the supreme kind of knowledge, which explains all phenomena by reference to the idea of the good. Aristotle described the dialectical method as having three stages: a statement or thesis, a number of arguments to prove or disprove it, and finally a resolution based on the balance of the evidence offered.

In modern European philosophy and social thought, dialectic has been central to the works of German philosopher Georg Wilhelm Friedrich Hegel (1770–1831) and to Marxist philosophy overall. Hegel understood dialectic as a constant interplay of thesis, antithesis and synthesis (see Figure 5), which was not only a method of reasoning, but also a principal driving force in thought, history and life more generally. Hegel's method

D

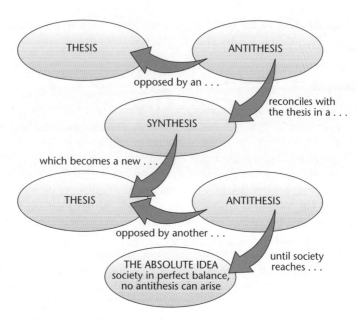

Figure 5   The Hegelian dialectic

was espoused and elaborated by Marxists in their philosophy of dialectical materialism, based on a fundamental belief that change in history occurs through the struggle of opposites, notably class struggle.

See also: **Marxism, Leninism, Western Marxism**

Dialogism

Although it figures prominently in nineteenth-century neo-Kantian philosophy, dialogism is today primarily associated with the work of the Russian literary scholar Mikhail Bakhtin. In his book *Problems of Dostoevsky's Poetics*, Bakhtin praised the Russian novelist for creating texts where several voices conversed and responded to each other, without any one of them dominating or silencing the others. According to Bakhtin, a 'plurality of independent and unmerged voices and consciousnesses, a genuine polyphony of fully valid voices is in fact the chief characteristic of Dostoevsky's novels' (1984 [1929]). Bakhtin contrasted the dialogic nature of Dostoevsky's novels with the monologism of traditional authorial texts, which tend to be dominated by a single voice. In Bakhtin's work, the logic of dialogism is applied not only to literary texts, but also to linguistic utterances, the social world, and individual consciousness.

The notion of dialogism is closely related to heteroglossia. While the latter should be understood as the conflicting multiplicity of languages that constitutes the 'condition of our existence', the former is the 'necessary mode of knowledge in such a world, a form of relationship between or among different languages that, like dialectics, defines a sort of logic' (Kershner 1989: 15–16).

Bakhtin's account of dialogism has had a profound impact on a number of disciplines, including linguistics, literary studies, anthropology, psychology and social theory. Most notably, it was the springboard for Julia Kristeva's theory of intertextuality, which replaces 'Bakhtin's idea of several voices inside an utterance with the notion of several texts within a text' (2002: 8). The concept of dialogism is also useful in theorizing new interactive technologies, which challenge the notion of knowledge as emanating from a single authoritative source.

See also: **Carnivalesque; Heteroglossia; Intertextuality; Text**

Further reading: Holquist (1990).

Diaspora

Deriving from Greek *dia*, meaning 'over', and *speírein*, meaning 'to sow or scatter', the term originally referred to the scattering of a population, within the broader context of colonization and migration. It has been traditionally deployed to designate the dispersal of the Jews since the time of Babylonian captivity in the sixth century BCE. Its meaning has since been extended to pertain more broadly to other forms of transnational mobility, such as those that resulted from the transatlantic slave trade, indentured labour and the more recent migratory patterns associated with globalization.

An authoritative account of global diasporas in a historical perspective has been provided by the British sociologist Robin Cohen (1987). Diasporas, argues Cohen, normally exhibit several of the following features: (1) an often traumatic dispersal from an original homeland; (2) alternatively, the expansion from a homeland in search of work, in pursuit of trade or to further colonial ambitions; (3) a collective memory and myth about the homeland; (4) an idealization of the supposed ancestral home; (5) a return movement; (6) a strong ethnic group consciousness sustained over a long time; (7) a troubled relationship with host societies; (8) a sense of solidarity with co-ethnic members in other countries; and (9) the possibility of a distinctive creative, enriching life in tolerant host countries (1987: 180). In an attempt to transcend the narrow definition of 'diaspora' in terms of the traumatic experience of

D

the Jewish people, Cohen has developed a more comprehensive typology of global diasporic movements, which includes the victim/refugee diaspora, the imperial/colonial diaspora, the labour/service diaspora, the trade/business/professional diaspora, and the cultural/hybrid/postmodern diaspora (1987: 78).

In cultural studies, 'diaspora' has been interpreted as having a critical edge similar to that attributed to the notion of hybridity. Diasporic experience challenges the essentialist accounts of identity as a fixed condition and the notion of culture as bound to a particular territory. In Paul Gilroy's influential book *The Black Atlantic*, for example, it is regarded as a 'privileged standpoint from which certain useful and critical perceptions about the modern world become more likely' (1993: 111).

See also: **Globalization; Hybridity; Identity, identification, identity politics; Nation, nationality, nationalism**

Further reading: Braziel and Mannur (2003), Cohen (1987).

Différance

Différance is a neologism that combines two meanings of the French verb *différer*, to differ and to defer. It was coined in the 1960s by French poststructuralist philosopher Jacques Derrida, to refer to the infinite displacement of meaning along a chain of signifiers. To quote Mark Currie, *différance* is a 'notoriously unpindownable concept, but in fact it means something very close to "unpindownability" . . . something like the opposite of presence, or even the opposite of concepthood' (2004: 45). The general thrust of *différance* – which Derrida in fact insists is neither a word nor a concept (1982: 7) – is to signal that linguistic signs are only meaningful in relationship with other signs, and that presence of meaning is always deferred from one sign to another in an endless sequence. Derrida's model of *différance* can also be understood as a critique of the fundamental orientation in structuralist analysis, which privileged the spatial or synchronic structure of the linguistic system over its temporal or diachronic dimension. It implies that signs are never fixed, but always contain the traces of the signs that surround them, that have preceded them, and that come after them.

See also: **Deconstruction; Poststructuralism**

Further reading: Derrida (1974 [1967]).

Difference

For ages, difference has been a fundamental organizing principle of Western culture. Class, race, ethnicity, gender and sexuality have provided a fertile ground for cultural self-definition. The notion of difference has underpinned identity politics, within which each group asserts its own distinct character and fashions its politics accordingly to address the interests of the group. In postmodern society, difference has become more fragmented and slippery than ever before, undermining any essentialized sense of identity. Within the consumer culture of late capitalism, difference itself has become commodified, in the sense that the styles and objects labelled as 'different' attract strong demand in today's market.

In structuralist and poststructuralist theory, difference is the fundamental force that governs the generation of meaning in language and society. In Saussure's structuralist linguistics, signs are meaningful only in so far as they are different from other signs within the language system. Structuralist anthropology applies the same principle to the study of cultural phenomena, such as kinship relations, customs, food preparation and rites of passage. These phenomena are understood as discrete units of culture, or signs, that are not meaningful in themselves, but draw their meaning from the system in which they operate. Poststructuralism challenged the structuralist assumption that the meaning of a sign can ever be self-present, arguing that it can only be understood as perpetually slipping from one sign to the next.

The nexus between difference and identity has been theorized in Lacanian psychoanalysis. Within this paradigm, identity is understood as a function of difference and is therefore always seen as multiple and under construction. Postcolonial critics have employed poststructuralist theories of 'difference' to destabilize and deconstruct Western liberal ideas of an 'essential' truth and humanity. Feminists have argued that men have repressed women's differences and employed them to maintain patriarchal rule. Feminism of sexual difference is based on a belief that women need to re-appropriate all their differences – not only in terms of sex, but also in terms of class, race, age, ethnicity, sexual preferences and lifestyles – in order to shatter the foundations of patriarchal society.

Within cultural studies, difference itself is understood as a fluid category, which is produced and reproduced in specific social circumstances. In contemporary society, difference is closely related to the forces of globalization and lacks a 'fixed political inscription: sometimes it is progressive, sometimes it is emergent, sometimes it is critical, sometimes it is revolutionary' (Hall 2000: 217). A positive re-inscription of difference, based on the principles of coupling and inclusion rather than exclusion, is associated with the notions of hybridity, creolization and diaspora.

D

See also: **Alterity; Binary opposition; Creolization; Diaspora; Hybridity; Identity, identification, identity politics; Poststructuralism; Psychoanalysis; Structuralism**

Further reading: Currie (2004).

Discourse

Deriving from Latin *discursus*, which means running to and fro, the term has a complex history and a wide spectrum of critical applications. In contemporary popular usage, it is commonly associated with the act of conversing, or speaking at length about a particular topic. As a critical concept, discourse has become standard currency in a range of disciplines, including linguistics, philosophy, sociology and cultural theory. In linguistics, it refers to an extended series of language utterances that constitute a single speech event, like a conversation, joke or lecture.

In the writings of Michel Foucault, 'discourse' refers to a distinct configuration of representations, institutions and practices through which meanings are produced and authorized. Discourse, according to Foucault, is the 'site of conjunction of power and knowledge', which alters 'its form and significance depending on who is speaking, her/his position of power, and the institutional context in which the speaker happens to be situated' (1980: 100). Foucault paid particular attention to the discourses of sexuality and madness, both of which he saw as socially constructed. There is, he contended, no such thing as madness or sexuality except as humans construct ideas about them through discourse. Discourses are, according to Foucault, neither the product of a single author, nor confined to any individual text or practice. Rather, they travel through different contexts and cut across a range of subject positions and areas of social and institutional practice. They always epitomize a particular configuration of power and knowledge and act performatively to naturalize and universalize a particular worldview. Discourse-specific 'regimes of truth' define what is considered legitimate and valid within a particular discourse. Discourse, in other words, 'defines and produces the objects of our knowledge. It governs the way that a topic can be meaningfully talked about and reasoned about. It also influences how ideas are put into practice and used to regulate the conduct of others' (Hall 2001: 72).

See also: **Agency; Discourse analysis; Governmentality; Panopticism, synopticism; Power**

Further reading: Macdonell (1986), Mills (1997), Wetherell et al. (2001).

Discourse analysis

The term refers to a range of qualitative research strategies that have their origins in linguistics, anthropology and literary studies. Discourse analysis has gained currency with the emergence of the concept of discourse as a key explanatory category from the 1960s onwards. Its principal aim is to interpret language as it is embedded in a social and historical context. There is no fixed set of rules the researcher needs to follow in analysing discourse. Rather, the tools and strategies of research always depend on the specific aims and research questions of each individual project. There are, however, several theoretical considerations and general guidelines that inform this type of research in varying degrees. Some of these are outlined below (Parker 1992: 6–20):

- Discourse lives in texts: Consider everything to be text and explore the connotations, allusions and implications that the text evokes.
- A discourse is about objects: Discourses are practices that systematically form the objects of which they speak.
- A discourse contains subjects: Specify what types of persons are talked about and speculate what rights they have to speak.
- A discourse is a system of meanings: 'Map' a picture of the world this discourse represents.
- A discourse refers to other discourses: Set different discourses against each other and see what objects they form.
- A discourse reflects on its own way of speaking: Refer to other texts to elaborate the discourse.
- Discourses are historically located: Look at how and where the discourses emerged and describe how they have changed.
- Discourses support institutions: Identify institutions that are reinforced when this discourse is used, and identify the institutions that are subverted when this discourse appears.
- Discourses reproduce power relations: Identify which categories of persons gain and lose from applying the discourse.
- Discourses have ideological effects: Show how a discourse connects with other discourses, which of them sanction oppression, and how dominant groups prevent those who use subjugated discourses from 'making history'.

D

To summarize, discourse analysis is concerned with identifying the internal features of discourses, the relation of discourses with each other, and the role of discourses in the constitution of identities, social hierarchies, practices and behaviours. Since discourses are not clearly delimited entities, they can only be studied in so far as they manifest themselves in a variety of texts, such as transcribed conversations, books, articles, policy documents, instruction manuals, laws, advertisements or movies. Discourse analysis tracks ideological discourses across a range of texts, practices, behaviours and institutions. In doing so, it seeks to destabilize and ultimately overturn the oppressive effects of institutionalized power relations.

See also: **Discourse; Method, methodology**

Further reading: Barker and Galasinski (2001), Gee (1999).

DiY culture

The term 'DiY (do-it-yourself) culture' refers to various counter-cultural forms of youth activism that have emerged in a number of countries worldwide since the 1990s. Some of the practices associated with DiY culture are raves, independent music, squatting, graffiti, culture jamming, hacktivism (computer hacking with a political purpose), and independent media. Rather than passively absorbing the products offered to them by cultural industries, participants in DiY cultures use interactive technologies and other means at their disposal to produce a culture of their own. They see their activities as a critique of and challenge to the dichotomy between producers and consumers, which underlies commercial culture. Furthermore, the spread of DiY cultures has had an impact on the evolution of citizenship, because it opened up new possibilities for self-determination based on voluntary cultural allegiances, rather than on an established set of obligations to a particular state (Hartley 1999).

See also: **Author, authorship; Citizenship; Consumption; Culture jamming**

Dominant, residual, emergent

In Raymond Williams' elaboration of Gramsci's theory of hegemony, cultural formations at any given historical moment are characterized by a dynamic interplay among dominant, residual and emergent cultural forces. The dominant are those tendencies that are most prominent in a particular cultural formation, such as the forces of capitalism at the present moment. The residual forces represent a residue 'of some previous social and cultural institution or formation' (1977: 122), but are still practised and experienced in the present. According to Williams, the residual should be distinguished from the archaic aspect of culture, which is 'wholly recognised as an element of the past' (ibid.). The emergent forces, on the other hand, are those that introduce meanings, practices, values and relationships that are distinctly novel, or genuinely different. Both the residual and the emergent tendencies can be alternative to the dominant culture, in which case they don't represent a real challenge and are largely tolerated by society. If, however, they are

D

oppositional to a dominant culture, they represent a genuine threat to the existing social order. Williams was alert to the difficulty of distinguishing between the properly emergent cultural forces, and those forms that are merely novel and thus remain within the dominant paradigm.

See also: Hegemony

Further reading: Williams (1977).

Doxa

Doxa is the Greek word for 'popular opinion'. In Pierre Bourdieu's work, the concept of doxa refers to the tendency of every society to naturalize, or take for granted, aspects of its own worldview and political order. A doxic society, according to Bourdieu, is one wherein the 'established cosmological and political order is perceived not as arbitrary, i.e., as one possible order among others, but as a self-evident and natural order which goes without saying and therefore goes unquestioned' (1977 [1972]: 166). Doxa needs to be distinguished from orthodoxy, which is understood as the endeavour to defend the doxa, and from heterodoxy, which is the effort to challenge the naturalized assumptions of the doxa.

See also: **Discourse**

Further reading: Bourdieu (1977 [1972], 1990).

D

Écriture Féminine

French for 'feminine writing', the term, developed primarily by the French writer, critic and feminist theorist Hélène Cixous, signifies a manner of writing that eludes the hierarchical binary logic inscribed in the patriarchal symbolic order. The concept of feminine writing, although not named as such, is also present in the work of the French philosopher Luce Irigaray and the Bulgarian-born linguist and psycho-analyst Julia Kristeva.

Feminine writing, argues Cixous, renounces the demands of the self and the dictates of the established order. It begins by assuming the position of the other and proceeds to faithfully inscribe life as it is. Cixous interprets the terms 'masculine' and 'feminine' as behavioural economies that are not simple reflections of biological sex. The mascu-line economy, she suggests, implies a logic of compliance, fear and yearning for control; by contrast, the feminine position is marked by generosity, openness and a refusal to destroy. These two economies are not stable categories, but rather, exist in a constant state of flux. Although they are accessible to men as well as women, Cixous believes that, on biological as well as cultural grounds, women are more prone to adopt a feminine position than men. Her examples of *écriture fémi-nine*, however, include male writers such as Shakespeare, as well as female writers such as the Russian poet Marina Tsvetayeva.

In psychoanalytic terms, *écriture féminine* involves establishing a connection with one's primordial state of being before socialization. This is a state of inclusivity, which is parallel to a feminine writer's refusal to discriminate between possible meanings and modes of repre-sentation. In her own writing, Cixous has employed unconventional vocabulary, syntax and typography to convey the multiplicity of meaning characteristic of feminine writing.

See also: **Binary opposition; Imaginary, symbolic, real; Patriarchy**

Further reading: Cixous (1994).

Ego

See **Id, Superego, Ego**.

Empire

Political philosophers Antonio Negri and Michael Hardt have used the term 'Empire' to describe a new global political order that undermines the old paradigm of national sovereignty under the influence of global-ization. Empire, according to Negri and Hardt, is not to be confounded with imperialism, which is intimately related to the now vanishing para-digm of national sovereignty and the struggle for territory and resources among the competing nation-states. Rather, Empire should be seen as the successor to the modern, imperialist form of control. Empire does not dismantle the existing nation-states, but rather subsumes them into its own 'mixed constitution', which is constituted by the interplay of different forms of political agency: 'monarchic' forms such as the global superpowers and major supranational institutions; 'aristocratic' forms represented by a majority of nation-states and multinational corpora-tions; and the 'democratic' forces represented by entities such as the United Nations General Assembly, religious organizations, the media, and non-governmental organizations (NGOs). Negri and Hardt regard the politics of hybridity as insufficient in itself to contest Empire, as it in fact represents the very driving force of the new imperial order. Empire can only be subverted by what Hardt and Negri, after Spinoza, call the 'multitude': a spontaneous association of free and productive singulari-ties outside of the rubric of any organizing body or ideology.

See also: **Agency; Globalization; Nation, nationality, nationalism; Postcolonialism, neo-colonialism**

Further reading: Hardt and Negri (2000 and 2004).

Encoding/decoding

In semiotics, the term 'encoding' refers to the generative process whereby signs are endowed with meaning and structured into codes in the course of the production of a specific text. 'Decoding' represents the interpretation of meaning in the process of consumption.

In a 1973 essay that is commonly regarded as a turning point in the conceptualization of the audience within cultural studies, Stuart Hall rejected the earlier theoretical paradigms, which saw communication as a one-way transfer of meaning from the sender to the receiver. He developed a model of the communicative process that involved four

E

distinct stages: production, circulation, distribution or consumption, and reproduction. Each stage, he argued, is relatively autonomous and marked by its own 'conditions of existence' (Hall 1980c: 129), which leave their imprint on the code itself. The possibilities of interpretation, however, are never unlimited, since each stage has the effect of constructing certain 'limits and parameters' within which the next stage in the circuit will operate. There has to be some degree of correspondence between encoding and decoding, 'otherwise we could not speak of an effective communicative exchange at all'. However, as Hall contended, this correspondence is never a given condition, but rather, a product of an 'articulation between two distinct moments' (p. 136). Furthermore, since each stage in the communication circuit is governed by its own structure of dominance, and since each stage delimits to some extent the possibilities of the next, the process of communication itself is deeply implicated in reproducing patterns of domination.

Hall identified three standpoints from which a message may be decoded: the dominant-hegemonic position, or the 'preferred' reading, in which the encoded meanings and the decoded meanings largely overlap; the negotiated reading, which privileges a dominant interpretation, while 'reserving the right to make a more negotiated application to local conditions' (p. 137); and finally the oppositional reading, which 'retotalizes the message within some alternative framework of reference' (p. 138). The three positions are never distinct or stable, and are always determined by the broader social cultural context.

See also: **Agency; Audience; Communication; Consumption**

Further reading: Hall (1980c).

Enculturation/acculturation

In cultural anthropology, the term 'enculturation' refers to the process of internalizing the basic knowledge, beliefs and patterns of behaviour of the surrounding culture. Anthropologists generally distinguish between enculturation, which refers to the life-long process of cultural learning, and acculturation, which involves contact between different cultures.

See also: **Transculturation, transculturality, transculturalism**

Enlightenment, the

Also referred to as the 'Age of Reason', the Enlightenment is a period in European intellectual and cultural history that was characterized by a strong belief in reason, distrust of religious and traditional authority, and a gradual formation of the ideals of a liberal and democratic society. The

Enlightenment worldview, which implied a strong faith in the possibilities of rationality and scientific knowledge, underpinned many fields of intellectual endeavour, including literature, the arts, science, religion, and philosophy.

The dawn of the Enlightenment can be traced back to the works of the English philosophers Francis Bacon and Thomas Hobbes and the French philosopher René Descartes in the seventeenth century. It is the eighteenth century, however, that is commonly put forward as the peak of the Enlightenment period. In Germany, the Enlightenment extended from the mid-seventeenth century to the early nineteenth century and included poets and philosophers such as Johann Wolfgang von Goethe, Friedrich Schiller and Immanuel Kant. In France, it was primarily associated with philosophers Jean-Jacques Rousseau, Denis Diderot, Charles Montesquieu and Voltaire, whose work provided the intellectual basis for the French Revolution. In Scotland, the philosopher David Hume introduced the experimental method into the study of the human mind; and the political economist Adam Smith theorized the benefits of a free-market economy.

The legacy of the Enlightenment project – its mechanisms of social control, utopianism, individualism, Eurocentrism and universalism – has been criticized from different perspectives from the early twentieth century onwards.

See also: **Capitalism; Eurocentrism, Westocentrism; Modernity, modernization, modernism**

Further reading: Adorno and Horkheimer (2002 [1947]).

Episteme

Epistêmê is the Greek word for knowledge, as opposed to *technê*, which is usually translated as either craft or art. Plato distinguished between *epistêmê* , or a superior knowledge based on absolute certainty or reality, and *doxa*, an inferior knowledge based on opinion, probability and appearances.

Episteme is a key concept in Michel Foucault's discourse analysis, especially in his study of the human sciences such as linguistics, psychology and sociology. In Foucault's work, 'episteme' refers to the structure of knowledge that unites the discursive practices at work during a specific stage in history. Foucault defined the episteme as the 'totality of relations that can be discovered, for a given period, between the sciences when one analyzes them at the level of discursive regularities' (1972 [1969]: 191). Although lacking any ultimate unity, episteme has the power to enable or delimit the discourse of the period. Foucault identified three epistemes: the 'sixteenth-century episteme', in which the world is conceived of as a divine 'text' bearing the imprint of God; the 'classical episteme', in which the function of knowledge is to order and classify the world; and the 'modern episteme', in which knowledge is structured into empirical sciences around 'man' as the knowing subject. At the end of the modern episteme, Foucault famously predicted, the human subject will disappear 'like a face drawn in sand at the edge of the sea' (1971 [1966]: 387).

See also: **Discourse; Discourse analysis; Doxa; Knowledge**

Further reading: Foucault (1971 [1966] and 1972 [1969].

Essentialism

Essentialism is the philosophical doctrine that all phenomena have essential properties that define their nature. Essentialists believe that it is possible to demonstrate the truth of a scientific theory by uncovering the essence that underlies the appearance of a phenomenon. For instance, Marxist theory is often criticized as essentialist because of its claim that all social phenomena are ultimately reducible to economic causes. Poststructuralist theory has disputed the essentialist worldview by claiming that theories are in fact socially constructed and dependent on the contingent structures of power.

Essentialism also presumes that groups or categories of objects have certain defining features shared by all members of the group. With regard to identity categories, such as race, ethnicity or gender, the features that are considered 'essential' within each category are described as primordial and immutable, and emphasized over all other 'non-essential' qualities. This kind of essentialism is based on ideas of a coherent totality of individual social identities, and of a mutual antagonism between them. Essentialist discourses, such as colonialism or Orientalism, have functioned to maintain and strengthen hegemonic control. The rejection of this form of essentialism is predicated on a belief that identities are neither stable nor unified, but rather fragmented and dynamic, and subject to negotiation.

The notion of 'strategic essentialism' refers to the political credo espoused by some feminist and postcolonial critics, who maintain that essentialist arguments have to be deployed strategically in order to counter the effects of patriarchal, colonial and neocolonial domination (see, for example, Spivak 1984–85).

See also: **Feminism; Hegemony; Identity, identification, identity politics; Marxism, Leninism, Western Marxism; Postcolonialism, neo-colonialism; Poststructuralism**

Further reading: Barker (2003).

E

Ethnicity

The Greek word *éthnos*, translated either as people, nation or tribe, typically signified non-Greek peoples, or foreigners. The Greek translators of the Bible used this term to refer to Gentiles or heathens. The original connotation of 'foreignness' is reflected in the rather objectionable popular usage of the word 'ethnic' in current English, as applied only to minority groups and never to the majority population.

As a critical concept, ethnicity manifests itself as a collective consciousness of shared origins and traditions, based on real or perceived commonalities in language use, way of life and forms of material and immaterial culture. The noun 'ethnicity' appeared in the English language as late as the 1940s, as a replacement for the word 'race' after the latter had become associated with the genocidal horrors of the Nazi regime. Later in the period following the Second World War, ethnicity itself came to be regarded as an unwelcome vestige of pre-modern times on its way to extinction. However, the rise of ethnic nationalisms in the 1980s was a clear sign that ethnicity remained a salient factor on the global political scene. Ethnicity has been the fundamental principle of identity formation among the formerly colonized peoples, and has been instrumental in mobilizing identities at a level below the nation-state in the face of globalization, as exemplified by the recent disintegration of countries such as the Soviet Union, Czechoslovakia or former Yugoslavia.

There are two distinct views on the nature of ethnic affiliation in the scholarly literature: primordialist approaches understand ethnicity as a stable category, rooted in deep-seated primeval sentiments; social constructionist or instrumentalist theories see it as a functional adaptation to changing socio-political circumstances. The relationship between ethnicity and nationalism is attracting much scholarly interest in political science and sociology. Some contend that nations are built around constructed myths of a common ethnic past, while others claim that nationalist movements can only flourish if they emerge from a genuine sense of belonging to a particular ethnic group.

The accounts of ethnicity within cultural studies have consistently argued that ethnic sentiments are historically, culturally and politically constructed. In a seminal essay entitled 'Minimal Selves' (1987), Stuart Hall placed ethnicity at the centre of debates about identity, representation and belonging. He praised those who have adopted a 'new conception of ethnicity as a kind of counter to the old discourses of nationalism or national identity' (1996a: 118). While insisting on their specific differences, Hall says his new ethnicities are 'not necessarily armour-plated against other identities'. They are neither 'tied to fixed, permanent, unal-

E

terable oppositions', nor 'wholly defined by exclusion' (p. 119). Hybrid in nature, they are increasingly the standard in postmodern societies.

See also: **Globalization; Hybridity; Identity, identification, identity politics; Nation, nationality, nationalism; Race**

Further reading: Hall (1987).

Ethnocentrism

The term signifies the predisposition to view another culture from the perspective of one's own. Ethnocentrism also often involves the belief that one's own ethnic group is in some way superior to other groups. Concrete expressions of ethnocentrism may involve proselytizing, discrimination, hostility and violence.

Ethnocentrism goes against the grain of the liberal worldview based on Enlightenment ideals, which attempts to downplay differences by appealing to a universal humanity. Social sciences have traditionally censured ethnocentrism as an impediment to comprehending other cultures. The pioneers of modern anthropology such as Franz Boas and Bronisław Malinowski argued that doing away with the ethnocentric understanding of other cultures was one of anthropology's principal tasks. The approach that seeks to avoid the cultural bias of the researcher is called 'cultural relativism'. More recently, poststructuralism has problematized the possibility of knowledge that is not culturally grounded. Under the sway of poststructuralist theory, US pragmatist philosopher Richard Rorty (1991) has criticized the liberal notion of cultural relativism and claimed that a self-reflexive ethnocentric outlook based on broad-mindedness, tolerance and solidarity, is not only possible, but also necessary.

See also: **Eurocentrism, Westocentrism; Poststructuralism; Pragmatism**

E

Ethnography

Ethnography is a methodological paradigm used in anthropology, sociology and cultural studies to produce in-depth accounts of the behaviours and practices of clearly defined social groups. Ethnographers typically employ qualitative research methods, such as participant observation, focus groups and in-depth interviews. Ethnographic data usually consist of the researcher's written field notes and the audio and video recordings of interviews, group discussions and informal conversations. Rather than relying on a predetermined analytical framework, ethnographers build their approach gradually, through continuous interactions with their informants. The myth that ethnography can provide a transparent account of a culture 'as it really is' has been dispelled in the wake of poststructuralism, which has emphasized the social and cultural contingency of knowledge construction.

Ethnographers have characteristically examined territorially bounded and relatively homogeneous cultural groups by immersing themselves in the host culture over an extended period of time. A notable example of such practice is Bronisław Malinowski's sojourn amongst the Trobriand Islanders in Melanesia in the early decades of the twentieth century. In the wake of accelerating globalization, the viability of the traditional dwelling-based ethnography has been increasingly challenged on a theoretical level. The US cultural anthropologist James Clifford, among others, has called for the development of new 'multi-sited ethnographies', or 'ethnographies of travel', which would be better suited to account for the fluid and hybrid nature of contemporary cultures.

See also: **Method, methodology; Thick description**

Further reading: Clifford (1988, 1997), Clifford and Marcus (eds) (1886).

Eurocentrism, Westocentrism

The two terms are roughly interchangeable, and refer to the way of thinking that consistently posits Europe or the 'West' – or rather, a certain constructed notion of the Western experience – as a universal ideal to be emulated by the rest of the world in most spheres of human existence. In contemporary popular usage, the notion of the 'West' does not designate geographical location, but rather, a 'type of society' or a 'level of development'. Although it may be true that what we mean by the 'West' today did first develop in Western Europe, the 'West' is 'no longer only in Europe, and not all of Europe is in "the West"' (Hall 1996b: 185).

The discourse of Eurocentrism seeks to corroborate the idea of Europe's uniqueness and universality by constructing commonalities based on Christian faith, Greco-Roman heritage, and the philosophical and political ideals of the Enlightenment. The Eurocentric discourse not only imagines the 'European West' as the world of 'material wealth and power, including military might'; the site of the 'triumph of the scientific spirit, rationality, and practical efficiency'; and the world of 'tolerance, diversity of opinions, respect for human rights and democracy, concern for equality . . . and social justice' (Amin 1989: 107).

The Eurocentric discourse was used to justify and promote Europe's colonial projects and maintain the hegemonic position of the West on

E

the global scale. A consistent critique of Eurocentrism is a central concern in postcolonial studies. The Indian-born historian and post-colonial theorist Dipesh Chakrabarty has coined the phrase 'provincial-izing Europe' (2000), to refer to the impetus, within postcolonial studies, to dismantle the Eurocentric discourse of modernity by demonstrating that its fundamental concepts are not transparent or universally valid, but rather, contingent and socially and politically motivated.

See also: **Colonialism; Enlightenment, the; Ethnocentrism; Orientalism; Postcolonialism, neo-colonialism; Tropicalization/s, tropicopolitan**

Further reading: Chakrabarty (2000), Hall (1996b).

Everyday

The generation and organization of meaning in everyday experiences as diverse as walking, talking, sleeping, shopping and telephone conversa-tions has traditionally been studied by a branch of sociology called microsociology. As a theoretical concept associated with popular culture, the everyday has been progressively gaining ground as a major object of research in cultural studies.

French Marxist sociologist Henri Lefebvre (1991 [1947]) argued that the separation of work, household and leisure under capitalism has had the effect of commodifying and alienating daily life. He emphasized the imperative of changing the social and cultural conditions of everyday life in order to overcome alienation. The promise of transformation, accord-ing to Lefebvre, could be found within the everyday itself, particularly in those instances of everyday experience such as festival or carnival, that can serve to destabilize cultural values.

A major contribution to the theory of the everyday has been given by French social critic and philosopher Michel de Certeau, who interprets the cultures of everyday life as resistant to representation and rational categorization. He understands the everyday in a psychoanalytic sense as the place of the Other, that is, excluded from the organized structures of culture and society and ultimately unknowable. The distinction between everyday life and the rationalized and institutionalized social system corresponds to de Certeau's distinction between the tactical and the strategic, where the tactic is a calculated action that 'must play on and with a terrain imposed on it and organized by the law of a foreign power'. The tactics, says de Certeau, 'must vigilantly make use of the cracks that particular conjunctions open in the surveillance of the proprietary powers. It poaches in them. It creates surprises in them. It can be where it is least expected. It is a guileful ruse' (1984 [1980]: 37). A strategy, on the other hand, is possible only when a 'subject with will and power (a business, an army, a city, a scientific institution)' delimits its own position in relation to 'an exteriority composed of targets or threats (customers or competitors, enemies, the country surrounding the city, objectives and objects of research, etc.)' (pp. 35–6).

Certeau thus imagines everyday life as a realm of resistance, which obstructs and disperses the flow of domination. However, the resistance of the everyday is not imagined here as the inverse of power, bur rather as a plurality of micro-powers that operate within the conditions imposed by the social system. Furthermore, the politics of the everyday can only be truly grasped through a critical and methodological practice that operates 'from within' the everyday itself and embodies its polyphonic quality. The pre-requisite for such an undertaking, according to Certeau, is the invention of a poetics that could articulate the resourcefulness of everyday activities.

See also: **Consumption; Mass culture, culture industries; Popular culture, folk culture; Space, place**

Further reading: de Certeau (1984 [1980]), Lefebvre (1991 [1947]).

E

Family

The family is a basic unit of social structure characterized by a specific set of household arrangements and systems of kinship. It is neither universal nor biologically determined, but rather, contingent and socially constructed. Some of the functions most commonly associated with the family are reproducing, protecting and socializing children, providing emotional reassurance for adults and regulating daily life and social behaviour.

The nuclear family, which consists of parents and their natural or adopted children living in the same household, is considered to be the standard in industrial societies. This family model is distinguished from the extended family, which, in addition to parents and their children, also includes different other relatives who share the household with them. In societies where divorce is widespread, common family structures include the single-parent family, and the compound or melded family, which includes children from the previous marriage or marriages of one or both of the partners. The patriarchal model of the nuclear family underwent a profound crisis in the twentieth century, with the considerable increase of female participation in education, the labour force, and politics.

Feminists have condemned the role of the nuclear family in establishing, maintaining and legitimating gender-based power disparities. Gay and lesbian campaigns for the legalization and equal treatment of homosexual partnerships have further destabilized the normative understanding of family relationships. More generally, it could be argued that, in late capitalism, the certainties of the nuclear family model have given way to a definitional crisis characteristic of the 'postmodern condition'.

In cultural studies, research into the production and consumption of cultural texts has taken into account the social processes at work in the family unit. A frequently quoted example is David Morley's study of television viewing as a family leisure activity (1986) that bears the imprint of the power structure within the family or household.

See also: **Audience; Feminism; Gender; Patriarchy; Queer, queer theory**

Further reading: Barker (2000), Morley (1986).

Femininity

The term refers to the culturally specific and normative constructions of womanhood, as opposed to the biological attributes of the female sex. Femininity is a fundamental concept in feminism, gender studies, sexuality studies and queer theory.

Angela McRobbie (1993) has identified a profound transformation of the 'modes of femininity', which has taken place among young British women over the last two decades. McRobbie finds evidence of an increased fluidity of the meaning of femininity at a number of levels, including social institutions, commercial mass culture and a range of youth subcultures. While upholding strongly feminist values in their everyday conversations, the young British women of the 1990s refused to be labelled as feminist and were in fact more prone to maintain an exaggerated image of conventional femininity, at least as an outward image. This has led McRobbie to conclude that the 'old binary opposition which put femininity at one end of the political spectrum and feminism at the other is no longer an accurate way of conceptualizing young female experience' (1993: 409).

See also: **Audience; Feminism; Gender; Patriarchy; Sexuality**

Further reading: McRobbie (1993).

Feminism

The term is used to refer to a vast array of interrelated political agendas and theoretical frameworks that share a fundamental interest in the experience and the status of women in society. By critically examining and revising the basic methods of knowledge construction and by elaborating new categories of analysis, feminist theory has made significant contributions to a range of disciplines. The feminist inflection in disciplinary practices is acknowledged in phrases such as 'feminist epistemology', 'feminist history', 'feminist literary theory', 'feminist psychoanalysis' and 'feminist cultural studies'.

It has become conventional to periodize feminism in terms of three major 'waves': the first wave, in the nineteenth and early twentieth centuries, was concerned mainly with the achievement of equal legal and political rights for women; the second, in the 1960s and 1970s, focused on the issues of reproductive and sexual freedom and consciousness raising through the establishment of women's studies in higher education; finally, the third wave, which emerged in the early 1990s, is characterized by its acknowledgement of diversity within its own ranks and its rejection of the possibility of a single feminist stand-point. This fragmentation is reflected in the widespread use of the plural form – feminisms – to refer to the myriad of traditions that anchor their political objectives in feminist values and ideals.

As the feminist social and political movement has gradually trans-formed from a basic struggle for women's franchise to a more far-reaching enterprise endeavouring to achieve equal opportunity in all spheres of life, so feminist analysis has evolved through a range of theoretical frameworks: liberalism, Marxism and postmodernism, to name only the most salient few.

Liberal feminism, aligned with Enlightenment ideals, interprets the exploitation of women in society as arising primarily from the lack of equal rights and opportunities for women to engage fully in mainstream social and political life. Liberal feminists therefore focus their energies upon changing gender-biased cultural assumptions, institutional regula-tory frameworks and social practices. The liberal feminist approach is sometimes criticized for its uncritical acceptance of the major forces at work in developed patriarchal societies, such as capitalism or mili-tarism. Critics of this approach also argue that liberal feminists seek equality based on a traditionally male lifestyle, which makes them complicit in devaluing those qualities, behaviours and practices that are perceived as traditionally female.

Unlike liberal feminists, Marxist feminists locate their political goals within the general framework of the class struggle. Marxist feminism considers women to be exploited in capitalism, both by their husbands in the household and by employers at the workplace. The most wide-spread criticism of Marxist feminism is that it overlooks the fact that patriarchy had existed in pre-capitalist societies, and is still at work in present-day communist countries, such as China, Cuba, Laos, North Korea, and Vietnam.

Radical feminism interprets the subordination of women as a funda-mental form of oppression in all societies past and present. This oppres-sion, it claims, is the result of a concerted male drive to dominate all spheres of political, social, economic, cultural and religious life. Violence against women, compulsory heterosexuality, and the structure of social institutions are all seen as ways to secure male dominance. Radical feminists see unity among women and a radical reconstruction of sexuality as the only possible means for overcoming patriarchy.

Wary of the essentialism of earlier feminist theories, postmodern feminists avoid claims to universal experience and knowledge. Rather than presenting a united political front, they rely on temporary coalitions based on plurality and difference. Drawing on poststructuralist and psychoanalytic theories, they understand gender as a contextualized performance and examine the way it is shaped by language and representation.

Feminist theory shares with cultural studies a fundamental concern with the social construction of subjectivity and the role this plays in cultural practices and everyday life. Yet, the relationship between these two tangential frameworks of inquiry has not always been one of synergy and mutual reinforcement. Charlotte Brunsdon has written about the difficulties of introducing a feminist perspective in the work of the Centre for Contemporary Cultural Studies at Birmingham University in the 1970s, which were, in her account, met with hostility, incomprehension and indifference. Despite the initial stalemate, feminist frameworks have since had a significant impact on cultural studies theories and practice. According to Stuart Hall (1992), the feminist notion that 'the personal is political' motivated a significant turning point in cultural studies, as it encouraged research into new spheres of social experience from radically different perspectives. Furthermore, the feminist understanding of power as functioning within the private sphere as well as the public domain motivated cultural studies scholars to revise their understanding of how hegemony was established, maintained and possibly opposed. Feminist cultural studies frequently focused on the cultural practices that are conventionally associated with female experience, such as shopping, reading romance fiction or watching soap operas. Rather than interpreting women's consumption of mass culture as a simple reflection of their passive subordination to hegemonic forces, feminist cultural studies scholars have explained it as a creative and potentially counter-hegemonic practice. Feminists in cultural studies have also examined specific women's experiences in relation to issues of class, race, ethnicity, sexuality and social and technological development.

See also: **Centre for Contemporary Cultural Studies (CCCS); Gender; Marxism, Leninism, Western Marxism; Patriarchy; Poststructuralism; Postmodern, postmodernity, postmodernism; Power; Public/private; Sexuality**

Further reading: Shiach (1999).

Fetish

The word originates from Portuguese *feitiço*, which means sorcery or black magic. Early Portuguese voyagers used the word to refer to amulets and other objects of devotion worshipped by the natives of the West African coast. The term has since been widely used in the study of primitive religion to denote a sacred object.

In psychology, the fetish signifies a sexual fixation on a part of the body or other object. In his *Three Essays on the Theory of Sexuality* (1975 [1905]), Freud explained the fetish as originating from the male child's horror of female castration: the child represses the mother's lack of penis and finds some object to substitute for it, thereby relieving the anxiety and reinstating the erotic attachment to the female. The process entails not only finding a substitute object, but also a subsequent act of forgetting the original substitution.

In Marxism, the concept of commodity fetishism is used to explain a fundamental feature of capitalist societies, whereby commodities are ascribed autonomous value divorced from both their origins in human labour and their practical use. Marxist-inflected theory understands fetishism as a certain de-contextualization and abstraction of the world of things. Most notably, French philosopher and social critic Jean Baudrillard (1981 [1972]) has explained postmodern society in terms of a fetishism of signs, which now have no meaning other than their value relative to other signifiers.

As an object that sits in the interstices of two different economic and cultural spaces and facilitates the exchange between them, the fetish is a useful conceptual category for cultural studies, postcolonial studies and gender studies.

See also: **Identity, identification, identity politics; Marxism, Leninism, Western marxism; Postmodern, postmodernity, postmodernism; Psychoanalysis; Simulacrum**

Further reading: Apter and Pietz (eds) (1993).

Fictocriticism

The term 'fictocriticism' refers to a genre-defying mode of critical writing, associated primarily with Australian cultural studies and closely related to what is elsewhere variously referred to as paraliterary writing, theory-fiction, paracriticism, postcriticism, confessional criticism or metafiction. Fictocritical writing moves back and forth between theoretical/essayistic and personal/poetic narrative fragments. While characterized by a strong presence of the author's personal voice, it is also rich with theory and typically follows academic conventions, such as footnoting, referencing and bibliography.

The discursive genealogy of fictocriticism includes French feminist ideas of embodied writing practices and the postmodernist notions of pastiche and hybridity. Over the last two decades, fictocriticism has had

considerable influence beyond Australian borders, and has been practised in creative writing across the globe. Some notable fictocritical
works are Stephen Muecke's *No Road: Bitumen all the Way* (1997), and
the anthology of feminist writing *The Space Between: Australian Women
Writing Fictocriticism* (1998), edited by Heather Kerr and Amanda
Nettelbeck.

Further reading: Kerr and Nettelbeck (eds) (1998), Muecke (1997).

Flâneur

The French word *flânerie* denotes the activity of strolling without a
specific purpose, while observing the surrounding scenery, people and
events. The person (typically male) who engages in this activity, the
flâneur, represents a social type associated with the Paris of the nineteenth century. As a cultural trope, this ambiguous city stroller and
observer has come to embody a way of existence under the conditions
of urban modernity.

The figure of the *flâneur* features prominently in the works of the
French poet Charles Baudelaire. For Baudelaire, the poet can read
aesthetic meaning into the spectacle of the metropolitan environment,
and gain a certain kind of existential fulfilment from it. Without the
public spectacle of the anonymous urban crowd, Baudelaire's *flâneur* is
deprived of his own reason for existence.

In Walter Benjamin's reading of Baudelaire (1983 [1969]), *flânerie* epitomizes the production of meaning in modernity, predicated on the
distance between the observer and the observed. Benjamin's *flâneur* is
the urban stroller who does not only 'read' the city, but also produces
metropolitan texts. He thus operates in the same way as the detective,
the journalist, the urban sociologist, the artist and the poet of modernity.
Benjamin saw *flânerie* as a desperate and ultimately fruitless attempt to
fill the emptiness imposed by the commodification of modern society
and intimated its demise with the development of Parisian grands boule-
vards and department stores in the latter half of the nineteenth century.

Feminist critics have taken issue with the concept of the *flâneur*,
maintaining that it defines modernity as an exclusively masculine experience. Janet Wolff, in particular, has argued that there is no female
counterpart of the *flâneur*, because the modern separation of the public
sphere and the private sphere 'was also one which confined women to
the private, while men retained the freedom to move in the crowd or to
frequent cafés and pubs' (1990 [1985]: 40). Wolff has appealed to feminist scholars to broaden the scope of modernist studies by examining
'life outside the public realm' and the 'experience of "the modern" in its

F

private manifestations' (47).

See also: **Modernity, modernization, modernism; Public/private; Public sphere**

Further reading: Benjamin (1983 [1969]), Wolff (1990 [1985]).

Focus groups

Focus groups, or moderated group discussions, are commonly used as a method of qualitative data collection in market research, politics, health and community work, education and the social sciences. Their main advantage over other data-collection methods is that they provide a reasonably natural, relaxed and stimulating setting, in which participants feel relatively free to express their feelings and opinions. This is why they are often used to collect data on difficult, sensitive and complex issues.

The focus-group discussion format is designed to emulate as closely as possible the way people naturally engage in everyday group conversations. They can be designed as relatively free-flowing brainstorming sessions on a broadly defined topic. Alternatively, they can be fairly structured, with participants taking turns to respond to a set of questions prepared by the researcher. Since the rigorously structured format tends to restrain the natural group dynamic, this type of group discussion is more common in projects with a relatively limited focus and scope.

Focus groups can be used at any stage of the research process. They are, however, particularly useful at the early stages of research, when they can provide a valuable signpost for framing the key questions to be addressed in the research project. At any time, they can serve to pursue in more depth any unexpected findings obtained through other data-collection methods. In activism and community work, focus groups are sometimes used to give a voice to disempowered social groups.

Participants of a focus group may be selected from already existing groups, for example employees of a particular company or institution. More commonly, however, they are purposely assembled as a representative sample of the population relevant to the research project. A preliminary screening process may involve a small number of questions designed to identify appropriate participants. When approaching potential participants, researchers need to explain the context and expected outcomes of the research project, clarify any privacy issues, and outline the planned structure and format of the focus group. A broad script with a set of core open-ended questions is usually prepared in advance.

Focus groups can be audio or video recorded. Video recording is usually preferable, as facial expressions, postures and gestures can

F

provide useful information. Whenever possible, researchers also take hand-written notes. At the beginning of the session, the moderator usually briefly re-states the purpose of the meeting, introduces herself or himself to the group, and invites all participants to do the same. Moderating focus groups takes a great deal of skill and sensitivity. The moderator needs to be flexible enough to allow a natural discussion flow, while ensuring that all research questions get adequately covered and that all participants have sufficient opportunity to express their opinion. A variety of props and group activities can be used to promote discussion.

See also: **Interview; Method, methodology; Questionnaire**

Further reading: Denzin and Lincoln (eds) (2000 and 2003), Johnson et al. (2004).

Fordism/post-Fordism

This term, used by Antonio Gramsci in his *Prison Notebooks*, refers to a form of industrial production that was pioneered by the US car manufacturer Henry Ford (1863–1947) in the years leading up to the First World War. Fordism combined an approach to industrial efficiency called Taylorism (after its architect, Frederick Winslow Taylor) with an extensive reform of production and marketing that involved standardized outputs, moving assembly lines, and an encouragement of market demand through low prices, higher income levels, advertising, and consumer credit. The heyday of Fordism in most industrialized countries lasted roughly from the end of the Second World War to the economic crisis of the early 1970s. As a concept in political science, 'Fordism' has been used to denote a 'regime of accumulation' in which mass production was sustained by mass consumption, trade unions negotiated with both capital and the state, and governments were committed to full employment and the development of the welfare state. In his dystopian fantasy *Brave New World* (1932), Aldous Huxley satirized Fordism as the dominant religion of the future, with its massification and standardization representing a dangerous menace to individual freedom and creativity.

F

The demise of Fordism and the dawn of a new era, variously called post-Fordism, disorganized capitalism and the post-industrial society, is associated with a combination of socio-economic factors related to the economic crisis of the 1970s. The term 'post-Fordism' refers to a form of production and accumulation characterized by flexibility of both labour and machinery, a large-scale casualization of the workforce, small-batch and just-in-time production and niche marketing.

The assemblage of social, political and cultural phenomena that have been developing hand in hand with post-Fordist flexible production has been referred to as 'New Times' (Hall and Jacques (eds) 1989). These phenomena include the customization of design and quality, niche marketing, consumer lifestyles, globalization, new social and political movements, state deregulation and privatization of welfare, the cultural configurations of postmodernism and a reconfiguration of class divisions (Barker 2000: 160).

See also: **Capitalism; Globalization; Postmodern, postmodernity, postmodernism**

Further reading: Hall and Jacques (eds) (1989).

Frankfurt school

See **Critical theory**.

F

Gender

'Gender' refers to the socially constructed distinction between men and women, as opposed to 'sex', which denotes the biologically determined anatomical and reproductive differences. As a social construct, gender changes over time and across different cultures.

As a critical and analytical tool in the humanities and social sciences, the term 'gender' was born out of the second wave of feminism in the late 1960s and early 10970s. Prior to then, the term 'sex roles' had been used to signify the socially constructed ideals of manhood and woman-hood. Feminist scholars introduced the term 'gender' to intimate the possibility of resistance to the conventional sex roles imposed on women and men in patriarchal societies. US feminist Gayle Rubin (1975) introduced the expression 'sex/gender system' to argue that all cultures ascribe symbolic meaning to the biological difference between the sexes. This symbolic meaning, according to Rubin, underlies the power relations at work in all societies.

Since the 1980s, feminist critics aligned with poststructuralist and postmodernist thought have disputed the salience of binaries such as sex/gender, nature/culture and mind/body. In her seminal book *Gender Trouble* (1990), Judith Butler has argued that it is impossible to theorize the sexed body outside of culture and asserted that the body itself is always discursively produced. According to Butler, gender is performative, that is, it has no ontological status 'apart from the various acts which constitute its reality' (1990: 136).

Butler's account of gender has had a crucial impact on feminist theory, queer theory and cultural studies. It has, however, been challenged by a number of feminist critics, who have argued that its anti-foundationalism undermines the possibility for agency and the 'normative vision of feminist politics and theory' (Benhabib 1992: 215).

See also: **Femininity; Feminism; Performativity, performative, performance; Postmodern, postmodernity, postmodernism; Poststructuralism; Queer, queer theory; Sexuality**

Further reading: Benhabib (1992), Butler (1990), Rubin (1975).

Genealogy

The word, which derives from Greek *genea*, meaning race or generation, is used in common parlance to denote the study of a person's line of descent, by tracing a family tree that spans several generations. Genealogical research is often undertaken with an eye to discovering evidence of distinction among the ancestors and thus casting a positive light on the present-day generation.

As a critical and methodological concept, 'genealogy' refers to a distinct approach to history writing that derives from Michel Foucault's reading of the German philosopher Friedrich Nietzsche (Foucault 1984 [1971]). The Foucauldian genealogy does not seek to uncover 'origins', or the transcendental 'essence' of things present. Rather, genealogy is a form of history that accounts for the constitution of discourses and modes of human subjectivity without making 'reference to a subject which is either transcendental in relation to the field of events or runs in its empty sameness throughout the course of history' (1980: 117).

If the assumed task of traditional history is to produce objective knowledge, the aim of genealogy is to affirm that all knowledge is perspectival and culturally situated. Knowledge, in other words, does not relate to a transcendental truth, but rather to what is given the highest value within a specific discourse or set of practices. Genealogy therefore does not seek to produce a coherent story of past events, but rather to excavate the numerous inconsistencies, disruptions, accidents and errors that have, over time, shaped the discourses that prevail in contemporary society.

See also: **Archaeology; Discourse; Poststructuralism; Subject, subjectivity**

Further reading: Foucault (1980).

Generation

The word has two principal meanings: a group of people of similar age, and a cohort that occupies the same position within a kinship system. Since there is always a continuity of births in a society, there are no clear boundaries between generations. Generations in history are usually defined in terms of significant events or specific historical conditions that mark the formative years of a specific age group, such as the 'silent generation' born during the Depression, or the 'baby boomers', born during the period of increased birth-rates following the Second World War. The distinct set of experiences of social reality that characterizes each of these periods is believed to shape, to some extent, the ideas, values and worldviews of the people of each generation. These are, however, never monolithic, as they depend on numerous other factors, including gender, sexuality, ethnicity and class. Generational identities also change as a generation grows older, as has happened, arguably, with the rebellious spirit of the baby boomers.

The young people of the 1970s have been described as the 'me generation', characterized by self-centredness, materialistic greed and an obsession with health and self-improvement. The generation that came of age in the 1980s is commonly referred to as 'generation X'. The term was popularized by Canadian novelist Douglas Coupland, who described the overall aimlessness, disillusionment and other symptoms shared by this generation in his cult novel *Generation X: Tales for an Accelerated Culture* (1991).

See also: **Family; Identity, identification, identity politics**

Further reading: Coupland (1991).

Genre

Genre is a French word that means type, kind or form. Understood as a category of text in art, literature and the media, the term 'genre' has had a perplexing variety of applications, ranging from the most fundamental literary divisions (e.g. lyric, epic and dramatic art), to their more narrowly defined subcategories, based on form (e.g. sonnet), length (e.g. epigram), intent (e.g. satire), effect (e.g. comedy) or subject matter (e.g. romance, detective fiction etc.). Filmic genres include the gangster film, the Western, the horror film, comedy and the like. Each of these can be further divided into sub-genres, such as romantic comedy or slapstick comedy. The word 'genre' can also denote identifiable patterns in any discursive formation, including everyday communication (e.g. a job interview).

The familiarity and repetitiveness of generic texts is often assumed to have therapeutic or consolatory effects on the reader. In contemporary society, generic texts tend to follow the rules of the market, by endeavouring to anticipate and incorporate the elements expected by the audience. Regulated by distinct sets of conventions, genres are also said to limit the possibility and scope of individual variations. They are, however, far from being stable categories, since their conventions change over time and from culture to culture. Also, individual texts can combine conventions from multiple genres. This blurring of generic boundaries is often seen as one of the defining features of postmodern textual forms.

G

See also: **Mass culture, culture industry; Narrative; Popular culture, folk culture; Text**

Further reading: Dowd et al. (eds) (2006).

Globalization

A catchphrase that has dominated the media and informed scholarly debates for nearly two decades, the term 'globalization' denotes the economic, political, social and cultural processes that increasingly operate at a level beyond that of the nation-state. At a personal level, these processes foster an increased awareness of the world as a whole. As an object of study, globalization traverses a range of disciplines, including economics, international relations, political science, sociology, environmental science, agriculture, communication studies and cultural studies. Although the roots of globalization can be traced back to empire building in the pre-modern period, its intensification and unprecedented spread are associated with the latter half of the twentieth century.

In economic terms, globalization works to intensify global flows of capital, labour, goods and services and has differential impacts upon individual regions and states. Transnational corporations move a large proportion of their manufacturing facilities to less developed countries, where production costs are cheaper. While the flows of goods and capital across national boundaries unfold largely without obstruction, the migrations of people become increasingly problematic, as is evident from the ever more stringent immigration policies adopted by various countries of the developed world. Anti-globalization activists struggle against the reduction of local autonomies and the erosion of state-based protection mechanisms under the sway of globalization. Anti-globalization campaigns are typically raised against unequitable labour conditions, child and slave labour, environmental destruction, social injustice and politically oppressive regimes.

In social and political terms, globalization encourages new understandings of identity and community, and promotes new forms of governance and political action. An important aspect of political globalization is the increased coordination of activities between nation-states at a variety of levels. Also, as the new technologies of communication and transportation undermine the state control of information flows, likeminded activists and other interest groups develop new forms of transnational civil society. In addition to facilitating the creation and day-to-day operation of numerous transnational non-governmental organizations, social movements and knowledge-based networks, globalization has also given rise to such destructive phenomena as the transnational networks of the drug trade, prostitution and pornography, as well as terrorist organizations.

In cultural terms, globalization is associated with the increasing homogenization, worldwide, of consumer goods and services.

According to Stuart Hall, new globalization manifests itself in a global mass culture which is not English, but American (1991). The traditional focus of cultural analysis on traditions tied to a particular territory or nation, is increasingly shifting to the hybrid forms that result from dislocation and cultural interaction. Globalization here is not 'understood as a simple process of homogenization in which everything becomes the same', because the forces of globalization 'do not simply impose themselves everywhere in just the same ways. . . . Instead, local societies, cultures, economies, and political formations respond in active and distinct ways to the changes that confront them' (Bennett et al. (eds), 2005: 149).

See also: **Capitalism; Fordism/post-Fordism; Hybridity; Network; Transnational, transnationalism**

Further reading: Hall (1991), Bennett et al. (eds) (2005).

Governmentality

'Governmentality', in Michel Foucault's thought, refers to a particular understanding of governance that developed in Western Europe around the eighteenth century, building on the various practices of social discipline that had emerged in the early modern period, including the institution of police. Within this paradigm, authorities took on the role of acting upon the conduct of the population, with a view to establishing and promoting order and a broad-spectrum wellbeing. Governmentality thus differs from both disciplinarity and sovereignty, in that it takes social prosperity as its principal target and guiding principle. Neither should governmentality be confused with state government in its narrow institutional guise, because governmentality emanates from a multiplicity of 'authorities and agencies, employing a variety of techniques and forms of knowledge, that seeks to shape conduct by working through our desires, aspirations, interests and beliefs' (Dean 1999: 11). The role of the state within the general framework of governmentality is to coordinate disparate technologies of governing that reside in multiple sites. Studies of governmentality focus on the development of particular regimes of truth that regulate people's conduct. Their aim is to offer a constructive critique of governmental strategies, assumptions, visions and blind spots.

Since the 1990s, the concept of governmentality has been instrumental in cultural policy studies, a strand within cultural studies that gained prominence in the 1990s, notably through the work of the Key Centre for Cultural and Media Policy Studies at Griffith University in Queensland, Australia. Cultural policy researchers sought to re-conceptualize culture in terms of governmentality, as constituting a specific field of social management. They refuted the neo-Gramscian approach in cultural studies as exceedingly concerned with the struggle over meaning at the level of the text, and not paying enough attention to the institutional frameworks, which regulate different cultural fields. Culture, they argued, should be understood as a 'historically specific set of institutionally embedded relations of government in which forms of thought and conduct of extended populations are targeted for transformation – partly via the extension through the social body of forms, techniques, and regimens of aesthetic and intellectual culture' (Bennett 1992a: 26).

See also: **Cultural policy; Discourse**

Further reading: Dean (1999), Bennett (1992a).

Grounded aesthetics

The concept of 'grounded aesthetics' was introduced by the British cultural theorist Paul Willis, to uphold the notion that aesthetic value does not 'naturally' pertain to any formal or structural quality inherent in cultural texts and practices. Rather, according to Willis, the aesthetic of culture resides in the 'sensuous/emotive/cognitive' (1990: 24) act of consumption, whereby common people use symbolic creativity to reconfigure their social world and make sense out of it. In other words, the aesthetic is no longer inscribed in objects themselves, but in the activity of giving meaning to existing symbols and practices through consumption. The word 'grounded' here points to the notion that this activity does not follow a universal pattern, but rather depends on the specific socio-cultural context within which each individual person operates.

See also: **Consumption; Value, value system**

Further reading: Willis (1990).

G

Grounded theory

Sometimes referred to as the 'constant comparative method', grounded theory is a qualitative research methodology, the aim of which is to construct theoretical propositions inductively and progressively from systematically collected and examined data. The grounded theory approach is used primarily in the social sciences, health work and education. The key advantage of grounded theory is its capacity to generate new concepts and theoretical frameworks that genuinely expand, rather than simply replicating, an existing field of inquiry.

Grounded theory was originally developed in the 1960s by American sociologists Barney Glaser and Anselm Strauss (1967), to challenge the deductive approach prevalent at the time. Deductive methodologies begin with a pre-established research problem, construed on the basis of existing theory, and use the subsequently collected data to verify the original hypothesis. Grounded theory, in contrast, begins with a broadly defined area of interest and develops the research problem progressively through inductive analysis. Since the problem is not predefined, the focus of research may change several times in the process of data collection and analysis.

Throughout the research process, the researcher writes memos about emerging relationships and potential research hypotheses. Theory generation typically unfolds through a combination of coding and sampling. The researcher examines the collected data, such as transcribed interviews, field notes and other documents, and identifies recurring concepts by using the strategy called 'open coding'. Concepts are further clustered into broader categories, and used as a basis for subsequent data sampling. The data are considered 'saturated' when they generate no further concepts. Selective coding is the process of identifying core categories, to which all other categories need to be related. The process of identifying the relationships between various codes and categories is called axial or theoretical coding.

See also: **Method, methodology**

Further reading: Denzin and Lincoln (eds) (2000 and 2003).

G

Habitus and field

In Latin, *habitus* means condition or disposition (from *habere*, to have, to consist of). As a theoretical concept, it can be traced back to the philosophy of Aristotle and medieval Scholasticism. In Pierre Bourdieu's theory of practice (1977 [1972]), the concept denotes an assemblage of acquired models of taste, behaviour, and thought that mediates between social structures and social practice or social action. According to Bourdieu, human action emerges from a dialectical relationship between individuals' thought and activity (habitus) and the objective social world (field) within which people operate. Habitus 'ensures the active presence of past experiences, which, deposited in each organism in the form of schemes of perception, thought and action, tend to guarantee the "correctness" of practices and their constancy over time, more reliably than all formal rules and explicit norms' (1990: 54).

Field, in Bourdieu's theory, represents a fluid and dynamic set of institutions and social positions (for example, a specific profession, industry or art scene) that constitute an operational hierarchy and produce and legitimate certain practices and discourses. Fields often overlap, and are continuously changed both through internal practices and through contact with other fields. The precise articulation of what constitutes cultural capital in a particular context is largely determined within, and sometimes limited to, a specific field. For example, certain styles of dress, behaviour and language use may possess 'exchange value' in some cultural fields, while being utterly devalued in others. Capital is also related to the wider field of power, which has an impact on all other fields and is based on deep-seated social divisions, including class, gender and ethnicity. A field can be imagined as a 'market', as it represents a set of interdependent and unequal relationships, and involves a degree of competition. It can also be envisaged as a game, with players competing for success while observing a set of rules, including the rules that determine their own position and power within the game. The rules of a field, however, are subject to a continuous revision by the players and can be both explicit, or codified, and tacit, or un-codified.

Both the specific positions of individuals and institutions within a field and the nature of their relations can be ontologically verified. The field and the habitus are in a relationship of mutual conditioning, as the habitus represents the embodiment of a field or set of fields, while at the same time endowing those fields and sets of fields with meaning and value.

Bourdieu's theory of practice has been criticized for its ostensibly mechanistic interpretation of power and domination and its overly deterministic view of human agency.

See also: **Agency; Cultural capital; Determinism; Value, value system**

Further reading: Bourdieu (1993).

Hegemony

The word derives from the Greek *hegemon*, which means chief, leader or ruler. In Leninist thought, hegemony signified the revolutionary strategy that the proletariat would employ as a means of winning popular support and ultimately overthrowing the Tsarist regime in Russia. The theory of hegemony widely used in the humanities and social sciences was developed by Antonio Gramsci in the 1920s and 1930s, to explain why fascism enjoyed such popularity in Italy although it severely restricted the liberties of most Italian people.

In Gramsci's work, hegemony provides a matrix for understanding the complex nature of authority in social relations. It refers to the production and dissemination of values and beliefs that sustain and are sustained by the interests of a dominant social group, through a diverse range of techniques and networks, including state apparatuses, cultural institutions such as education, civil society, religion and the family; and, at a micro-level, the common practices of everyday life. Hegemony is thus both coercive and depending on consent, or the seemingly spontaneous acceptance of the status quo. While appealing to popular desires, hegemony is always at risk of overstepping its own boundaries and activating fantasies that may well work against it. According to Gramsci, hegemonic forces condition and are conditioned by an equally malleable set of counter-hegemonic responses. Hegemony is thus different from power, because it always contains within itself the imperative for resistance and change.

Gramsci's notion of hegemony has had wide currency in cultural studies scholarship since the first publication of his works in the English language in the late 1960s. The theory of hegemony provided cultural studies with a more sophisticated and fluid paradigm of social critique than that offered by the traditional Marxist base/superstructure model.

H

It also allowed scholars to move beyond the then prevalent semiotic analysis of cultural texts, and study the practices, uses and feelings involved in the production and consumption of popular culture. Popular culture was seen as a conduit that not only could promote hegemony, but could prompt resistance to it. Hegemony has also been central to the study of the 'rituals of resistance' associated with a range of working-class and youth subcultures (Hall and Jefferson 1993 [1976]). A notable example of the use of hegemony as an analytical tool in cultural studies is Stuart Hall's account of Thatcherism in the British culture and society of the 1980s (1983).

See also: **Base and superstructure; Centre for Contemporary Cultural Studies (CCCS); Intellectuals; Marxism, Leninism, Western Marxism; Polysemy; Popular culture, folk culture; Subculture; Thatcherism**

Further reading: Gramsci (1971), Hall and Jefferson (eds) (1976 [1993]).

Hermeneutics

The word, which derives from the Greek verb *hermēneúein* (to make something clear, to interpret), refers to theories of interpretation, in terms both of textual interpretation and of our interpretation of the world more generally. Originally applying to the reading of the Greek classics, and of biblical and juridical texts, it was extended to the humanities more generally by German philosophers Friedrich Schleiermacher (1768–1834) and Wilhelm Dilthey (1833–1911). The main proponents of twentieth-century hermeneutics are Martin Heidegger (1889–1976), Hans-Georg Gadamer (1900–2002) and Paul Ricœur (1913–2005). A central postulate of hermeneutics is that, since our interpretation of texts is always shaped by our individual social and cultural context, there can be no definite 'true meaning' inherent in the text itself.

Heidegger (1962 [1927]) is credited with bringing about an 'ontological turn' in hermeneutics. Rather than interpreting hermeneutics as a matter of understanding linguistic communication, he saw it as deeply implicated with issues of our being in the world. Understanding, for Heidegger, is not a product of our conscious reflection, but rather a mode of our pre-reflective 'being there' (German *Dasein*).

Drawing on Heidegger's ontological approach, Gadamer (1975 [1962]) interpreted human being as a being in language, arguing that it is only through language that we know the world. This, he argued, has implications for our understanding of the human sciences. Since we are always embedded in our own tradition, texts do not reveal themselves to us as value-free objects of inquiry. Rather, they are inevitably part of

H

the horizon through which we develop our worldview and cannot be 'objectively' reconstructed. Tradition, for Gadamer, always evolves through the rich and ever-growing web of interpretations.

Gadamer's hermeneutics has been criticized by Habermas (1976 [1971]), on the grounds that it places too much emphasis on the authority of tradition, downplaying the power of critical judgement. Hermeneutics, Habermas argues, must be compounded by a critical theory of society, based on a set of 'quasi-transcendental principles of communicative reason' that can be used to evaluate the tradition. The humanist underpinning of hermeneutics is also at odds with poststructuralist theory, which regards any meaning or identity, including that of the reader, as transient and always 'deferred'.

Hermeneutics had a major impact on reader-response theory, developed in the 1960s and 1970s by German literary theorists Wolfgang Iser and Hans-Robert Jauss (1921–97). Cultural studies that draw on this theoretical strand usually do so to bring to the fore the agency involved in the consumption of cultural texts.

See also: **Agency; Audience; Consumption; Critical theory;** *Différance*, **Poststructuralism; Reader-response criticism, reception theory**

Further reading: Wilson (1993).

Heteroglossia

The word comes from Greek and signifies a plurality of voices. Its synonym, polyphony, derives from Latin. It is used in English translations of the writings of the Russian literary theorist Mikhail Bakhtin, as an equivalent of his Russian term *raznorechie*, to indicate the variety of voices within any instance of linguistic activity, in particular a literary text.

See also: **Dialogism**

Heterotopia

H

The word is of Greek origin and literally means a 'place of otherness'. In the humanities and social sciences, its meaning derives from a lecture delivered by Foucault in 1967 and published only after his death (1986 [1967]). Foucault used the word 'heterotopia' to describe sites, both physical and symbolic, where incongruous elements coalesce in disquieting and usually transgressive ways. Foucault's heterotopia, in other words, is a space of hybridity, associated with 'time in its most flowing, transitory, precarious aspect', with 'time in the mode of the festival' (1986 [1967]: 26).

The concept has been deployed by Kevin Hetherington (1997) to describe the ordering of modernity in terms of an incessant oscillation between ideas of freedom and control. Heterotopia, in this sense, is the space 'in between', the space of deferral, where 'ideas and practices that represent the good life can come into being, from nowhere, even if they never actually achieve what they set out to achieve – social order, or control and freedom' (p. xviii).

See also: **Carnivalesque; Hybridity; Modernity, modernization, modernism**

Further reading: Foucault (1986 [1967]).

Historical materialism

The term refers to the Marxist theory of history, which regards the material basis of society, or the modes of material production, as the primary force that motivates societal change. The historical modes of production that Marx and Engels identified were: primitive communism, the 'Asiatic' mode of production, slavery, feudalism and capitalism. They also intimated an inevitable overthrow of capitalism and a future development of two more modes, socialism and advanced communism. They saw each mode of production, except primitive and advanced communism, as characterized by a hierarchy of social classes, in which the ruling class owns the means of production. Changes in the forces of production, brought about by technological progress, then produce conflict between the classes, from which new types of social organization emerge.

Critics within cultural studies have argued that historical materialism downplays the autonomous role of culture in driving societal change (Hall 1977; Hall and Jacques 1989). Historical materialism is also widely criticized as being historicist, because of its claim that there are certain universal laws that drive historical progress. Furthermore, it is considered to be teleological, because of its assumption that history will come to an end when it reaches its final stage, advanced communism.

See also: **Base and superstructure; Historicism, new historicism; Marxism, Leninism, Western Marxism**

Further reading: Hall (1977) and Hall and Jacques (1989).

Historicism, new historicism

The word 'historicism' has been deployed to convey at least two meanings, which are to a considerable degree mutually exclusive: on the one hand, it refers to a relativist approach to history, which argues that all historical events are unique and unrepeatable and therefore need to be interpreted on their own terms; on the other, it signifies those theories that interpret historical progress in terms of an intrinsic logic or *telos* that operates through identifiable trends, patterns or laws. Austrian-born British philosopher Karl Popper employed the term 'historism' to refer to the former usage, and 'historicism" to connote the latter.

Aspects of historicism, in the former sense of the term, are at work in contemporary theories of poststructuralism and postmodernism, which emphasize historical contingency and generally distrust claims to universal knowledge.

Popper criticized historicism, in its teleological guise, claiming that history could not be predicted, because it depended on human knowledge. He argued that it was impossible to predict knowledge, since to do so would mean, paradoxically, to possess it already. In particular, he rejected the economic determinism and historicism of traditional Marxist theory. He also criticized a range of teleological theories of modernity and modernization. Historicism, he further argued, is potentially conducive to totalitarianism, because it tends to suppress and erase alternative points of view.

New Historicism is a specific approach to literary theory and criticism, which developed in the USA in the 1980s and is mostly associated with the work of literary theorist Stephen Greenblatt. New Historicism draws on Clifford Geertz's concept of 'thick description' and Foucault's genealogy to develop a methodological framework that relies on close reading of seemingly minor events that can throw light on the power relations at work in greater social and cultural formations. Furthermore, it makes use of Marxist criticism to foreground the significance of political and social context. It does not, however, assume that literature mirrors reality, or that readers can grasp the 'truth' about past events without distortion arising from their own social context.

See also: **Genealogy; Marxism, Leninism, Western Marxism; Thick description**

Further reading: Gallagher and Greenblatt (2001).

H

Hybridity

The word 'hybrid' is of Latin origin and denotes an amalgamation of different elements: in biology, for example, a hybrid is the offspring of two plants or animals of different species or varieties; in linguistics, hybrid words are composed of elements taken from different languages (*COED*). More recently, hybridity has become a key concept in postcolonial studies and cultural studies, where it refers to the processes of intercultural mixing and the attendant formation of new types of subjectivities, which characterize the cultural politics of globalization. The principal semantic cognates of hybridity, in this sense, are creolization, diaspora and *mestizaje*.

While the biological and linguistic applications of the word signal a relatively stable condition, in the humanities and social sciences hybridity is seen as a fluid set of processes that are both generated and contested through complex relations of power. It has been widely recognized that a position of hybridity can be both empowering and disempowering, depending on the specific relationships of power in which it partakes. As flows of people, information and commodities increase, the binary between 'self' and 'other', prevalent in the dominant discourses of modernity, is becoming increasingly difficult to sustain. Identities which have traditionally depended on ostensibly 'stable' variables, such as territorial belonging, nationality, ethnicity, race, class or gender, are becoming more fluid. The spaces of hybridity are thus conceived in terms of flows, rather than bounded territories.

Recent scholarship has interpreted hybridity as a potential challenge to existing hierarchies and essentialist worldviews. Postcolonial theorist Homi Bhabha, for example, has argued that hybridity works to disrupt hegemonic colonial narratives of culture and identities (1994). According to Bhabha, hybridity occupies a 'third space' in between the subject positions of the colonizer and the colonized. This space in between does not recuperate the essence of its constitutive elements, but rather enables new positions to emerge.

British postcolonial theorist and historian Robert Young (1995) has distinguished between two rather different types of hybridization: hybridization as creolization, which fuses different identities into new forms that may assert some identifiable cultural 'essence' in an endeavour to achieve a greater degree of empowerment; and hybridization as 'restless chaos', which 'produces no stable new form but rather something closer to Bhabha's restless, uneasy, interstitial hybridity: a radical heterogeneity, discontinuity, the permanent revolution of forms' (25). The former type of hybridization is associated with nineteenth-century racial theories, while the latter emerged later, as part and parcel of contemporary globalization. Both types co-exist in contemporary society, in a tense relationship of continuing mutual contestation.

See also: **Creolization; Diaspora; Globalization; Identity, identification, identity politics; Mestizaje**

Further reading: Bhabha (1994).

H

Hyperreality

Deriving from a Greek word that means above or over, the term 'hyper-reality' signals something that is 'more real than real'. In computer science, the concept refers to a technological capacity to blend virtual reality with physical reality, and artificial intelligence with human intelligence, in a way that is perceived as seamless or 'real'.

In social and cultural theory, the concept connotes a condition of postmodern society in which simulations of reality tend to supplant and erase reality itself. In his famous essay entitled 'Travels in Hyperreality' (1997 [1975]), the Italian semiotician, cultural critic and literary author Umberto Eco explores the blurring of the distinction between real worlds and possible worlds in such iconic places of American popular culture as Disneyland and Las Vegas. Hyperreality, for Eco, is the defining feature of the American imagination, which, demanding the 'real thing', paradoxically needs to 'fabricate the absolute fake' in order to obtain it (8).

In the work of French social critic and postmodernist philosopher Jean Baudrillard (1983, 1995), hyperreality characterizes the production, exchange and consumption of signs and symbols in a consumer society. Baudrillard explains the notion of hyperreality by way of a story by Jorge Luis Borges, in which the cartographers of an empire create a map so realistic and detailed that it exactly covers the territory it represents. When the empire wanes, the map itself deteriorates. To serve as an allegory of the hyperreal, says Baudrillard, Borges's story has to be inverted, so that it is the map that precedes and produces the territory, and it is the territory that is now wasting away. According to Baudrillard, both maps and territories – or, both representation and reality – have now in fact lost their ontological essence and have been supplanted by simulacra. In contemporary society, media and cultural texts fabricate social relations to the extent that the latter become mere simulations of social reality. It ensues that the referents deployed in social science, such as gender, class and the like, now have no real grounding in anything but their own 'reality'.

H

See also: **Consumption; Postmodern, postmodernity, postmodernism; Simulacrum; Spectacle**

Further reading: Baudrillard (1983, 1995).

Id, superego, ego

The terms 'id' and 'ego' derive from the Latin personal pronouns 'it' and 'I' respectively. The triad of the id, the ego and the superego constitutes the mechanism of the human psyche, as it is theorized in Freudian psychoanalysis. According to this model, the id represents the domain of primal human instincts; the superego embodies internalized parental and social control; and the ego mediates and maintains equilibrium between the first two domains and constitutes the rational part of the psyche, which governs processes such as memory, problem solving, inference making and reality testing. The categories of the ego, the superego and the id loosely correspond to Lacan's concepts of the Imaginary, the Symbolic and the Real, although Lacan's account of the function of these three realms of the psyche is in no way equivalent to Freud's.

See also: Identity, identification, identity politics; Imaginary, symbolic, real; Oedipus complex; Psychoanalysis

Further reading: Freud (1960 [1923]).

Identity, identification, identity politics

Deriving from the Latin noun *identitas*, which means sameness (from *idem*, the same), identity implies a 'core' similarity between a number of elements, which is said to exist despite apparent differences. The Danish-born psychologist Erik Erikson (1902–94) developed the concept of identity to describe psychological development over the life course: personal identity, in Erikson's work, refers to the notion of self-same-ness over time. There are two main directions that studies of identity have taken over the last century or so: on the one hand, psychology and psychoanalysis focus on identity as a person's essential self, or the subjective idea of oneself as an individual; on the other, social sciences emphasize the communal and cultural aspects of identity formation.

Freud's theory of identification postulates that a child develops his or her identity by gradually assimilating external persons or objects, especially the parental superego. Drawing on Freud's work on narcissism, as well as on the structuralist theory of language, Lacan's theory foregrounds a specific stage in early childhood, the so-called 'mirror stage', as the first instance of a child's self-identification, which occurs when the mother holds the infant in front of the mirror, and the child imagines an illusive unity with the mother (1977). This moment, which belongs to the realm of the Imaginary, does not last long, for the child then realizes the differences and similarities between him/herself and the mother, and begins to experience the 'lack', or the loss of the mother. The second part of the mirror stage is coterminous with the Symbolic, when the original illusion of unity with the mother is forever foreclosed through the intervention of the father. This is when the child enters the realm of the language and order, and the process of socialization begins. The primary instance of misrecognition in the early mirror stage provides a template for identity formation, which, according to Lacan, is characterized by a fundamental split between an external 'ideal ego', or the mirror image, and the internalized 'ego ideal'.

Until the latter half of the twentieth century, social sciences interpreted collective identities as relatively stable categories, related to social groupings such as class, gender, ethnicity, nationality or race. With the advent of structuralism and poststructuralism, however, language and representation came to be seen as major factors in the formation of identity. In the work of Michel Foucault, for example, discourses provide the framework within which identification operates. Foucault has emphasized that each individual occupies multiple and at times even contradictory identities, which interact with each other and provide the individual with different possibilities for agency. Judith Butler's notion of identity as 'performative', in the sense that it 'constitutes as an effect the very subject it appears to express' (Butler 1998: 725), has had a significant impact on the understanding of identity in contemporary social and cultural theory.

An important insight that social and cultural inquiry has gained from psychoanalysis is that 'identities are constructed through, not outside, difference'. This, according to Stuart Hall, 'entails the radically disturbing recognition that it is only through the relation to the Other, the relation to what it is not, to precisely what it lacks . . . that the "positive" meaning of any term – and thus its identity – can be constructed' (Hall 1996c: 4–5). Also, Lacan's theory has provided an influential paradigm for film studies (see, for example, Žižek 1991), and studies of visual culture more generally. In film studies, the screen has been taken to have analogies with the mirror stage: the screen represents the mirror with which spectators identify, imagining themselves as unified beings.

They then perceive their difference and become aware of the 'lack'. Finally, they come to comprehend themselves as perceiving subjects. Within this paradigm, each film viewing represents a re-enactment of the unconscious processes of identification.

The increased traffic of people and ideas under globalization has further problematized the notion of identity as a stable and unified whole. The intensified contact between cultures has given rise to new types of subjectivities, associated with diasporic or hybrid identities. People today increasingly 'belong to more than one world, speak more than one language (literally and metaphorically), inhabit more than one identity, have more than one home'. They have learned to 'negotiate and translate between cultures' and to 'live with, and indeed to speak from, difference' (Hall 1995: 206).

Identity politics refers to any political activity mobilized around issues relevant to a specific identity group, including racialized minority movements, ethnic minority groups, the women's movement, the gay pride movement and the like. Identity politics is generally considered to be an effective form of struggle for the equal treatment of marginalized social groups.

See also: **Alterity; Diaspora; Hybridity; Id, superego, ego; Imaginary, symbolic, real; Performativity, perverformative, performance; Psychoanalysis**

Further reading: Du Gayl and Hall (eds) (1996).

Ideologeme

This term denotes the minimum intelligible unit of ideology, in the same manner in which 'phoneme', for instance, refers to the smallest intelligible unit of phonetics, and 'seme' to the smallest unit of semantics. In Bakhtin's account of dialogism (1981), 'ideologeme' signals a unique ideological discourse, or worldview, expressed by a specific character in the novel. Ideology is understood here as a system of ideas that serves as a symbolic source of identification within a specific social and historical context.

In Julia Kristeva's (1980 [1970]) account of intertextuality, the ideologeme operates both as a textual or thematic unit in a narrative text, and as a conceptual unit within the extra-textual ideological field, or, to use Kristeva's own terminology, in the 'historical and social text'. Texts, according to Kristeva, have no unified meaning of their own. Rather, each text should be understood as a temporary rearrangement of ideologemes, or elements with socially pre-existent meanings.

In Fredric Jameson's analysis of the politics of literary form, the ideologeme represents the 'smallest intelligible unit of the essentially antagonistic collective discourses of social classes' (1981: 76). Ideologemes, according to Jameson, can manifest themselves either as 'pseudoideas' or belief systems, or as 'protonarratives', or individual or collective narrative fictions. For example, we could think about market liberalism as an ideologeme of mass culture, or about multiculturalism as an ideologeme of globalization. The conceptual paradigms associated with these two ideologemes lend themselves to representation in the form of narrative fiction, which is why it is possible to identify them in a range of literary and media texts.

See also: **Dialogism; Discourse; Ideology; Intertextuality**

Further reading: Bakhtin (1981), Jameson (1981), Kristeva (1980 [1970]).

Ideology

The term (in French, *idéologie*) derives from French Enlightenment philosophy, where it was originally used to describe a rigorous 'science of ideas', untainted by religious and metaphysical prejudices. The word has since been associated with a variety of different meanings, not all of which are mutually compatible (Eagleton 1991). In everyday usage, it refers to a set of beliefs characteristic of a social group or individual (*COED*). It may also have negative connotations, and refer to a biased worldview that does not correspond to reality, or one that is motivated by a hidden agenda.

In classical Marxist theory, 'ideology' refers to a set of ideas that not only constitute the worldview of the dominant class, but also serve its interests. Ideology is interpreted here as a form of false consciousness, which distorts social reality by presenting a historically contingent social order as necessary and universal. Within this paradigm, ideology is perceived as standing in sharp contrast to objective knowledge, which is said to derive from an understanding of the material basis of society.

Twentieth-century Marxist accounts broadened the meaning of 'ideology', to include not only the ideas of the dominant class, but also class-consciousness more generally. Most importantly, the consciousness of the proletarian class was seen as a necessary precondition for revolutionary action. Gramsci foregrounded the role of culture as the principal field of ideological struggle. Class domination, according to Gramsci, is achieved and maintained through the ideological hegemony of the dominant class, which is embedded in everyday life and culture.

Building on Gramsci's ideas, Louis Althusser (2001 [1970]) developed the concept of ideological state apparatuses (ISAs), or mechanisms of the state that sustained the existing social hierarchy not by coercion, but through cultural reproduction. These state apparatuses included institutions such as religion, education, the media, the legal system and the family. Althusser used the term 'repressive state apparatus' (RSA) to refer to the institutions that operate by violence rather than by ideology, such as the police, the army, the courts and the prisons. The function of ideology, in Althusser's account, is to constitute concrete individuals as subjects. Althusser distinguished between practical and theoretical ideologies: he understood the former as shaping the latter, and reflecting the material conditions of a society.

Since the 1980s, poststructuralists have focused on the ways in which discourse reflects and reproduces ideological formations. Their studies have expanded the meaning of ideology beyond the class paradigm, to examine how other social divisions – such as race, ethnicity, gender or sexuality – produce, assimilate or contest ideological codes.

The concept of ideology has had wide currency in cultural studies. According to one critic, 'British Cultural Studies could perhaps be described just as easily, and perhaps more accurately, as ideological studies for they assimilate, in a variety of complex ways, culture to ideology' (Carey 1989: 97). Cultural studies characteristically focus on ways in which cultural texts, institutions and practices produce, sustain, disseminate and contest meanings. Drawing primarily on Gramsci's insight that the relations of power and domination extend beyond state institutions, and on Foucault's theory of discourse, cultural studies seek to examine the relations of power in the cultural domain.

See also: **Base and superstructure; Centre for Contemporary Cultural Studies (CCCS); Discourse; Hegemony; Historical materialism; Interpellation; Imaginary, symbolic, real; Marxism, Leninism, Western Marxism; Poststructuralism; Subject, subjectivity**

Further reading: Centre for Contemporary Cultural Studies (2006 [1978]).

Imaginary, symbolic, real

In Jacques Lacan's psychoanalytic theory, the Imaginary, the Symbolic and the Real are the three interrelated orders through which individuals relate to self, other and the world (1977). The Imaginary and the Symbolic develop during certain significant episodes in early infancy, namely the mirror stage and the acquisition of language respectively. The three orders, however, continue to co-exist and interrelate with each other throughout a person's adult life.

The Imaginary is the realm of internalized perceptual representations, or pre-linguistic images, which is set in motion during the so-called mirror stage in early infancy, approximately at six months of age. It is then that the child begins to identify with its own image in the mirror.

The fundamental split between the child's fragmented internal self and its deceptively coherent external image lies at the very heart of human subjectivity and identity. In the Marxist-poststructuralist theory of Louis Althusser (2001 [1970]), ideology operates within the realm of the Imaginary. Ideology, for Althusser, has the function of the mirror, in which individuals (mis)recognize themselves as autonomous subjects.

The Symbolic represents the sphere of language and social regulation, which gives meaning to our experience of the world. The Symbolic, for Lacan, is the sphere of the Other. It is constituted by an essential lack, because to enter the Symbolic order means to lose a good deal of our pre-symbolic existence. Lacan draws on the work of structuralist linguistics to argue that meaning, in the Symbolic order, is a consequence of relations between different signifiers.

The Real, for Lacan, is the realm that resists representation. It is both pre-imaginary and pre-symbolic, and it exists as a 'residue' that is left over after the process of symbolization. In the Real, there is neither meaning nor lack: the Real can be said to simply exist. According to Žižek, it is the very process of symbolization that 'introduces a void, an absence in the Real. But at the same time the Real is in itself a hole, a gap, an opening in the middle of the Symbolic order – it is the lack around which the Symbolic order is structured' (1989: 169–70). Žižek has interpreted ideology as an effect of the lack in the Symbolic order, a 'scenario filling out the empty space of a fundamental impossibility, a screen masking a void' (p. 126).

Lacan's account of subjectivity has been influential across a range of disciplines, especially in feminist literary theory and cultural and media studies. In French feminist theory, Julia Kristeva (1980 [1970]) renamed Lacan's 'Imaginary' the 'Semiotic' and emphasized its association with the feminine, the repressed and the marginal. In Kristeva's account, the Symbolic suppresses the Semiotic, but does not entirely displace it. Rather, the Semiotic continues to exist in non-traditional forms of language use, such as avant-garde poetry.

See also: **Avant-garde; Identity; Identification, identity politics; Ideology; Interpellation; Subject, subjectivity**

Further reading: Lacan (1977).

Intellectuals

In social sciences, intellectuals are broadly defined as people who by occupation or profession perform intellectual, as opposed to manual, labour. People whose role in society is to use their minds in pursuit of knowledge, truth and social wellbeing have existed since the dawn of civilization. Initially, they may have been shamans and priests. In more advanced societies, philosophers, scholars, professionals, literary authors and artists have all performed intellectual labour. Arguably, mass education and new media technologies have worked to undermine the aura of intellectual work in contemporary society.

The word 'intellectual' entered common usage in the last decade of the nineteenth century, in relation to a political scandal that shook France and Western Europe at the time, known as the Dreyfus Affair. The protest against the unjust imprisonment of a Jewish army captain Alfred Dreyfus, initiated by Émile Zola in his famous open letter entitled 'J'accuse', mobilized support among people of letters beyond France's borders, ready to intervene in the name of justice. From the outset, this willingness and capacity to exercise authority in the public sphere became a defining feature of the word 'intellectual'. Public intellectuals are commonly perceived as an opposition group, capable of amending social injustice and challenging traditional values and ideas. Also, right from the beginning, the word was open to negative connotations, when used to signal a gratuitous interference in matters supposedly beyond one's jurisdiction or expertise. The close association of the origin of the term with a nineteenth-century historical event has caused disagreement in the ranks of historians as to whether it is possible to talk about intellectuals in earlier historical periods.

In his seminal book *The Treason of the Intellectuals* (1928 [1927]), French philosopher and novelist Julien Benda asserted that intellectuals represented a social category of their own: they differed from other people, because their activity was not aimed at serving practical or material interests. Writing in the 1920s, Benda lamented that intellectuals had abandoned their original commitment to justice and truth, in order to serve the interests of their class, nation or race.

Gramsci challenged Benda's notion of intellectuals representing an autonomous social category. Each social group, he argued, 'creates together with itself, organically, one or more strata of intellectuals which give it homogeneity and an awareness of its own function not only in the economic but also in the social and political fields' (1971 [1929–35]: 5). Gramsci distinguished between these 'organic' intellectuals and 'traditional' intellectuals, who serve to validate the status quo in society, while misleadingly presenting themselves as independent from the dominant social group.

Michel Foucault rejected the view that intellectuals, in contemporary society, can profess to speak a universal truth at all. He believed, however, in the revolutionary potential of 'specific' intellectuals, who can grasp and contest the impact of general truth regimes within the particular social settings in which they operate (Foucault and Deleuze 1973).

Pierre Bourdieu (1988 [1984], 1989) theorized the role of intellectuals in contemporary society within the larger context of what he called the 'intellectual field'. This field, according to Bourdieu, is heterogeneous and conflictual. Despite their differences, actors in the field also have a shared interest in acquiring and exploiting a specific form of capital, which Bourdieu named 'cultural capital'. Being the dominated fraction of the dominant class, intellectuals – according to Bourdieu – often sympathize with the subordinated classes and act on their behalf. Bourdieu called for a renewal of solidarity among contemporary intellectuals, in the interests of their own social group. Only by protecting their own interests, he asserted, will intellectuals be able to engage in promoting universal ideals.

See also: **Author/ship; Cultural capital; Discourse; Episteme; Habitus and field; Hegemony; Knowledge; Power**

Further reading: Said (1994).

Interdisciplinarity

The term 'interdisciplinarity' refers to research that integrates theories and methodologies across different disciplines. Although clear-cut boundaries between academic disciplines are becoming increasingly difficult to sustain, the traditional divisions persist within institutional frameworks, including discipline-specific departments at tertiary institutions, scholarly journals, symposia and funding bodies.

Interdisciplinarity is a defining feature of cultural studies. In fact, it has been argued that cultural studies are not merely interdisciplinary, but indeed, 'actively and aggressively anti-disciplinary' and therefore in a 'permanently uncomfortable relation to academic disciplines'. The choice of research practices in cultural studies is 'pragmatic, strategic and self-reflective', in the sense that it always depends on the specific questions that are asked in each individual project (Grossberg, Nelson and Treichler 1992: 2). The resources that provide important insights to cultural studies research are drawn from assorted interfaces between disciplines such as philosophy, social theory, economics, political science, law, anthropology, sociology, psychology and psychoanalysis, history, geography, literary theory, literary criticism and linguistics; as well as from a range of tangential interdisciplinary strands, such as feminism, gender studies, media and communication studies, postcolonial studies and queer studies.

See also: **Discourse; Knowledge; Power**

Interpellation

In Louis Althusser's theory of ideology, 'interpellation' refers to the process by which individuals are summoned to become subjects, that is, to assume specific positions and roles within a social system. Althusser's famous example of interpellation is the 'most commonplace everyday police (or other) hailing: "Hey, you there!"' (2001 [1970]: 174). By recognizing and acknowledging the call, the person who is being hailed positions herself/himself as a subject of state power. The 'call' does not refer here to a factual real-life occurrence, but to the process of internalizing a specific subject position. The concept has been widely criticized for downplaying the possibility of human agency and resistance.

See also: **Agency; Ideologeme; Ideology; Subject, subjectivity**

Further reading: Althusser (2001 [1970]).

Intertextuality

The term was coined by Julia Kristeva in the 1960s. It refers to a relationship between different texts, which may quote one another, hint at one another, or otherwise interrelate. Building on Bakhtin's concept of dialogism, Kristeva argued that each text was a 'mosaic of quotations': an 'absorption and transformation' of other texts (1980 [1970]: 66). In other words, no text exists in isolation. Intertextuality is most obvious in anagrams, allusions, parodic texts, pastiche, textual adaptations, imitations and translations. The concept of intertextuality has gained currency across a range of scholarly fields, such as literary criticism, architecture, visual arts, film, media, music and cultural studies.

According to Roland Barthes (1974 [1970]), intertextuality does not only exist between different texts, but is also inscribed in the active process of reading. The reader, according to Barthes, approaches each text from the perspective of a multitude of other texts she or he has read, or is indirectly familiar with.

Intertextuality is a common feature of postmodern texts, such as popular genre literature or televisual fiction. John Fiske has distinguished between horizontal intertextuality, which operates 'between primary texts that are more or less explicitly linked, usually along the axes of genre, character, or content', and vertical intertextuality, which is at work 'between a primary text, such as a television program or series, and other texts of a different type that refer explicitly to it', such as 'studio publicity, journalistic features, or criticism, or tertiary texts produced by the viewers themselves in the form of letters to the press or, more importantly, of gossip and conversation' (1987: 108).

See also: **Dialogism; Text; Mass communication and mass media; Postmodern, post-modernity, postmodernism**

Further reading: Barthes (1974 [1970]), Fiske (1987), Kristeva (1980 [1970]).

Interview

The interview is a data collection method used in qualitative research in a range of academic disciplines. It is considered to be among the most resource-intensive data collection methods, since the researcher needs to obtain information from respondents on a one-to-one basis. The key advantage of the interview is that it can give the researcher an in-depth understanding of the nature and significance of issues under scrutiny. Interviews are usually conducted face-to-face or by telephone. The latter are more appropriate for shorter and more structured interviews targeting a large number of respondents.

Interviews can involve varying degrees of structure. In unstructured interviews, the researcher proposes one or more broad areas of discussion, but gives the respondent a considerable freedom to decide how the discussion will unfold. In semi-structured interviews, the researcher has a limited number of pre-defined questions and areas of discussion, while still allowing the respondent to have some creative input. Finally, the structured interview gives the researcher an absolute control over the content, format and order of questions, which are carefully planned in advance. Regardless of the interview type, researchers usually prepare a list of key issues that need to be covered during the interview.

When planning a structured or semi-structured interview, researchers usually group questions into clusters organized around specific issues or themes. It is considered good practice to familiarize the respondent with the planned structure of the interview at the beginning of the interview session. The interview is usually structured by using a 'funnelling' technique. This means that both the thematic clusters and the questions within each cluster should move from the more general to the more specific areas of interest. Piloting the interview design with a small number of people before the interview itself is a good strategy for identifying possible ambiguities and inconsistencies.

Since interviews can sometimes last for more than an hour, handwritten notes taken during or after the interview session are a less effective recording technique than audio recording or video recording. Interviews are usually audio-recorded or video-recorded. It is common today to use digital recording technologies, which facilitate data manipulation and transcription.

It is very important, in the planning stage, to select a representative sample of interviewees. Exactly who, and how many people, will be included in the sample will depend on the research questions asked in a specific project. If several interviewees belong to the same institution, it is a common practice to approach them in order of seniority.

At the beginning of the interview session, a researcher should briefly introduce her or himself, and explain the context of the research project, the aim of the interview and its planned structure and format. It is also good practice to specify how the interview findings will be utilized, and whether anonymity will be respected. Seating arrangements during the interview session will depend on the level of formality required in specific circumstances.

Interview questions can be either closed or open-ended. The latter type is more effective in retrieving in-depth and unsolicited information. During the session, it is important for the interviewer to provide attention cues to the interviewee, such as nodding the head or establishing eye contact. Memory cues can be used to help the interviewee to recall past experiences.

The researcher will usually conclude the interview session by summarizing what has been discussed. This also gives an opportunity to the interviewee to clarify certain issues or provide additional information. The researcher may also offer to provide written documentation of the interview, or access to the published outcomes of the research project.

The recorded data then need to be transcribed and meaningfully arranged for qualitative analysis. This may involve cutting and pasting from different interview transcripts, following a logical structure of relevant thematic clusters. Different commercial and open-source software packages, designed specifically for qualitative research, can greatly assist data transcription and analysis. They typically rely on a coding structure that needs to be designed by researchers before they proceed with qualitative analysis.

See also: **Focus group; Method, methodology; Questionnaire**

Further reading: Denzin and Lincoln (eds) (2000 and 2003), Johnson et al. (2004).

Irony

The word derives from Greek *eironeia*, which means 'dissimulation'. In everyday usage, it refers to a rhetorical strategy, common in both literature and everyday life, in which a 'false' statement is used not in order to deceive the listener, but rather to draw her or his attention to a concealed meaning. The extreme form of irony known as 'sarcasm' is at work when a speaker says the direct opposite of what she or he means, in order to ridicule, mock or show contempt for another person's views.

As a strategy of dialectic used by the Greek philosopher Socrates (470–399 BCE) and rendered famous by Plato (c. 427–c. 347 BCE) in his Socratic dialogues, Socratic irony involves feigning ignorance about a particular topic, in order to reveal the flaws in a dogmatic belief, or in the arguments put forward by another speaker. The Socratic irony requires a split in the audience, between those who feel sorry for Socrates and desire to enlighten him, and those who know the rules of the game and are able to anticipate Socrates' triumph in the debate. The opposition between the ostensible meaning and the underlying meaning is central to the ironic experience, and its ultimate resolution is said to produce the effect of joyous enlightenment through the release of tension.

Literary irony can be achieved by way of a naïve character or unreliable narrator, whose understanding of her or his circumstances is clearly at odds with the 'real' situation implied by the author and recognized by readers. Dramatic irony occurs in a play when the audience knows facts about a character's situation that the character is unaware of, and is thus able to predict a resolution contrary to the character's expectations. A well-known example of dramatic irony is Sophocles' *Oedipus Rex* (c. 425 BCE), in which Oedipus endeavours to find the murderer of King Laius, only to learn that the murderer is in fact no other than Oedipus himself, a truth the audience has been aware of all along.

Critics have interpreted irony as a trope that goes hand in hand with the scepticism of the postmodern era, because it collapses the boundaries between truth and simulation. 'Today', Claire Colebrook has argued, 'we wear 1980s disco clothing or listen to 1970s Country and Western music, not because we are committed to particular styles or senses but because we have started to question sincerity and commitment in general' (2003: 2).

The US philosopher Richard Rorty (1989) has theorized irony as the only viable ethic of modern liberalism. Irony, for Rorty, involves an understanding that the fundamental moral and political concepts that underpin the liberal worldview, such as justice, freedom, humanity or democracy, have no intrinsic meaning or universal foundations. According to Rorty, irony is a private attitude that does not preclude the use of these concepts in the public domain. It gives us an awareness of the plurality of competing narratives, and thus enables us to occupy our own social position, while acknowledging and accepting the existence of others.

Though acknowledging the potential of irony to destabilize the foundational narratives of Western thought, the Canadian theorist of postmodernism Linda Hutcheon (1994) warns that it may also represent yet another gesture that allows the West to speak of and for itself, albeit from a distance, or, so to speak, 'in quotation marks'. She gives the example of a Canadian museum exhibition, which took an ironic approach to colonialism, by presenting a series of colonial images that were characteristically objectifying the indigenous population in a patronizing and demeaning way. Many of the indigenous viewers of the exhibition either missed the irony or were offended by it, seeing the images as one more instance of colonial arrogance. The self-referentiality of irony, in Hutcheon's account, forecloses the possibility of a dialogue between the West and its significant others.

See also: **Parody, pastiche; Postmodern, postmodernity, postmodernism; Pragmatism; Trope**

Further reading: Hutcheon (1994), Rorty (1989).

Iterability

In the poststructuralist theory of Jacques Derrida, iterability is a defining feature of all linguistic forms, which allows them to be repeated or performed again and again in different contexts. Derrida explained his coinage as deriving from the Sanskrit word *itara*, which means both 'once again' and 'other', and thus simultaneously implies both repetition and alterity (1981: 90).

Expanding on John Langshaw Austin's theory of speech acts, Derrida argued that language, in order to be performable, had to contain traces of past performances, while at the same time being open to deviations and alterations in each new performance. Because the possibility of distortion is a necessary condition of intelligibility, language continually produces meanings that never generate perfect reproduction, but rather produce further dispersal or, to use Derrida's terminology, endless dissemination.

Derrida's concept of iterability is central to Judith Butler's theory of gender performativity (1990, 1993). According to Butler, the reiteration of norms exists before the emergence of the subject and interpellates the subject into the symbolic order. In order to function in society after the original interpellation, the subject has to cite and perform the very norms that brought it into existence. For Butler, meaning is generated through the continuous performative reiteration of norms, which both produces a set of material effects on the body and makes bodies socially intelligible. Social change, in Butler's account, depends precisely on the iterability of the speech act, which explains both the persistence of relatively stable hegemonies, and the possibility of innovative enactments within new contexts.

See also: **Alterity; Deconstruction;** *Différance*; **Imaginary, symbolic, real; Interpellation; Logocentrism, phonocentrism,** *écriture*; **Poststructuralism; Subject, subjectivity**

Further reading: Butler (1990 and 1993), Derrida (1981).

Jouissance

Jouissance is a French word that means 'enjoyment' and can connote sexual gratification. As a concept in psychoanalysis and cultural theory, *jouissance* signals a transcendent bliss or rapture, which disrupts normative subjectivity, as opposed to pleasure (French *plaisir*), which is seen as comfortable and reassuring.

In the work of French semiotician Roland Barthes, the experience of reading can afford two types of fulfilment: one of these is pleasure (*plaisir*), which is associated with reading those texts that confirm the cultural assumptions of the reader, or, in Barthes's terminology, readerly texts; the other is bliss (*jouissance*), which characterizes the experience of reading what Barthes calls writerly texts, which disrupt their readers' expectations and challenge them to create new meanings while reading.

In Lacanian psychoanalysis (see Lacan 1977), *jouissance* is akin to what Freud called the 'death drive', which exists beyond the pleasure principle. *Jouissance* here belongs to the domain of the Real, the primeval and the feminine. The individual's entry into the symbolic order is predicated on the loss of *jouissance*. The ensuing lack drives people in vain pursuit of the primeval state of fullness. Lacan's concept of the '*jouissance* of the Other' refers to the notion that, in this pursuit, people tend to believe that the Other (understood not as a person, but as a domain of alterity produced by language) possesses the plenitude, or *jouissance*, which they themselves lack.

Lacan's concept of *jouissance* is central to French feminist theory (Irigaray 1985 [1974] and 1985 [1977]), where it is deployed to foreground the *jouissance féminine*, or the feminine libidinal drive repressed by the symbolic order, as the basis for feminine creativity.

See also: **Desire; Identity, identification, identity politics; Imaginary, symbolic, real; Text**

Further reading: Irigaray (1985 [1974] and 1985 [1977]), Lacan (1977).

Kitsch

The word came to use in late nineteenth-century Germany, as a derogatory label for cheap and low-quality artworks, designed as souvenirs for an undiscerning tourist market. It entered the English language in the early decades of the twentieth century. A truly international term, the word 'kitsch' – in its original or domesticated form – is today widely used in many world languages. Its etymology, however, is far from certain. According to one hypothesis, the German word derives from the English word 'sketch', used by the Anglo-American tourists who bought cheap art at the markets of Munich. A second hypothesis relates the word 'kitsch' to the verb *verkitschen*, which in a particular German dialect means 'to render something cheap'. A third explanation links 'kitsch' to the German verb *kitschen*, used in the south-west of Germany to refer to collecting rubbish from the street.

In common usage, the word 'kitsch' usually signals some form of bad taste, or aesthetic inadequacy. It can apply to almost anything that is susceptible to judgements of taste, including painting, sculpture, literature, film, TV programmes, music, architecture and everyday objects of material culture. Stylistically, kitsch has been defined in terms of predictability, as art that 'has established rules' and a 'predictable audience, predictable effects, predictable rewards' (Rosenberg 1959: 266). Classifying something as kitsch, however, is never a mere aesthetic judgement, but always entails considerations of context and purpose. For example, an original Picasso painting displayed ostentatiously in a rich person's garage would unmistakably produce a kitsch effect.

Despite the apparent incompatibility between modernity, with its belief in progress and change, and kitsch, with its dependence on banality and repetition, the emergence of kitsch as a social and cultural phenomenon is commonly associated with the modern era. It is variably linked to the sentimentalism and aesthetic escapism of the Romantic period, and to the massification and commodification of culture in the late nineteenth and early twentieth centuries. Adorno (1984 [1970]) explained kitsch as a 'parody of catharsis' that offers a hallucination of escape from the dreary monotony of modern life. Sociologically, kitsch has been interpreted as the expression of the hedonistic lifestyle and the consumer mentality of the middle class.

In the first half of the twentieth century, avant-garde movements such as Dada and surrealism used a variety of techniques and elements borrowed from kitsch, in an ironic gesture that served as a comment on the exclusionary nature of aesthetic judgement. More recently, the US artist and sculptor Jeff Koons has become famous for his use of kitsch imagery in his installations, which are often of extremely large proportions. Kitsch has come to enjoy a considerable prestige as part and parcel of camp sensibility, which cultivates bad taste as a form of resistance to dominant aesthetic codes. More broadly, kitsch has been interpreted as one of the key elements of the postmodern aesthetic (Jameson 1991 [1984]: 2–3).

See also: **Authentic culture; Mass culture, culture industry; Value, value system**

Further reading: Olalquiaga (1998).

Knowledge

Theories of the nature of knowledge, or epistemologies, have varied throughout history and across different cultures. Objectivist theories postulate the existence of a universal knowable truth, which can be grasped either through observation (empiricism) or through reason and logic (rationalism). Relativist theories assume that both knowledge and truth are relative to a person, a time, a place or a socio-cultural setting.

The notion that knowledge and truth are historically and socially contingent, now widely accepted across the humanities and social sciences, can be traced back to the work of German philosopher Georg Wilhelm Friedrich Hegel (1770–1831). For Hegel, the key problem was to comprehend how it might be possible to transcend one's historical perspective and access what he called 'absolute knowledge' (see Hegel 1977 [1807]). He intimated that the attainment of this absolute knowledge would eventually come as a result of the dialectical movement of mind or spirit through history.

Marxist theory introduced a materialist approach to Hegel's account of knowledge as historically specific. It explained the social origins of knowledge in terms of the economic basis of society, and in terms of class interests. In Marxism, the theory of knowledge is inextricably linked with the theory of ideology, which explains how power relations influence people's beliefs and identities.

In the philosophy of Friedrich Nietzsche (1844–1900), knowledge is not class-bound, but rather, motivated by human desire and 'will to

K

power' (see Nietzsche 1967 [1901]). Nietzsche was not interested in the possibility of the existence of an absolute trans-historical truth, but rather in the effects that the situated forms of knowledge produce in a specific historical period.

Nietzsche's approach to knowledge has exercised decisive influence on poststructuralist epistemologies, which concur in claiming that knowledge systems are socially and culturally contingent, and dependent on power relations and desire. Furthermore, they shift their focus of interest from the contents of knowledge to the forms and practices of knowing and the ways these shape, and are in turn shaped by, political, cultural, and institutional discourses. According to Michel Foucault (1972 [1969]), what is deemed to constitute knowledge in any given moment in history is determined by the power of specific discursive practices.

The notion of the contextual conjunction between knowledge and power, as well as an understanding of the capacity of knowledge to amend hegemonic power relations, provide the epistemological foundations for cultural studies research. According to Lawrence Grossberg, cultural studies is neither universalist nor particularist: rather, it 'seeks new forms and articulations of authority, built on the effectivities of knowledge . . . rather than the status of the producer'. While having 'no pretensions to totality or universality', Grossberg argues, cultural studies does 'seek to give a better understanding of where "we" are so "we" can get somewhere else, hopefully somewhere better' (1997a: 253–4).

See also: **Base and superstructure; Discourse; Episteme; Historical materialism; Ideology; Marxism, Leninism, Western Marxism; Poststructuralism; Power**

Further reading: Pollock and Cruz (1999 [1986]).

K

L

Language

The word denotes both the 'method of human communication, either spoken or written, consisting of the use of words in a structured and conventional way' and 'any method of expression or communication', for example, body language (*COED*). In both senses of the term, language lies at the heart of every culture. Through language, people assign meaning to human experience. Through language, they create, manipulate, contest and communicate knowledge. Language also helps classify people into relatively distinct speech communities, which can be based on locality, ethnicity or nationality, but also on class, gender, age, profession, occupation or lifestyle. Furthermore, language utterances – such as, promises or oaths – can literally perform meaningful actions.

The scholarly discipline concerned with language study is called linguistics. It has a number of subfields that deal with specific aspects of language, including phonetics (sounds), phonology (sound systems), morphology (word structure), syntax (sentence structure), semantics (meaning) and pragmatics (context). Language studies also include subdisciplines such as sociolinguistics (study of the relationship between languages and societies), dialectology (study of dialects), psycholinguistics (study of the psychological and neurobiological foundations of language) and applied linguistics (primarily language education and second-language acquisition). Generative linguistics, pioneered by Noam Chomsky (1965), posits that human beings possess an innate competence that enables them to perform an infinite number of complex utterances, based on a finite set of structural rules – the so-called 'deep structure' – that are common to all languages. In contrast, behaviourist linguistics argues that linguistic competence is not innate, but rather acquired through a person's exposure to a specific language or languages in early life.

In structuralist linguistics, pioneered by the Swiss linguist Ferdinand de Saussure (1983 [1915]), language (French *langue*) is a system of signs, the meaning of which is fixed not by reference to any extra-linguistic reality, but by their relationship with each other within the system. It is distinguished from language-in-use, or actually occurring linguistic utterances (French *parole*). Saussure's notion of differential systems of meaning provided the basis for the structuralist approaches in disciplines other than linguistics, including anthropology, literature studies, sociology, history, and social and cultural theory and critique. The French anthropologist Claude Lévi-Strauss (1966 [1962]) deployed Saussure's theory to interpret the myths, symbolic systems, and traditional practices in tribal societies; and the semiotician Roland Barthes (1984 [1957]) applied it to the analysis of the cultural texts and practices of contemporary Western societies.

In cultural studies, culture itself is regarded as a 'signifying practice', which has 'its own determinate product: meaning' (Hall 1980a: 30). A study group within the Birmingham Centre for Contemporary Cultural Studies (CCCS), called 'Language and Ideology', critically examined the different traditions of contemporary linguistic theory and research. The strands of language-related analysis of particular interest for cultural studies are Barthes's semiotics, Lacan's psychoanalytic theory of language, Derrida's poststructuralism, Marxist theories of language and ideology and Foucault's theory of discursive formations.

See also: **Centre for Contemporary Cultural Studies; Discourse; Myth; Poststructuralism; Psychoanalysis; Semiology, semiotics; Sign (CCCS); Structuralism**

Further reading: Yarbrough (1999).

Leavisism

The term 'Leavisism' refers to an aesthetic and moralizing view of culture promoted by the British literary critic F. R. (Frank Raymond) Leavis (1895–1978) and a group of his associates in the period from the 1930s to the 1970s. Leavisites argued that the 'great tradition' in literature reflected the organic properties of social life, and thus had an important role in educating young people to become balanced and responsible members of society. For Leavis, pre-industrial England was a model of 'organic community', which had an authentic common culture of the people and a minority culture of the educated social strata. Standardization and cultural levelling associated with industrialization, he argued, all but obliterated the organic nature of society. He saw a potential antidote to this degradation in the assumed capacity of a selected canon of English literature to liberate the minds of the young from the damaging influence of popular fiction, film and commercial advertising. The Leavisite canon included works that carried a moral message, by writers such as George Eliot, Jane Austen or Alexander Pope, but ruled out more experimental authors, such as Virginia Woolf or James Joyce. Leavisism played an important role in shaping the

L

English curricula at British schools and universities in the period following the Second World War. Furthermore, the disdainful Leavisite view of
mass culture provided the discipline of English studies with its own
moral rationale and intellectual responsibility.

The emergence of British Cultural Studies at Birmingham University in
the 1960s can be seen as an outgrowth of 'left Leavisism', associated
primarily with Raymond Williams and Richard Hoggart. The Leavisism of
early British cultural studies should be understood as an attempt to
'address the manifest break-up of traditional culture' and to 'come to
terms with the fluidity and the undermining impact of the mass media'
(Hall 1990b: 12). While upholding the Leavisite belief in the socially
redemptive value of literature, and its commitment to literary criticism
as a social responsibility, Hoggart – who was the first director of the
Birmingham Centre for Contemporary Cultural Studies (CCCS) – also
endeavoured to expand the field of cultural studies to 'popular arts',
including television, photography, fashion and pop music.

See also: **Authentic culture; Centre for Contemporary Cultural Studies (CCCS); Literacy;
Value, value system**

Further reading: Milner (1994).

Left, New Left

As a spatial metaphor for a set of political ideas, the term 'left' originates
from the seating arrangement in the National Constituent Assembly in
the early years of the French Revolution (1789–91), when Jacobin radicals sat on the left side of the King; moderates in the centre; and royal-
ists and the clergy on the right. Left-wing politics has since been
associated with struggle for equality and popular sovereignty in social,
political and economic life. In contemporary society, the notion of the
political left encompasses a range of agendas that typically include
social egalitarianism, demands for broad-spectrum welfare provision,
support for the working class and other marginalized social groups,
some degree of state regulation of the economy, and opposition to
nationalistic defence and foreign policies.

Precisely what constitutes left-wing political ideas depends on
cultural context. In nineteenth-century Europe, the left consisted of
middle-class radicals, mobilized mainly around the demand for universal suffrage, and a nascent working class, operating under the banner of
socialism and interested primarily in achieving greater control over the
capitalist economy. In the twentieth century, the term was variably
deployed to describe the political position of socialist, social democratic, labour and communist parties, and of feminist, anti-nuclear, anti-

war and anti-globalization movements. Over the last two to three decades, the progressive dismantling of welfare provisions in most Western countries and the downfall of authoritarian communism in countries of the former Soviet bloc have arguably worked to destabilize traditional left-wing party politics across the globe and prompted a move towards a spectrum of more dispersed modes of counter-hegemonic resistance.

The expression 'New Left' refers to a radical movement that brought together humanist dissidents from communist parties and supporters of Western Marxism during the Cold-War period. The origin of the term is associated with the establishment, in 1960, of the London bi-monthly journal *New Left Review* by a group of left-wing intellectuals disillusioned with Soviet-style politics. These included Edward Thompson, Raymond Williams and the journal's first general editor, Stuart Hall. The focus of the *New Left Review* was on issues related to culture, such as the social impact of consumerism and the mass media. The group associated with the journal has made a major contribution to contemporary Marxist theory, both by encouraging the translation into English of unorthodox Western Marxists such as Antonio Gramsci, Louis Althusser, Theodor W. Adorno and György Lukács, and by critically engaging with their work.

As a movement, the New Left emerged in the 1950s and 1960s, particularly in Britain and the US, both in response to revelations about the horrors of Stalinist dictatorship and in protest against the suppression of the Hungarian revolution (1956) and the Prague Spring (1968) by Soviet troops. In contrast to orthodox Marxism, the New Left saw the revolutionary potential of social groups other than the industrial working class, such as students, women and people of colour. By the late 1960s, the movement spread across Western Europe and the US, mobilized particularly around demands for university reform and the withdrawal of US troops from Vietnam. It is now widely recognized that the movement contributed to the development of anti-militarist and anti-racist sentiments in Europe and the US, remaining a source of inspiration for subsequent radical theory and activism.

See also: **Centre for Contemporary Cultural Studies (CCCS); Marxism, Leninism, Western Marxism**

Further reading: Davies (1995).

Liberalism, neoliberalism

The word derives from Latin *liberalis*, 'of a free person', and ultimately from *liber* (*libera*, *liberum*), which means 'free'. As a concept in political and social science, 'liberalism' refers to a range of political positions and doctrines, which assert a commitment to individual freedom and equality. Some of the individual rights traditionally defended by liberalists are the right to life, the right to property, freedom of association, freedom of expression, freedom of religion and freedom from state interference in people's private lives. Liberalism assumes that rights and freedoms are, or should be, universal to the human species regardless of the social and cultural context. Liberalism is commonly considered to be the dominant ideology of contemporary Western democracies. It does not, however, constitute a monolithic worldview, but rather, manifests itself in a variety of positions that are not always mutually compatible.

Historically, liberalism emerged in Western Europe during the Enlightenment period, in opposition to state and church authoritarianism. Classical liberalism is usually identified with the works of philosophers John Locke (1632–1704), David Hume (1711–76), Jeremy Bentham (1748–1832), and John Stuart Mill (1806–73). It is also strongly associated with the belief that trade should be freed from state control, a belief promoted in eighteenth-century England by political economists such as Adam Smith (1723–90) and David Ricardo (1772–1823). The liberal worldview received a considerable impetus in the years following the Second World War, when critics such as Karl Popper (1966) argued for the superiority of a liberal 'open society' over the authoritarian control of fascist and communist states. The collapse of communism in Eastern Europe since 1989 has been interpreted by Francis Fukuyama (1992) as evidence of a decisive and irreversible victory of liberalism in contemporary society.

There are two main strands of liberal philosophy: the utilitarian strand, which emphasizes that government policy should be guided by the principle of the greatest good for the greatest number of people; and the rights-based strand, which posits that the rights of an individual should not be alienated under any circumstances and that government should be based upon the consent of individuals, who enter into the social contract in order to protect their fundamental rights. Another distinction can be made between economic or conservative liberals, who advocate the *laissez-faire* doctrine, and social liberals, who believe that, in developed industrial societies, genuine equality and freedom cannot be achieved without considerable intervention by the welfare state.

Liberalism has been a target of critique from a number of theoretical perspectives, notably Marxism and feminism. Traditional Marxists tend to see liberalism as an ideology that sustains and reinforces capitalist society by encouraging the individual accumulation of wealth and obscuring the social and political conditions under which individuals operate. Feminists have criticized the male-centred underpinning of contemporary liberal democracy, with origins in the social contract predicated on women's subjugation through marital rights (Pateman 1988). Espousing the postmodernist distrust in the possibility of universal truth, contemporary liberal thinkers such as John Rawls (1993) and Richard Rorty (1989) tend to emphasize the relative and contextual rather than universal scope of the liberal worldview.

Neoliberalism is associated with the emergence of the New Right in a number of countries across the globe, following the economic crises of the 1970s. Invoking the *laissez-faire* doctrine of economic liberalism, the theorists of the New Right argue that the swift distribution of resources associated with free markets boosts human welfare. Neo-liberalism is linked, in particular, with the political hegemony of Margaret Thatcher (Prime Minister 1979–90) in the UK and President Ronald Reagan (1980–8) in the US. The call for a free market and the cutting down of the role of the nation-state has been given a further impetus by globalization and the growing dominance of multilateral regulatory institutions, such as the International Monetary Fund (IMF) and the World Trade Organization (WTO).

See also: **Capitalism; Enlightenment, the; Fordism, post-Fordism; Globalization; Modernity, modernization, modernism; Patriarchy; Postmodern, postmodernity, postmodernism; Pragmatism; Thatcherism.**

Further reading: Pateman (1988), Rorty (1989).

Lifeworld and system

The concept of the lifeworld (German *Lebenswelt*) derives from the phenomenology of German philosopher Edmund Husserl (1859–1938). It refers to the world as it is experienced by people in their daily lives, as opposed to the construed and idealized world of science. The lifeworld, for Husserl, constitutes a pre-representational and pre-analytic foundation of all our assumptions, beliefs and practices. In the theory of Austrian-born philosopher Alfred Schütz (1899–1959), the lifeworld is seen as socially constructed and governed by assumptions and habitual points of reference that underlie our actions.

The concept of the lifeworld is central to Jürgen Habermas' theory of communicative action. Habermas draws on Schütz's work to interpret the lifeworld as a repository of shared beliefs, values and practices that make communication possible. The function of the lifeworld, according to Habermas, is to legitimate and reproduce the cultural patterns at work in a given society. Habermas distinguishes between the lifeworld, which governs direct communicative interactions between social

L

agents and is motivated by a desire for mutual understanding; and the system, which underpins the impersonal and functional exchanges that pertain to the economy and the state. The 'colonization of the lifeworld' refers to the uneven relationship between these two domains of society, reflected in the progressive commodification and bureaucratization of everyday life.

See also: **Capitalism; Everyday; Phenomenology**

Further reading: Habermas (1984 and 1987 [1981]).

Literacy

The word signifies the skills of reading and writing, and the pedagogical practice that aims at imparting those skills to an individual, or a constituency of learners. The concept of cultural literacy has been deployed to signal the mastery of ideas, values and codes of behaviour of a given culture, usually in so far as they are embedded in a selected textual canon. Literacy is conventionally regarded as a path to emancipation and social empowerment, and was – before the spread of mass education in the latter half of the twentieth century – often limited to the privileged social strata. Until quite recently, literacy was used as a rallying point to circumscribe culture to a repository of selected texts, and to ban or devalue popular, socially marginal or oppositional elements of culture. In his seminal book *The Uses of Literacy* (1958), Richard Hoggart argued in favour of free education and universal literacy, and against the commercialization of culture.

Within contemporary cultural studies, it is typically assumed that literacy pertains not only to the institutionally sanctioned cultural canon, but also to the full range of popular texts and practices that inform a person's everyday life. This means that literacy can no longer be seen as a principle of hierarchy and exclusion, but rather, as one of equality in difference. In other words, 'to be literate is to undertake a dialogue with others who speak from different histories, locations and experiences'. From that perspective, literacy is defined as a discursive practice 'in which difference becomes crucial for understanding not simply how to read, write or develop aural skills, but to also recognize that the identities of "others" matter as part of a broader set of politics and practices aimed at the reconstruction of democratic public life' (Giroux and Trend 1992: 65).

See also: **Class; Culturalism; Leavisism; Value, value system**

Further reading: Hoggart (1958).

Logocentrism, phonocentrism, *écriture*

The Greek word *logos*, which means 'word', is deployed in philosophy to refer to a fundamental principle of reason, logic or truth. In Christian theology, it stands for the Word of God, as the origin of all creation. The French poststructuralist thinker Jacques Derrida coined the term 'logocentrism' in his deconstructive critique of Western thought (1974 [1967]). Logocentrism signals the 'metaphysics of presence' that, according to Derrida, has underpinned Western philosophy since Plato. It is manifested in an undue faith in the stability of meaning, which is supposed to be guaranteed by a transcendental fixed point, such as the 'Divine Father', Man, or Truth.

Western thought, Derrida argued, conceives of the world in terms of binary oppositions such as good/evil or man/woman, in which the first term of the binary always occupies a privileged position, as it is held to possess higher presence and therefore to represent truth or logos. Derrida sought to demonstrate how logocentric thinking works to suppress difference in favour of presence and identity.

The most evident case of logocentrism, according to Derrida, is phonocentrism, or the tendency in Western thought to privilege speech over writing. Phonocentrism is based on a belief that speech possesses an integral meaning, guaranteed by the presence of the real speaker.

Derrida introduced the concept of *écriture* (a French word that literally means 'writing') as a metaphysical paradigm opposed to logocentrism, based on the assumption that meaning is generated through an endless process of difference and deferral. The metaphor of writing is deployed to underscore the physical and metaphysical separation between the original creator or 'Father' of the utterance and its many differential meanings.

See also: **Deconstruction**; *Différance*

Further reading: Derrida (1974 [1967]).

L

Marxism, Leninism, Western Marxism

Marxism is a set of economic, social and political doctrines originally developed by the German theorists Karl Marx (1818–83) and Friedrich Engels (1820–95), which was further expanded and revised by Marxist thinkers in the twentieth century, notably in Germany, Italy and France. The three fundamental influences on Karl Marx's thought were German ideology, French utopian socialism, and British classical economic theory. Althusser emphasized a fundamental difference between Marx's early writings (1840–4), in which Hegel's ideology is a major influence, and his later work (1857–83), which was decidedly anti-humanist and oriented towards providing a 'scientific' foundation for his theory.

Marxist theory forecast an eventual breakdown of capitalism, the emergence of a classless communist society and the 'withering away' of the state. This was the foundation of Marx's 'scientific socialism', which postulated the existence of a universal dynamic in human history, which could be understood in terms of the conditions of material production in a given society. Marx and Engels believed that the triumph of the proletariat would end the dialectic of history, since there would be no more conflict between the upper class and the subordinate classes.

Leninism is an outgrowth of Marxism associated with the Russian revolutionary Vladimir Ilyich Lenin (1870–1924). Lenin assumed the need for immediate proletarian revolution in Tsarist Russia, rather than awaiting the auspicious constellation of economic relations to unfold naturally within capitalism itself, as orthodox Marxists had predicted. He also promoted the establishment of an elite party of professional revolutionaries that would serve as the vanguard of the proletarian revolution. Leninism became the guiding doctrine of the Soviet Union, providing a model for communist-style regimes in other countries across the globe. Today, Marxism persists as the official state ideology of the People's Republic of China, North Korea, Vietnam and Cuba. In the twentieth century, Marxism had a significant impact on national liberation and anti-colonial struggles in Asia, Africa and Latin America.

The term 'Western Marxism' refers to a softer version of Marxist thought, developed by twentieth-century Marxist thinkers based mainly in Western and Central Europe. The main proponents of Western Marxism are the philosopher and literary critic György Lukács (1885–1971), the political activist and theorist Antonio Gramsci (1891–1937), the thinkers associated with the Frankfurt school, the existentialist philosopher Jean-Paul Sartre (1905–80), the Marxist sociologist Henri Lefebvre (1901–91) and the structuralist Marxist Louis Althusser (1918–90).

The Western Marxists endeavoured to bypass the teleology, economic determinism and class reductionism of orthodox Marxism and to foreground the role of culture in society (see Thompson 1966 [1963]; Williams 1977; Hall 1992).

See also: **Alienation; Base and superstructure; Centre for Contemporary Cultural Studies (CCCS); Critical theory; Hegemony; Historical materialism; Ideology; Left, New Left; Post-Marxism**

Further reading: Milner (1994).

Masculinity

'Masculinity' refers to the normative and socially and culturally constructed patterns of manhood. What precisely constitutes masculine appearance and behaviour varies from culture to culture, but strength, activity, assertiveness, competitiveness and aggression are some of the most common stereotypes. Men are typically socialized to conform to what is considered the masculine norm.

As a discursive category, masculinity intersects with other identity categories, such as gender, class, race, ethnicity and sexuality. It cannot, however, be understood as fully belonging to any of these groupings. Most importantly, as Eve Kosofsky Sedgwick has convincingly argued, 'when something is about masculinity, it isn't always "about men"' (1985: 12). It is now widely acknowledged that there are female versions of masculinity (an obvious example is the butch lesbian variant) and, by the same token, male modes of femininity (for example, drag).

The conventional understanding of masculinity and femininity in patriarchal societies takes for granted a simple binary opposition between men and women, based on the assumed biological differences between the two sexes. Heterosexual masculinity is typically constructed as the normative standard and the foremost source of empowerment in patriarchy. Discourses that privilege some people by associating them with the socially defined patterns of maleness are referred to as hegemonic masculinities: 'Hegemonic masculinities define successful ways of "being a man"; in so doing, they define other masculine styles as inadequate or inferior' (Cornwall and Lindisfarne 1994: 16).

M

Over the last three decades, there has been an upsurge of interest in the study of men and masculinity, strengthened by the establishment of Men's Studies as a distinct area of inquiry within social sciences. Moreover, cultural critics in the fields of feminism, gay/lesbian and queer studies have endeavoured to destabilize normative social roles, challenging thereby the logic of patriarchy itself. Within cultural studies, critics have focused on the ways in which media and cultural texts and cultural practices construct and disseminate representations of men and maleness, and on the role these representations play in negotiating notions of the masculine in society.

See also: **Femininity; Feminism; Gender; Queer, queer theory**

Further reading: Gardiner (2002).

Mass communication and mass media

The term 'mass communication' refers to the transmission of information and entertainment content by skilled professionals to a large, diverse and anonymous audience, by way of advanced technologies. It is achieved through the mass media, that is, print, screen, audio and broadcast media such as newspapers, magazines, comic books, film, music, radio and television. It is now widely recognized that the media play a crucial role in the negotiation and dissemination of contemporary culture. We are witnessing the emergence of a media culture 'in which images, sounds, and spectacles help produce the fabric of everyday life, dominating leisure time, shaping political views and social behavior, and providing the materials out of which people forge their very identities' (Kellner 1995: 1).

Before the 1970s, most media theories assumed that the media were powerful forces that unilaterally imposed a dominant ideology on their audiences. Moreover, the traditions deriving from the Frankfurt School and Leavisite criticism shared a pessimistic view of the mass media as instruments of social oppression and indicators of spiritual degradation in industrialized societies.

In the early stages of the British tradition of cultural studies, the most prominent critic of this scornful view of the media was Stuart Hall (1980a, 1980b, 1980c). Drawing on the Gramscian notion of hegemony, Hall argued that media texts should be analysed in terms of opposition and struggle, as much as domination and control. Furthermore, the Gramscian paradigm allowed Hall to move beyond the class-based Marxist analysis and interpret media texts in terms of their engagement with the complex relationships of power and hegemony. Hall's influen-

M

tial theory of encoding/decoding challenged the notion of a passive audience uncritically absorbing the messages contained in media texts.

See also: **Audience; Class; Consumption; Critical theory; Encoding/decoding; Hegemony; Leavisism**

Further reading: Gurevitch et al. (eds) (1982).

Mass culture, culture industry

Until quite recently, the cultural sphere used to be conceptualized in terms of an opposition between a mass-produced popular culture, supposedly imposed from above on powerless and passive audiences, and an elite culture, which was believed to emanate from the genius of the individual artist and to be genuinely capable of revealing social reality. Most notably, this distinction informs the cultural theories that go under the rubrics of Leavisism and the critical theory of the Frankfurt School. Mass culture theories were a critical response to the industrialization and commodification of popular culture that occurred on a large scale in the early decades of the twentieth century.

Some of the defining features of mass culture, according to its critics, are triviality, superficiality and formulaic repetitiveness. The phrase 'culture industry' was coined by Theodor Adorno and Max Horkheimer in their book *Dialectic of Enlightenment* (2002 [1947]), to refer to the downright commodification of cultural forms in industrialized societies. The culture industry, according to Adorno, 'intentionally integrates its consumers from above. To the detriment of both, it forces together the spheres of high and low art, separated for thousands of years' (1991: 85).

Since the 1950s, mass culture theories have been criticized for their elitism, and for their tendency to homogenize popular culture and downplay the agency of the audience. Critics have also challenged the viability of a value hierarchy that extends from 'high' to 'low' culture, and of its correspondence with a stratification of social classes. It is also widely acknowledged that, in late modernity, the so-called 'high' culture itself has been absorbed within commodity regimes.

See also: **Critical theory; Leavisism; Value, value system**

Further reading: Strinati (2004).

Material culture

'Material culture' refers to objects used in everyday life, including art, craft and household utensils, furniture, clothes, technical devices and many others. It plays an important role in human existence, assisting people in their everyday activities and providing a medium of communication and exchange. Propelled into the social sphere, material objects develop histories of their own, which provide useful insights into social change, individual and group identities, and the patterns of consumption and value creation.

Material culture studies are an interdisciplinary field of inquiry into the social meaning of things. The emergence of material culture studies is associated with the appearance of ethnographic collections in European museums and the consolidation of anthropology as a discipline in the nineteenth century. Studies of material culture were originally motivated by a belief that artefacts could reflect the stage of social progress of a particular people or nation, in the same way that fossil remains signalled the different phases of biological evolution. Material culture studies thus reinforced the modernist worldview entrenched in the notions of progress and linear evolution. Politically, they bolstered Europe's belief in its own superiority, and its self-avowed mission as a civilizing force. The appearance of ethnographic collections coincided with the rise of consumerism: the glass cabinets and shop windows of the early European department stores were similar to the museum cabinets of curiosities, in that they could also be read as evidence of Western progress. The anthropological interest in material culture subsided somewhat with the rise of social anthropology, with its preference for participant observation over the museum-based study of material objects, and its interest in the structure of social systems, rather than their position on the scale of evolution. However, it did not disappear altogether. In fact, concerns over the loss of 'authenticity' through the growth of industrialization gave a new impetus to the study of material culture in the early decades of the twentieth century. A significant theoretical shift occurred in the 1970s, with structuralist and poststructuralist theories offering a compelling critique of the role of objects of material culture in symbolic systems and social structures.

See also: **Authentic culture; Consumption; Museum**

Further reading: Buchli (ed.) (2002).

Mediasphere

The term was coined by British media and cultural theorist John Hartley to describe the 'whole universe of media, both factual and fictional, in all forms (print, electronic, screen), all genres (news, drama), all taste hierarchies (from art to entertainment) in all languages in all countries' (1999: 217). Hartley builds on Yuri Lotman's (1922–93) notion of the semiosphere, the 'semiotic space necessary for the existence and functioning of languages' (Lotman 1990: 123). Lotman argued that the principal mechanism of meaning generation was not a specific language *per se*, but rather the entire semiotic space of culture. He considered the semiosphere to be analogous to Vladimir Vernadsky's notion of the biosphere, or the 'totality and the organic whole of living matter, and also the condition for the continuation of life' (p. 125).

Hartley imagines the mediasphere as existing within the semiosphere, as a storehouse of factual and fictional mediated content. The mediasphere can be understood as the space which brings together diverse 'cultural domains' for audiences, thus creating the self-perception of the audience itself as a community. Hartley revises the notion of the public sphere, which Jürgen Habermas relates to politically delimited national communities. In contrast, Hartley imagines the public sphere as a Russian doll, which is contained within a larger mediasphere and which in turn contains 'further countercultural, oppositional or minoritarian public spheres' (1999: 218).

See also: **Mass communication and mass media; Semiology, semiotics**

Further reading: Hartley (1999).

Memory

The term refers to the sense of the past in the present, both in the mind of an individual, and in the collective consciousness of a social group. As a social phenomenon, memory is in a close relationship with tradition, custom, myth and historical consciousness. It is the primary medium through which identities are constituted, maintained and contested.

Memory studies traverse multiple scholarly disciplines, including sociology, anthropology, psychology, history, cultural studies, literary criticism, art history and political science. Concepts such as collective memory, popular memory, vernacular memory and cultural memory are typically deployed to highlight the social nature of recalling, constructing and commemorating past experiences.

Critics have argued that our understanding of memory depends, to a large extent, on the material means of memory transmission. For example, the French historian Jacques Le Goff (1992) has identified five distinct periods in the history of human memory: prehistory, in which 'ethnic memory' is preserved in oral tradition; Antiquity, in which writing becomes a mnemonic device that facilitates commemoration and documentary recording; the Middle Ages, characterized by a divi-

M

sion between a circular liturgical memory and a lay memory; the period from the Renaissance to the latter half of the twentieth century, defined by the progressive exteriorization of individual memory, beginning with the invention of the printing press in the fifteenth century and culminating in the nineteenth-century emergence of archives, libraries and museums; and finally, the current moment, in which electronic means of recording and transmitting information have radically changed our ways of remembering the past.

A notable precursor to the study of memory as a social phenomenon was the French philosopher and sociologist Maurice Halbwachs (1877–1945). In contrast to the psychological interpretations of memory as an inherent property of individual consciousness, Halbwachs argued that 'it is in society that people normally acquire their memories. It is also in society that they recall, recognize, and localize their memories' (1992 [1941]: 38). Halbwachs interpreted history as a dead memory, which preserves pasts to which people no longer have an organic relation. He distinguished history from historical memory, which – although not part of our personal experience – could be kept alive by social institutions. He used the term 'collective memory' to refer to the active past that shapes our identities. Collective memory, he argued, eventually yields to history as people lose touch with their past.

The relationship between nationalism and social memory has been analysed by a number of critics. Perhaps the most important contemporary theorist of memory is the French historian Pierre Nora. In his multi-volume study *Realms of Memory* (1996–98 [1984–92]), Nora has argued that, in modern society, real environments of memory (in French, *milieux*) have been replaced by specific memory sites (French *lieux*). In contemporary society, Nora contends, memory is no longer upheld by a meaningful continuity of social reproduction. Rather, it now resides in explicit signs, or consecrated sites, which are not experienced organically by people. Nora's project is to register all of these sites of memory in French society. He considers the nation-state to be the last bastion that could guarantee a convergence between memory and history. But, the salience of the nation, he maintains, has dwindled as the state has ceded power to society: the nation itself, previously buttressed by memory, is now no more than a mere memory trace.

In *Twilight Memories*, postmodernist Andreas Huyssen has argued that, despite the widespread popularity of memory sites and practices in contemporary society, historical consciousness is in decline. This resurgence of memory differs from the modes of remembering associated with the nation-state. Rather, it is a sign of the 'evident crisis of the ideology of progress and modernization' and an attempt 'to slow down information processing', 'to recover a mode of contemplation outside the universe of simulation and fast-speed information and cable networks' and 'to claim some anchoring space in a world of puzzling and often threatening heterogeneity, non-synchronicity, and information overload' (1995: 7).

The increased interest in social or collective memory, since the early 1980s, has been attributed to three strands of thought that dominated the intellectual culture of the 1960s and 1970s: the interest in the historical narratives of repressed groups, which went hand in hand with the rise of multiculturalism; the postmodernist distrust in linear historicity and stable identities; and the neo-Gramscian understanding of memory as a potentially counter-hegemonic practice (Schwartz 1996). The neo-Gramscian approach, in particular, informed the work of the Popular Memory Group at the Centre for Contemporary Cultural Studies in Birmingham in the 1980s. The group sought to examine popular memory as an ongoing process of negotiation between official and unofficial, public and private, dominant and oppositional forms of memory.

See also: **Centre for Contemporary Cultural Studies (CCCS); Identity, identification, identity politics; Museum**

Further reading: Hodgkin and Radstone (eds) (2003).

Mestizaje

The Spanish-language term *mestizo* (French *métis*, Portuguese *mestiço*, Italian *meticcio*) derives from Late Latin *mixticius* or *mistitius*, and ultimately from *mixtus*, which means mixed. It originally referred to the peoples of mixed European and Amerindian race and culture, inhabiting the territory that spans Mesoamerica and South America. Initially associated with the early Spanish and Portuguese colonization of the Americas, the term is now sometimes deployed to refer more broadly to racially mixed people. In its cultural uses, *mestizaje* is semantically related to concepts such as hybridity, transculturation, creolization and diaspora, but it has a distinct character, because of its historical associations with questions of race in a specific colonial context.

M

Despite its origins in the colonial discourses of racial purity, which discriminated against native populations, the term has since acquired more positive overtones. In 1925, Mexican educator José Vasconcelos argued for a pan-Latin American embrace of cultural and racial mixture as a linchpin of local identities, albeit predicated on a progressive 'whitening' of the indigenous element. In countries of Latin America with significant *mestizo/a* populations, 'mestizaje has been adopted by architects of the nation as an official discourse', to imply 'that the state is based on a mythic foundation of racial tolerance, diversity, and plural-ism' (Allatson 2007). Furthermore, it has been used more recently in diasporic cultural discourses to describe the vitality and subversive potential of mixed cultural forms. A notable example is Gloria Anzaldúa's (1999 [1987]) celebration of the 'new mestiza conscious-ness', as a 'mode of identification that embraces Indian ancestry, and any other socially disparaged or marginalized identity' (Allatson 2007).

See also: **Creolization; Diaspora; Globalization; Hybridity; Transculturation, transcul-turality, transculturalism**

Further reading: Audinet (2004).

Metaculture

The prefix derives from Greek *meta*, meaning 'with, across, or after', and denotes, in this compound noun, something of a higher or second-order kind. 'Metaculture' therefore refers to 'culture about culture', or cultural discourses that comment on the nature, significance and other aspects of culture. According to Francis Mulhern, metacultural discourse is 'that in which "culture" addresses its own generality . . . and historical condi-tions of existence' (2000: 181–2). Cultural studies clearly fit that defini-tion. According to US anthropologist Greg Urban, metaculture functions as a supplement to culture, and may act as an 'accelerative force', aiding cultural products in their motion through the discursive space of the public sphere (2001: 4). For example, appreciative reviews of a cultural text may promote its circulation and social impact.

See also: **Culture; Discourse; Text**

Further reading: Mulhern (2000).

Metaphor, metonymy, synecdoche

Metaphor and metonymy are figures of speech, common both in creative literature and in everyday language. While metaphor is considered to be a key rhetorical device in poetry, metonymy is more commonly associ-ated with prose. Those metaphorical expressions that are so firmly rooted in common usage that they typically pass unnoticed are referred to as dead metaphors (for example, a leg of a table). In contrast, new and unexpected metaphors can cause people to stop and think, and to develop novel ways of dealing with the world that surrounds them.

The term 'metaphor' derives from a Greek word that literally means 'transfer' or 'carry over'. In linguistics and literary studies, metaphor is a rhetorical figure, in which an object, concept or action is referred to by a word or expression that commonly denotes something quite different, implying that the two share a common quality. The primary literal term in a metaphor is called the tenor, while the secondary figurative term is referred to as the vehicle. For example, in the metaphor the 'light (of faith)', the tenor is faith, and the vehicle is the light. While a simile expresses a resemblance between two terms, for example, 'my love is like a red, red rose' (Robert Burns), a metaphor assumes an imaginary identity between them, as in 'love is a rose', or 'he is an angel'. Usually, though not always, something quite abstract is identified with something concrete, that renders it more 'palpable'. Metaphors may be nouns, as in the above examples. They may also be adjectives (someone's enthusiasm may be infectious), verbs (a career may blossom), or idiomatic expressions (to take a step in the right direction). A mixed metaphor, or catachresis, is one in which the combination of terms appears illogical, as in 'the voice of your eyes is deeper than all roses' (e. e. cummings).

Metonymy is a figure of speech that substitutes a quality or attribute of something for the thing itself, for example in referring to the judiciary as the bench. A related rhetorical figure is that of synecdoche, in which a part is substituted for the whole (as in 'crown', to mean the King), or a whole is substituted for a part (Italy, to mean the Italian soccer team).

In the work of the Russian-American linguist Roman Jakobson (1896–1982), metaphor and metonymy – governed respectively by the principles of similarity and contiguity – are interpreted as the basis of all language and thought. This assumption underlies the work of later critics in disciplines including psychoanalysis, literary criticism, philosophy, feminist studies and cultural studies. In contemporary philosophy, there is increasing recognition that language is never purely denotative, as it never refers to a transcendental reality.

See also: **Connotation/denotation; Rhetoric; Trope**

Further reading: Lakoff and Johnson (2003 [1980]).

M

Method, methodology

The word 'method' derives from the Greek words for 'road' or 'way' (*hodos*) and 'after' or 'about' (*meta*). Method, therefore, is the 'route down which you go to pursue something' (Couldry 2000: 8). The application of the word 'methodology', in academic discourse, is twofold: on the one hand, 'methodology' refers to the overall epistemological paradigm adopted within a particular discipline or tradition, or within a specific research project, which may be interdisciplinary, multidisciplinary or transdisciplinary; on the other, it is sometimes used to designate a set of actual research practices, or methods, used to gather, process and interpret data.

Considerations of methodology within cultural studies are remarkably complex. Many accept that cultural studies 'in fact has no distinct methodology, no unique statistical, ethnomethodological, or textual analysis to call its own' (Grossberg, Nelson and Treichler 1992: 2). Rather, what constitutes method in cultural studies is described as *bricolage*, or a pragmatic and strategic selection of different methods, predicated on the specificities of each research project. Research into culture deploys a variety of paradigms borrowed from disciplines such as sociology, anthropology, history, psychology, linguistics and literary studies. Some have argued that 'without some shared commitment to methodological debate, cultural studies risks being no more than a trail of political interventions by authoritative voices' (Couldry 2000: 9). As a bare minimum, one can say that what makes cultural studies distinct from other disciplines is its primary concern with questions of culture and power and its 'insistence on certain democratic values at the heart of its method' (p. 5).

It is customary to think about methods of research as being either quantitative (concerned primarily with numbers and statistics) or qualitative (concerned with interpretation and meaning). Quantitative methods, originally associated with the natural sciences, are now used extensively in social science research. Within studies of culture, the most common quantitative method is content analysis. Qualitative methods are more widespread in humanities-related disciplines. The most widespread qualitative methods in the study of cultural texts are semiotic analysis, discourse analysis and deconstruction. In the study of culture industries and specific audiences, the commonly used methods of data collection include observation, participant observation, questionnaires, interviews, focus groups and oral history. Any research project typically encompasses several of these strategies or techniques.

See also: **Content analysis; Deconstruction; Discourse analysis; Ethnography; Focus groups; Grounded theory; Interview; Observation; Oral history; Questionnaire; Semiotic analysis.**

Further reading: Denzin and Lincoln (eds) (2000 and 2003), Stokes (2003).

Mirror stage

See **Identity, identification, identity politics; Imaginary, symbolic, real**

Modernity, modernization, modernism

The word 'modern' derives from Late Latin *modernus*, from Latin *modo*, which means 'just now'. The underlying logic of modernity is based on the idea of rupture between the current moment in history, which is seen as enlightened, scientific and progressive; and the preceding ages, which are considered to be dark, backward and superstitious. Another assumption of modernity is that history follows a linear progress, upon which people can have a creative impact.

The precise form of modernity has changed over time and across different societies. Even though historians sometimes argue that modernity emerged for the first time as early as the Christian Middle Ages (Calinescu 1987), its origins are typically traced back to the European discovery and colonization of the 'New World', since it was then that the colonizers were in a position to compare themselves with other societies and develop a sense of superiority in relation to them. Subsequently, the Enlightenment worldview – with its belief in reason and progress – had a significant role in shaping the ideals of modernity. Finally, modernity was set into full swing by the processes of industrialization, urbanization and secularization, characterized by rapid change, transience and alienation. From a post-colonial perspective, modernity is often criticized as profoundly Eurocentric, since it takes Europe as the model of progress that the rest of the world has to emulate. On the other hand, feminists have identified a pervasive masculinism at the very core of modern rationality.

Modernization refers to the multiple processes of social, economic and technological change that have ensued in the wake of industrialization. It was used by American social scientists in the latter half of the twentieth century, to refer to the processes of change, in which less developed societies attain features that are prevalent in more developed societies. Modernization theory underpinned the programmes of economic aid that followed the Second World War, with expectations that economic progress in developing countries would also bring about their ideological and political harmonization with the liberal West.

M

The term 'modernism' (or, more commonly, 'modernisms') is used to describe the various expressions of the cultural experience of modernity, which flourished in philosophy, religion, literature, theatre and fine arts in the period from the mid-nineteenth to the mid-twentieth century. The key representatives of modernism are, among others, James, Conrad, Proust, Mann, Kafka and Joyce in fiction; Strindberg, Pirandello and Brecht in drama; Baudelaire, Mallarmé, Yeats, Eliot, Pound and Rilke in poetry; and Picasso, Matisse, Kandinsky and Miro in painting. The most prominent features of modernism are experimentation, formalism, complexity, and a desire to produce a 'tradition of the new'.

See also: **Avant-garde; Colonialism; Enlightenment, the; Eurocentrism, Westocentrism**

Further reading: Habermas (1987); Hall, Held, Hubert, and Thompson (eds) (1996).

Monoculture

The prefix derives from Greek *monos*, meaning 'alone'. The notion of monoculture refers to a lack of diversity in the cultural sphere. The term has wide currency in agriculture, where it refers to the practice of relying on a single type of plant for commercial farming. In social science, it is used to denote a homogenization of cultural practices, for example under the influence of globalization.

See also: **Culture; Globalization**

Multicultural, multiculturalism

The adjective 'multicultural' refers to the identifiable quality of a particular socio-cultural community (for example, a multicultural society is one that includes diverse cultural communities; a multicultural school has students from different cultural backgrounds); or of a body of texts and cultural practices (for example, multicultural music or film). The adjective 'multiculturalist', on the other hand, describes the supportive attitude to cultural diversity at a personal, communal and institutional level, most notably that of the nation-state. In a broader sense, it may signal the appreciation of diversity in terms of class, gender, sexual orientation or lifestyle, since none of these categories can be understood as isolated from its cultural context. In a more circumscribed sense, prevalent in common usage, it refers to ethno-cultural diversity within a specific society. In both of these senses, multiculturalism signals an attitude that sustains difference, as opposed to monoculturalism, which encourages assimilation into the dominant culture. Multicultural societies can thus be either multiculturalist or monoculturalist in their ethos and orientation. Multiculturalist societies tend to support, to varying degrees, difference in the private sphere. They also often encourage cultural practices of ethnic minorities in education and the arts, while demanding compliance with a single set of rights and responsibilities in the public sphere.

Contemporary multicultural societies reflect the history of human mobility over the past centuries, and are related in particular to colonization, decolonization and, most recently, to the complex processes of economic and cultural globalization. The global spread of the mass media, the Internet and communication technologies have also undermined the possibility of maintaining self-contained and relatively homogeneous cultural communities.

Multiculturalism has been a target of critique from a number of perspectives. On the one hand, the liberal focus on diversity has been criticized for upholding the existing power relationships within multicultural societies and commodifying cultural diversity (Mitchell 1993). Also, critics across a range of disciplines have argued that the idea of multiculturalism, as well as the policies and practices that stem from it, essentialize cultural identities, failing to recognize their dynamic and fluid nature.

See also: **Essentialism; Globalization; Hybridity; Identity, identification, identity politics**

Further reading: Goldberg (1994).

Museum

The Greek term *mouseion* originally referred to the shrine of the Muses. The word 'museum' has found its way into numerous modern languages, to denote a public or private institution that collects, preserves, studies and classifies objects from the natural world and things made by humans. Both educational and entertaining, museums bring together the public and the personal, the objective and the subjective, the world of science and art, and the everyday life of ordinary people.

The birth of the museum has been associated with the emergence of the bourgeois public sphere in late eighteenth-century Europe. It was then that new cultural institutions such as museums, literary journals, debating societies and coffee houses came into being, as mediators between the 'state and the court on the one hand and, on the other, civil society and the sphere of private intimacy formed by the newly constituted conjugal family' (Bennett 1995: 25).

Museums are intimately bound with memory, because they delimit what is valued and remembered at the institutional level, as well as engaging the personal memory of their visitors. The historical museum and the heritage museum in particular have played a major role in constructing and sustaining discourses of national identity.

M

See also: **Cultural policy; Identity, identification, identity politics; Memory**

Further reading: Bennett (1995).

Myth

The Greek word *mythos* means 'story'. Classical Greek philosophy postulated a distinction between *logos* (reason) and *mythos* (story), with the former occupying the privileged position in the dichotomy. In common parlance, 'myth' can denote a widely accepted, but false belief (*COED*).

As a concept in literary theory, myth can be defined as a 'sacred narrative explaining how the world and man came to be in their present form' (Dundes 1984: 1). In contrast to folktales, which are secular and fictional, myths are held to express sacred truths about a range of matters fundamental to human existence, such as the origin of the world, the purpose of life, the nature of death and the like. They are also often associated with rituals, especially those that mark transitional stages in life, such as birth, puberty, marriage or death. Myths have provided one of the most fertile sources of inspiration for art and literature across the globe. They have also been an important topic of scholarly analysis, in disciplines such as psychology and psychoanalysis, anthropology, religion and literary studies.

In the work of Roland Barthes, myth is a form of metalanguage, or a system of meaning that builds on a pre-existing chain of signification. In his influential collection of essays, *Mythologies* (1984 [1957]), Barthes gave a satirical analysis of the numerous myths that make up contemporary French society. Myth, Barthes argued, operates by way of transforming what constitutes a sign (in structuralist linguistics, the relationship between a signifier, or word, and a signified, or the concept or idea associated with the word) in the first-order language system, into a mere signifier in the second-order system. Barthes's famous example of this second-order signification is a photograph of a black Algerian soldier saluting the French flag, which appeared on the cover of the French magazine *Paris-Match*. In this example, the mythic signifier – a black soldier giving a salute – assumes a new signified, which is a 'purposeful mixture of Frenchness and militariness' (p. 116). This in turn generates new meanings, related to the idea that France is such a great empire 'that all her sons, without any color discrimination, faithfully serve under her flag, and that there is no better answer to the detractors of an alleged colonialism than the zeal shown by this Negro in serving his so-called oppressors' (p. 116). Mythology, in Barthes's account, has an ideological function, since it turns culturally specific content into ideas that appear natural and universal.

See also: **Code; Ideology; Narrative; Poststructuralism; Semiology, semiotics; Sign; Structuralism**

M

Narrative

A narrative recounts a chain of events in a temporal and causal sequence, thereby applying an order and a viewpoint to human experience. The etymology of the word can be traced back to the Sanskrit root *gnâ*, which means to know, via the Latin adjective *gnarus* (*narus*), knowledgeable or skilled, and the Latin verb *narrare*, to tell or relate. The key function of narrative, therefore, is to articulate, store and communicate knowledge. Since narratives define what counts as knowledge in a given society (Lyotard 1984 [1979]), they are always bound up with relations of power and domination. Also, since they assign meaning to experience, they play a crucial role in identity formation. In fact, critics have argued that social life, and meaningful human action as such, can be conceived of as an enacted narrative (MacIntyre 1981, Ricœur 1984, 1985, 1988).

Narratives appear in a myriad of different genres. They can be 'carried by articulated language, spoken or written, fixed or moving images, gestures, and the ordered mixture of all these substances'. Furthermore, narrative is 'present in every age, in every place, in every society. . . . All classes, all human groups, have their narratives, enjoyment of which is very often shared by men [sic] with different even opposing, cultural backgrounds' (Barthes 1977 [1966]: 79).

Although the interest in narrative analysis can be traced back to the hermeneutic studies of the Bible, Talmud and Koran, the contemporary narrative theory owes its origins to four twentieth-century traditions: Russian Formalism (in particular, Propp, Shklovsky, Jakobson), new criticism (Frye, Scholes), structuralism (Barthes, Todorov), and hermeneutics (Gadamer, Iser, Jauss, Ricœur). Narrative theory typically distinguishes between the pre-literary events that inform a narrative (called *fabula* in Russian Formalism; *histoire* or story in structuralism), and the way in which these events are represented in the narrative (*sjuzhet* in Russian Formalism; discourse in structuralism).

The contemporary interest in narrative transcends the boundaries of literary theory and spreads across a range of humanities and social sciences. The US historian Hayden White, for example, has interpreted narrative as the principal mode of knowledge articulation in history writing. According to White, 'histories gain part of their explanatory effect by their success in making stories out of mere chronicles' (1973: 223). The historical narrative, in White's account, mediates between the reported events and a set of pre-generic plot structures that give them meaning.

French philosopher Jean-François Lyotard (1984 [1979]) differentiated between the narrative forms of knowledge, prevalent in pre-modern societies, and scientific knowledge, which is typical of modernity. He maintained that scientific knowledge relied on narrative to portray itself as valid, while at the same time denying narrative its legitimacy as a mode of knowledge in its own right. According to Lyotard, the defining feature of the postmodern condition is incredulity toward grand narratives or metanarratives, which serve to legitimate knowledge, such as the 'dialectic of Spirit' or the 'emancipation of humanity'. In contrast, it is the 'little narrative' (French, *petit récit*) which 'remains the quintessential form of imaginative invention, most particularly in science' (1984 [1979]: 60).

See also: **Discourse; Genre; Hermeneutics; Knowledge; Nation, nationality, nationalism; New Criticism; Postmodern, postmodernity, postmodernism; Poststructuralism; Russian Formalism; Structuralism**

Further reading: McQuillan (2000).

Nation, nationality, nationalism

Etymologically related to the words 'native' and 'nature', the word 'nation' derives from Latin *natio*, which means birth or race, from *natus*, the past participle of the verb *nasci*, to be born. In classical Latin, *natio* was typically used to refer to resident aliens living in port cities. In medieval universities, it designated groups of students distinguished by their birth in a specific city or region. In contemporary common usage, the term brings together the assumption of common descent, culture or language, with the idea of a political community that may be connected to a specific real or symbolic territory.

There are two distinct meanings of the term 'nationality': on the one hand, it may refer to the cultural belonging of an individual or group; on the other, it may signal the official status of being attached to a particular state for purposes of international law.

Nationalism is a doctrine that sustains and legitimizes the modern notion of nationhood. Although attachment to the native culture and land has existed throughout history, it was not until the French Revolution that nationalism emerged as a significant political force. Philosopher and social anthropologist Ernest Gellner (1925–95) defined nationalism as a 'theory of political legitimacy, which requires that ethnic boundaries should not cut across political ones, and, in particular, that ethnic boundaries within a given state . . . should not separate the power-holders from the rest' (Gellner 1983: 1). Critics have distinguished between nationalism and patriotism, describing the latter as the 'affection that a people feel for their country understood not as native soil, but as a community of free men living together for the common good' (Viroli 1995: 57).

Contemporary accounts of nationhood are typically seen as falling under one of four rubrics: primordialism, perennialism, ethno-symbolism and constructivism/modernism. Primordialist theories, now largely considered flawed and outmoded, view the nation as a primeval and natural aspect of the human condition, based primarily on genetic descent, kinship and ethnicity. Perennialist theories, which are also extensively disputed, claim that nations have existed throughout history, even though they are not inscribed in the natural order. Ethno-symbolist interpretations recognize the modernity of nationalist ideology, but foreground its roots in the symbols, myths, traditions and values that can be traced back to pre-modern ethnic communities or *ethnie* (see Smith 1986, 1991). Finally, constructivist/modernist theories, which have had a major impact on cultural studies, interpret the nation as contingent, socially produced and 'imagined', and deny the existence of the nation before the modern period (Gellner 1983; Anderson 1983).

As early as the nineteenth century, critics emphasized the subjective and voluntary character of national belonging. French historian Ernest Renan (1823–92) defined 'nation' as a daily plebiscite: 'the desire, clearly expressed, to continue the communal life' (1994 [1882]: 17). The nineteenth-century German sociologist Max Weber (1864–1920) defined nation as a 'community of sentiment' that tends to produce a state of its own (1947: 176). More recently, the American sociologist Benedict Anderson has defined the nation as an imagined political community: imagined, because the 'members of even the smallest nation will never know most of their fellow-members, meet them, or even hear of them, yet in the minds of each lives the image of their communion'; and because the 'nation is always conceived as a deep, horizontal comradeship', regardless of the 'actual inequality and exploitation that may prevail' in individual nations (1983: 6–7).

Over the last two decades, critics have challenged the essentialist interpretations of nationhood in contemporary theory. In particular, Homi Bhabha has argued that national culture is not unitary, but rather, ambivalent and disruptive. In Bhabha's work, the nation is constituted through narration, which entails the conversion of a particular territor-

N

ial space into a place of historical experience. At the same time, the narratives of the nation inevitably bring to the fore the diversity and inequality within it (Bhabha refers to this phenomenon as dissemiNation). According to Bhabha, the 'political unity of the nation consists in a continual displacement of its irredeemably plural modern space, bounded by different, even hostile nations, into a signifying space that is archaic and mythical' (1990: 300).

Within cultural studies, critics have examined the ambiguities of nationhood through the study of literary texts, arguing that nations are 'imaginary constructs that depend for their existence on an apparatus of cultural fictions in which imaginative literature plays a decisive role' (p. 49). The narrative genre, which is considered to constitute the foremost cultural representation of the nation, is the novel (Anderson 1983; Brennan 1990).

See also: **Essentialism; Ethnicity; Globalization; Hybridity; Identity, identification, identity politics; Narrative**

Further reading: Huchinson and Smith (1994).

National-popular

The concept of the national-popular originates from the work of Italian Marxist Antonio Gramsci (1891–1937). It refers to a nation-wide provisional alliance between disparate social groups with parallel interests, which has the power to accomplish social change. In the French Revolution, for example, the radical Jacobin bourgeoisie established a temporary hegemony by expanding its class interests to include those of the peasantry and the artisans. In the Italy of the 1920s, the Fascists effectively merged the interests of the industrial bourgeoisie, petty bourgeoisie and big landowners, while at the same time intensifying state control and manufacturing popular consent in civil society. Gramsci held that the failure to build a broad oppositional alliance between the industrial proletariat of Italy's developed north-west, peasantry in the south and the islands, and organic intellectuals, had enabled the Fascists to seize power.

In Gramsci's thought, the concept of the national-popular has a political as well as cultural dimension. Gramsci argued that the Italian literary production had long been out of touch with the Italian people: 'In other words, the feelings of the people are not lived by the writers as their own, nor do the writers have a "national educative" function' (Gramsci 1985 [1929–35]: 206–7).

Arguably, the national-popular has now been to some extent supplanted by an international-popular culture – a global folklore sustained by the transnational reach of communications – in which communities of consumers are formed across both national and class boundaries.

Within cultural studies, the concept of the national-popular has been deployed to describe counter-hegemonic struggles and patterns of identity construction that cut across class boundaries.

See also: **Common culture; Hegemony; Intellectuals; Nation, nationality, nationalism; Popular culture, folk culture**

Further reading: Gramsci (1985 [1929–35]).

Network

A network is a system of interconnected components which exchange resources with each other. The term has wide currency in computer science, business and management, sociology and media studies. In computer science, it refers to a system of computers (referred to as terminals or nodes), which are linked together by transmission media (links). The quintessential example of network structure is the Internet, a 'network of networks' that enables multiple networks to communicate with each other.

Social networks exist between individuals or groups linked together by a variety of social relationships, such as friendship, family ties, professional affiliation, political orientation, activism and lifestyle preferences. In social sciences, the network approach assumes that the agency and status of individual nodes depend more on their location within the network than on their inherent qualities.

Arguably, the network is the dominant structure of today's globalized world. The term 'network society' was coined by Catalan sociologist Manuel Castells. Castells has argued that networks 'constitute the new social morphology of our societies, and the diffusion of networking logic substantially modifies the operation and outcomes in processes of production, experience, power, and culture'. According to Castells, the network paradigm at work in information technology 'provides the material basis for its pervasive expansion through the entire social structure' (1996: 469). Networks are constituted by a space of flows, which works to destabilize patterns of identity construction based on specific physical, social, cultural and functional characteristics. Contemporary society, Castells argues, is characterized by a growing polarization of networked elites in relation to those who exist outside the reach of global networks.

See also: **Globalization; Deterritorialization/reterritorialization; Power**

Further reading: Castells (1996).

New Criticism

The term 'New Criticism' refers to a prominent paradigm of literary criticism, which emerged in the US in the 1920s and exercised profound influence upon classroom practice in English departments worldwide until the 1960s. Its major proponents were John Crowe Ransom (1888–1974), Allen Tate (1899–1979), Cleanth Brooks (1906–94) and Robert Penn Warren (1905–89). Other critics commonly associated with it are Kenneth Burke (1897–1993), René Wellek (1903–95) and Austin Warren (1899–1986).

The New Critics argued that criticism should focus on the form and structure of the literary work, rather than trying to explain it in terms of the life of the author, reader response, or its socio-cultural context. The proponents of the New Criticism shared a pessimistic view of the modern world, an idealized perception of the rural past, and a belief in the redeeming potential of quality literature and creative imagination. Since the 1960s, the New Criticism has been challenged from a range of theoretical perspectives, including psychoanalysis, Marxism, feminism and poststructuralism, mainly on the grounds of its ahistorical formalism and cultural elitism.

See also: **Literacy; Value, value system**

New Economy

The term refers to the nature of the global economy in the post-industrial era. The principal features of the new economy are the increasing commercialization of information and knowledge, and the relocation of manufacturing facilities from the developed countries to the developing ones.

See also: **Fordism/post-Fordism; Globalization**

New Times

See **Fordism/post-Fordism; Globalization**.

Nomad

Deriving from the Greek verb *nemein*, which means 'to pasture', the term 'nomad' refers to a member of a people that continually moves to find fresh pasture for its animals and has no permanent home (*COED*). Bedouins and the Roma people stand as quintessential examples of nomadic existence.

In *A Thousand Plateaus* (1987 [1980]), Deleuze and Guattari deployed the figure of the nomad to theorize the limits of Western 'sedentary' thought, based on the notion of a stable centre, from which truth can be ascertained and judged. The nomad here embodies all the dispersed forces that defy centring and codification. Nomads have no stable identity, as their identities materialize only provisionally, out of the constant play of resources, roles and relationships. While sedentary space is seen as marked by enclosures and paths between enclosures, the territory of the nomad is a smooth surface without any stable boundaries or fixed patterns of dissemination. Since the journey of the nomad has no point of origin and no fixed destination, the nomad exists beyond history, or temporal chronology. History, Deleuze and Guattari argue, 'is always written from a sedentary point of view and in the name of a unitary State apparatus, at least a possible one, even when the topic is nomads. What is lacking is a Nomadology, the opposite of a history' (p. 23).

Poststructuralist and postmodern critics have deployed the notion of nomadic deterritorialization to challenge disciplinary and canonical boundaries, as well as a range of other hegemonic discourses. Feminist philosopher Rosi Braidotti, for example, has proposed a 'new nomadism' in which ideas function as 'mobile, specific strategies, which are resistant to systematization', as a blueprint for a new feminist subjectivity (1991: 279). Teshome Gabriel (1990) has developed the notion of 'nomadic aesthetics' to describe the emergent aesthetics of black independent cinema.

See also: **Desire; Deterritorialization/reterritorialization; Rhizome, rhizomatics; Schizoanalysis**

Further reading: Deleuze and Guattari (1987 [1980]).

N

Observation

'Observation', in common usage, refers to the act or skill of gaining information by using the senses of sight, touch, smell, hearing, or taste. In social sciences, observation is a systematic strategy of data collection based on a researcher's aptitude to retrieve meaningful information through her or his senses. Observation is not a monolithic research method, but rather a complex strategy that involves a variety of methods.

Any observational study involves rigorous planning. In the planning stage, it is important to: take into account the issues of access to the environment under scrutiny; anticipate possible obstacles and devise ways of overcoming them; define the role of the researcher and identify areas of potential bias; define the criteria of observation, techniques of recording the data, and strategies for data analysis; design an observation schedule or checklist (this is not a requirement for unstructured observation); consider any ethical issues, and obtain ethics approval from the relevant institution. This original plan needs to be consistently reviewed and refined in the process of subsequent observations. The most common techniques for data recording are note-taking, journals, data sheets, photographs and audio and video recordings. Data interpretation typically involves one or more systematic strategies of data analysis, including statistics, semiotics, hermeneutics, grounded theory, content analysis, conversation analysis, discourse analysis and narrative analysis. Finally, findings should be considered in view of their significance; the original questions, hypotheses, aims and objectives, and limitations of the research project and existing research literature.

Since observational research focuses on perceptible phenomena, it is important to ensure that the observed environment remains as unaffected by the presence of the researcher as possible. A key obstacle in the search for reliable data through observation is the personal or cultural baggage of the researcher, that is, her or his past experiences, expectations and interests.

In non-participant observation, the researcher does not seek to become an integral part of the environment under observation. Non-participant observation typically entails watching people's behaviour and interaction from a reasonably secluded position, such as the corner of a room where a meeting is taking place, or a bench in the street during a local celebration. In non-participant observation, researchers endeavour to be as unobtrusive as possible. Non-participant observation is typically highly structured and undertaken over a set time period.

Participant observation is considered to be the principal data collection strategy in ethnography. Researchers engaging in participant observation are or become an integral part of the community they are observing. They may work at a particular workplace, dwell in a specific neighbourhood, or join a lifestyle group, religious community, or political organization. Their aim is to uphold the genuine dynamic of the community and to develop empathy with its members. Participant observation is typically less structured, and entails longer research periods and considerable emotional engagement. It also requires a rigorous discipline from the researcher, as active immersion in the activities of the community may result in a conflict of interest, or impose bias on the observation process.

In candid or overt observation, researchers are expected to provide full disclosure of the nature, aims and expected outcomes of the observation process. Despite the fact that full disclosure always to some extent affects the natural behaviour of the observed community, transparency is a standard requirement of ethical research.

In concealed or covert observation, participants either do not realize that they are being observed at all, or are not aware of the nature and the aims of the observation. Covert observation can be both non-participant and participant. Despite being problematic from the point of view of research ethics, concealed observation is sometimes considered necessary, especially when studying underground and illegal communities and activities. Ensuring the anonymity and confidentiality of those observed is considered to be the minimum ethical requirement of covert observation.

Observational techniques can involve varying degrees of structure and planning. A structured observation may be used to gather both quantitative and qualitative data. It always entails a set of clearly defined criteria, a viable observation schedule and a checklist of the intended areas of observation. In an unstructured observation, researchers initially record as many of their observations as possible. Any recurrent patterns are identified at a later stage, providing a template for subsequent observations.

See also: **Content analysis; Conversation analysis; Discourse analysis; Ethnography; Grounded theory; Hermeneutics; Semiotic analysis; Method, methodology; Thick description**

Further reading: Denzin and Lincoln (eds) (2000).

Oedipus complex

In Freud's psychoanalysis, the Oedipus complex represents a crucial step in the development of male sexuality, which occurs in the so-called phallic stage of early childhood, usually between the ages of three and six. The Oedipus complex manifests itself as a male child's erotic attachment to his mother, which goes hand in hand with feelings of intense rivalry and hostility towards his father. The Swiss psychoanalyst Carl Gustav Jung (1875–1961) introduced the term 'the Electra complex' to refer to a parallel step in the development of female sexuality. Both terms derive from Greek myth, as recast by Sophocles (c. 497–406 BCE) in his celebrated tragedies *Oedipus Rex* and *Electra*. In Greek mythology, Oedipus is the king of Thebes, who unwittingly killed his father and married his mother; Electra is a Mycenaean princess, who persuaded her brother to kill their mother in revenge for their father's murder.

According to Freud, resolution of the Oedipus complex is motivated by castration anxiety, or the boy's fear that the father might put a stop to his relationship with his mother by cutting off his penis. This fear then prompts the child to begin to identify with the father, and to renounce his libidinal interest in the mother. Freud considered the Oedipus complex the cornerstone of the superego and the constitutive force in the development of human subjectivity.

In Lacanian psychoanalysis, the Oedipus complex is related to the symbolic order, and exists beyond the boundaries of biological kinship and the nuclear family. For Lacan, castration represents a symbolic cut, which results from a person's compliance with the rules of language, or, in Lacan's terminology, the name of the father. Drawing on Lacan's theory, feminist theorists have emphasized the importance of language for the development of gendered subjectivity (see Grosz 1990).

In their seminal book *Anti-Oedipus: Capitalism and Schizophrenia* (1977 [1972]), French theorists Gilles Deleuze and Félix Guattari have disputed the universality of Oedipal subjectivity, interpreting the Oedipus complex as a typically modern form of familial and cultural guilt.

See also: **Desire; Id, superego, ego; Identity, identification, identity politics; Imaginary, symbolic, real; Psychoanalysis; Schizoanalysis; Subject, subjectivity**

Further reading: Deleuze and Guattari (1983 [1972]).

Oral history

Oral history has been defined as the 'interviewing of eye-witness participants in the events of the past for the purposes of historical reconstruction' (Ronald Grele, quoted in Perks and Thomson 1997: ix). It avails itself of research strategies from a range of related disciplines, most notably psychology, sociology and anthropology. As a supplementary but not necessarily subordinate method of historical investigation, oral history has gained considerable prestige and popularity over the last four decades. Some of its key advantages, according to a number of critics, are its power to bring recognition to marginalized social groups, whose voice is not discernible from mainstream historical documents; and to shed light on activities that are typically hidden from the public eye, such as family life, housework and personal relations. Also, it is considered to be a useful tool in the study of historical memory, capable of revealing 'how people make sense of their past, how they connect individual experience and its social context, how the past becomes part of the present, and how people use it to interpret their lives and the world around them' (Frisch 1990: 188). The most common charges against it, typically raised by conventional documentary historians, are the unreliability of personal memory and the possibly unrepresentative nature of individual testimony.

Oral history involves a human relationship between the researcher and her or his respondent, and an understanding that our past is always to some extent liable to personal interpretation. In some oral history projects, the underlying aim has been to empower or heal individuals or social groups by allowing them to remember and reconstruct past experiences.

The principal technique of data collection in oral history is the individual life story, in which the respondent recounts a comprehensive story of her or his entire life. Another common technique is the single-issue interview, which focuses on a specific aspect, event or period in the life of the respondent. In addition to individual interviews, data can also be collected in focus groups, community interviews or by diary interviewing. Life-story interviews are typically conducted in a series of one-to-one meetings between the researcher and the respondent, in a location that the respondent perceives as comfortable, private and familiar. Single-issue interviews are usually shorter and more detailed than life-story ones. Diary interviewing entails selecting a group of respondents, who contribute diary entries over an extended period of time, as part of a continuing study of social and cultural trends. Diary entries may be written or recorded, and may involve interviews at specific points in time, defined by the researcher. Focus groups are particularly useful in obtaining testimony from people who may lack confidence in a one-to-one situation, but draw confidence from being in a familiar group. They can be conducted in one or more sessions, each lasting between one and two hours. Focus groups typically consist of a smaller number of participants (between five and twelve), and are relatively homogeneous in terms of gender, social status and experience. The researcher in a focus group acts as a moderator, rather than an interviewer. Community interviews involve larger groups of respondents (usually around thirty people) and at least two interviewers performing predefined complementary roles. Since community interviews involve a large gathering at one time, they are particularly useful as a review technique to examine the validity of the basic tenets and findings of the project. A show of hands, for example, may serve as an indicator of how many people share the experiences or opinions expressed in individual interviews.

In order to facilitate the respondents' memory, researchers often use mnemonic prompts, such as old objects, maps, charts or photographs. Revisiting a memory site or performing role-play are among the other techniques that can be used by the researcher to refresh the memory of her or his respondent.

See also: **Focus groups; Interview; Memory; Method, methodology**

Further reading: Dunaway and Baum (eds) (1996).

Orality

The term 'orality' refers to verbal rather than written communication, and to the socially embedded cognitive patterns associated with spoken language. Critics have distinguished between orality as the primary mode of communication in pre-literate societies (primary orality), and the forms of oral communication advanced in recent times by modern media technologies (secondary orality). Some of the patterns of thought associated with orality are presence and participation as opposed to objective distance; and circularity, abundance and a formulaic structure as opposed to linearity.

See also: **Literacy**

Further reading: McLuhan (1962).

Orientalism

The term 'Orient' has been used in Western cultural discourses to designate the area east of the Mediterranean, including the Near East, Middle East, and Central and South Asia. 'Orientalism' refers both to the study of Middle Eastern and Asian cultures; and to the tendency among

Western scholars and artists to homogenize and objectify the 'Orient' and construct it as the exotic Other, or the inverse of an essentialized Western 'self'.

Orientalist scholarship and art flourished in Britain, France and Germany in the nineteenth century, thus coinciding with the growing imperialist drive in these countries. It was then that the study of distant cultures represented the core of a range of new academic disciplines, most notably philology, anthropology and ethnology. As European scholars endeavoured to gain knowledge of Eastern languages, religions, philosophies and cultural practices, bureaucrats and military officers needed their insights to impose and effectively maintain control over subordinated populations.

An influential critique of Orientalism was offered in 1978 by Palestinian American literary theorist, critic and political activist Edward Said (1935–2003). Said interprets Orientalism in terms of Michel Foucault's theory of discourse, as 'an enormously systematic discipline by which European culture was able to manage – and even produce – the Orient . . . during the post-Enlightenment period' (1995 [1978]: 3). He points out that the Orient is not real and has no fixed boundaries; rather, it is a projection of Western fantasies about the East. For Europe, the Orient is also the place of its 'greatest and richest and oldest colonies, the source of its civilizations and languages, its cultural contestant, and one of its deepest and most recurring images of the Other' (p. 1).

Drawing on the work of Antonio Gramsci, Said explains the hegemonic power of Orientalism in terms of its capacity to reproduce itself through non-coercive social institutions, such as education, art and the media. By analysing a variety of nineteenth- and twentieth-century sources, including scholarly texts, literary prose, poetry, travelogues and political writings, Said argues convincingly that all of them were complicit in generating and propagating forms of knowledge that sustained colonial domination. He highlighted the ways in which Orientalist discourse generated and disseminated stereotypical representations of the Orient as romantic and exotic, but at the same time irrational, backward, dangerous, violent and despotic. In contrast, the West constructed itself as an embodiment of rationality, progress and individual freedom.

Said's work on Orientalism has left a profound impact on postcolonial studies and the humanities more broadly. The main criticism raised against it has been that it does not provide an adequate account of the heterogeneity of Orientalist discourse (Aijaz 1992), nor of the multiple resistances against it that emerge from colonial texts (Pratt 1992).

Secondly, Said's work has been criticized for lacking a gendered dimension (Lewis 1995).

See also: **Alterity; Colonialism; Identity, identification, identity politics; Postcolonialism, neo-colonialism; Tropicalization/s, tropicopolitan**

Further reading: Said (1995 [1978]).

Other

See **Alterity**.

O

Panopticism, synopticism

Deriving from the Greek prefix *pan-*, which means all-encompassing, and *optikós*, from *optós*, seen or visible, the word 'panopticon' refers to a system or mechanism that facilitates universal visibility. English jurist and political philosopher Jeremy Bentham (1748–1832) used the term 'panopticon' (or the 'inspection house') to refer to an innovative prison design originally developed by his brother Samuel. Bentham's panopticon consisted of a circular building with a central watchtower, from which it was possible to observe all the cells arranged along the perimeter (see Figure 6). The cells were kept illuminated but the central tower was dark, so that prisoners could be watched at all times but could not tell when they were being observed. The desired effect of this system was for the inmates to learn to act as if they were continuously under surveillance. Once this was achieved, they could be released from prison with the hope that they would continue to regulate their own behavior in society at large.

Michel Foucault (1979 [1975]) deployed the image of Bentham's panopticon as a metaphor for the functioning of modern disciplinary society, in which a sense of surveillance is an integral part of human subjectivity. According to Foucault, the systems of social control that emerged in the seventeenth and eighteenth centuries resemble the

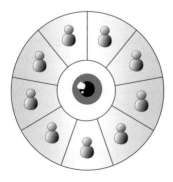

Figure 6   A simplified model of Bentham's panopticon.

panopticon, since they involve the division of society into legible categories – the sick, the insane, the criminal; or conversely, the healthy, the
sane, the socially respectable – which function as cells that can be
observed from a privileged standpoint.

New technologies, such as closed-circuit television (CCTV), global
positioning systems (GPS), Internet search engines, databases and
biometrics, to name only a few, allied with the proliferation of reality TV
shows such as *Big Brother*, *Temptation Island* or *Survivor*, have arguably
transformed the nature of surveillance in contemporary society.
According to some critics, surveillance has now become rhizomatic
(Haggerty and Ericson 2000) and there are no clear boundaries between
the observer and the observed. Thomas Mathiesen (1997) used the term
'synopticon' (from Greek *sún*, which means 'together'), to describe those
mediated practices through which the many watch the few, rather than
the other way round.

See also: **Discourse; Governmentality**

Further reading: Foucault (1979 [1975]).

Parody, pastiche

Deriving from Greek *pará-*, which can mean both beside and counter or
against, and *Ōide*, meaning ode or song, the word 'parody' refers to a
form of intertextuality, which is based on imitation of an earlier text,
style or genre. It has been defined broadly as the 'generic term for a
range of related cultural practices, all of which are imitative of other
cultural forms, with varying degrees of mockery or humour' (Dentith
2000: 193). As a 'repetition with difference', parody is related to, but not
synonymous with, such intertextual forms as satire, pastiche, burlesque,
travesty, allusion, appropriation, quotation and plagiarism. Over the
ages, the historically specific types of parody have involved varying
degrees of critical distance and a range of different desired effects. It is
impossible, therefore, to give any single definition of parody that would
reflect all of its historically specific varieties, from ancient Greek comedy
to postmodern textual forms.

The French word *pastiche* derives from the Italian *pasticcio*, which
designates a pie made of various ingredients. Both the French and the
Italian versions were first used in music and the visual arts to describe a
musical composition or a work of art pieced together from different fragments. In contemporary art criticism, literature and cultural studies,
'pastiche' denotes imitation of another style, genre or author without
critical distance.

In his account of the 'cultural logic' of late capitalism, Fredric Jameson distinguished between parody and pastiche, arguing that the latter represents a typically postmodern cultural form. Parody, for Jameson, has a critical dimension, as it seeks to challenge and ultimately subvert that which it imitates. Pastiche, on the other hand, is a 'blank parody', 'amputated of the satiric impulse' and 'devoid of laughter and any conviction that alongside the abnormal tongue you have momentarily borrowed, some healthy linguistic normality still exists' (1991 [1984]: 17).

The Canadian literary theorist and cultural critic Linda Hutcheon disagrees with Jameson's understanding of parody as a ridiculing imitation that always implies a polemical edge; and with his claim that, in postmodernism, parody has lost much of its earlier momentum. In contrast, she considers parody to be a 'privileged mode of postmodern formal self-reflexivity' (1988: 35), and defines it as 'repetition with critical distance' that 'allows ironic signalling of difference at the very heart of similarity' and 'paradoxically enacts both change and cultural continuity' (p. 26).

See also: **Irony; Postmodern, postmodernity, postmodernism**

Further reading: Dentith (2000), Hutcheon (2000 [1985]).

Patriarchy

Deriving from the Greek word *patriá*, which means family or clan (from *pater*, father), and *-arkhēs*, ruler, the term 'patriarchy' designates the structure of male dominance over women, both in the family and in society at large. It can be deployed to signify male dominance at the institutional level, in everyday life, or at the level of representation. Patriarchal societies have existed in a variety of historically specific forms. Throughout history, they have extended substantial legal, political and economic privileges to men as a group and maintained women in a marginalized position.

The concept of patriarchy has had wide currency in feminist theory and activism. Radical feminists describe it as a universal system, at work in all societies throughout history and across cultures. Marxist feminists focus on the intersections between patriarchy and capitalism, arguing that capitalism exacerbates gender division by relegating women to the private sphere. Drawing on poststructuralist theory, some contemporary feminists have contested the utility of the concept, arguing that it fails to account for the historical specificities of different systems of male dominance. Rather than understanding patriarchy as a homogeneous system of male authority, they have argued that it is in fact historically contingent and grounded in discursive practices.

P

See also: **Feminism; Gender; Public/private; Public sphere**

Further reading: Murray (1995).

Performativity, perverformative, performance

The concept of performativity derives from the theory of speech acts, developed by British philosopher of language John Langshaw Austin (1962). Speech act theory distinguished between two principal types of utterances: constative utterances, which simply describe or assert a fact; and performative utterances, which serve to perform an action, such as naming a ship, apologizing, promising or concluding a marriage, to name only a few. While constatives can be judged as either true or false, performatives can only be evaluated in terms of their 'felicity', or successful performance. Austin maintained that the success of a performative was determined by context.

While acknowledging the importance of Austin's theory for foregrounding the extra-referential aspects of language, Derrida (1988 [1972]) argued that context was never stable, since speech acts are subject to iterability. Furthermore, he claimed, all utterances contain a performative element. Performatives themselves are never 'pure', because they always contain, in their very structure, a possibility of failure. For instance, for someone to make a promise it is indispensable that she or he might be untruthful, or joking, or might die before keeping the promise. Derrida's notion of the 'perverformative' (1987 [1975]) highlights the risk of failure that underlies all performative language.

The concept of performativity is of central significance in Judith Butler's theory of gender. For Butler, there is 'no gender identity behind the expressions of gender', since 'identity is performatively constituted by the very "expressions" that are said to be its results' (1990: 25). She argues that there is no prediscursive identity, and that even our notion of biological sex is a product of discourse. Butler distinguishes between performance, which assumes a pre-existing subject, and performativity, which challenges the very idea of the subject. Butler's theory is open to criticism for ostensibly discounting the agency involved in gendered acts. According to Butler, however, agency is found in variations of the gender performances we are forced to repeat; that is, it is only within the sphere of cultural norms that the destabilization of these norms becomes possible (1990: 145).

See also: **Deconstruction; Gender; Iterability; Queer, queer theory; Sexuality**

Further reading: Butler (1990).

Phallus, phallocentrism, phallogocentrism

Deriving from the Greek word *phallós*, the word 'phallus', in contemporary usage, has symbolic rather than purely anatomical connotations. It refers, in the first instance, to the representation or image of the erect penis as a symbol of the generative force in nature (for example, the phallic effigies associated with the Dionysiac festivals in ancient Greece). In Freud's psychoanalytic theory, the phallic stage is the third stage of psychosexual development, in which the genitals are said to be a child's primary source of pleasure. The notion of phallic symbolism derives from psychoanalytic dream interpretation, where it is used to describe anything that can be seen as having the form of an erect penis, such as a pencil, a snake, or a cigarette.

In Lacanian psychoanalysis, the phallus is interpreted as an effect of the Symbolic Order. It is one of the few universal transcendental signifiers, which – being apparently beyond any doubt – serve to anchor the system of signification. It has a crucial role in dividing humankind into two categories, defined respectively by its presence or absence. Other binaries, such as active/passive, hot/cold or culture/nature, can be seen as ensuing from this primary dichotomy. Lacan interpreted the phallus in terms of absence or lack. He argued that no one could in fact possess a phallus; one could only be believed by others to have one. According to Lacan, all positions of patriarchal authority, such as the Father, the Judge, or God, are phallic in nature.

A concept in feminist theory, phallocentrism refers to the patriarchal order of representation, which takes man and masculine experience as the norm according to which woman is measured. According to Elizabeth Grosz, phallocentrism typically takes one of three possible forms: the first is based on the notion of identity between the two sexes; the second on the idea that the two sexes form a binary opposition; and the third on the assumption that they are complementary to each other (1989: 105).

The term 'phallogocentrism' (a combination of the words 'phallocentrism' and 'logocentrism') was coined by Jacques Derrida (1987 [1975]), to bring together the notions of male-centredness and the metaphysics of presence in Western thought. Phallogocentric discourse is characterized by dichotomous reasoning, linearity and order. French feminist theorists such as Hélène Cixous and Luce Irigaray have theorized a specifically feminine way of speaking and writing, which eludes the binary logic of phallogocentrism.

P

See also: Écriture féminine; Identity, identification, identity politics; Imaginary, symbolic, real; Logocentrism, phonocentrism, écriture; Oedipus complex; Psychoanalysis

Further reading: Derrida (1987 [1975]), Grosz (1989).

Phenomenology, cultural phenomenology

Deriving from the Greek word *phainomenon*, which means 'that which appears or is seen', the term 'phenomenology' denotes a branch of philosophical inquiry which describes how phenomena are experienced in individual human consciousness. As a qualitative research method in the humanities and social sciences, phenomenology takes the individual subject as its starting point. It aims to provide a description of conscious experience while suspending any preconceived ideas or explanations. In practical terms, it seeks to describe events and occurrences from the points of view of the relevant actors.

German philosopher Edmund Husserl (1859–1938) is generally considered to be the architect of modern phenomenology. Husserl argued that our experience of the world, including everything we perceive through our senses and everything we learn from our intellectual pursuits, is constituted in and by consciousness. In a somewhat revised form, Husserl's paradigm was elaborated by his student and assistant Martin Heidegger (1889–1976), and had a considerable impact on existentialism and modern hermeneutics. In literature studies, the Geneva school of literary criticism, which was active in the 1950s and 1960s, analysed literary texts as representations of deep structures of an author's characteristic modes of awareness. Other phenomenological approaches to literary criticism have focused on the reader's consciousness of literary texts.

French philosopher Maurice Merleau-Ponty (1908–61) defined phenomenology as a 'science of beginnings' (1962 [1945]), which should be taken as the starting point for philosophical and cultural investigations. Merleau-Ponty argued that culture does not solely reside in objects and representations, but also in the bodily processes of perception by which those representations come into being.

Drawing on Merleau-Ponty and others, contemporary cultural phenomenology endeavours to integrate the immediacy of embodied experience with the layers of cultural meaning in which we exist and operate. It thus subverts the strict division between biology (nature) and society (culture) and offers a more nuanced understanding of both. Certain aspects of contemporary socio-cultural and technological change lend themselves readily to cultural–phenomenological investigation grounded in embodiment. Most notably, cyberspace, virtual reality and cyborg identities have challenged the traditional boundaries between the 'social person and the persona interacting in a community defined by shared computer linkups'; 'between perception and the technological simulation of perception that is virtual reality'; and 'between humans as biological organisms and machines' respectively (Csordas 1999: 143).

See also: **Actor-network theory; Body; Cyborg; Lifeworld and system; Senses; Virtual, virtual community, virtual reality**

Further reading: Csordas (1999), Haber and Weiss (1999), Merleau-Ponty (1962 [1945]).

Polysemy

'Polysemy' refers to the capacity of signs or texts to carry multiple related meanings. A parallel concept in the philosophy of language and cognitive linguistics, 'homonymy', designates a plurality of meanings that are not mutually related. An example of polysemy is the word 'window', which can refer either to an opening in a wall or to the framed glass in that opening; an example of homonymy is the word 'bark', which can be understood either as the bark of a dog, or as the bark of a tree. Polysemy is at work at both the denotative (literal) and the connotative (metaphorical, symbolic) levels of meaning. It is the multiplicity of meaning in the domain of the symbolic that is of particular interest to semiotics, psychology, literary theory and criticism and cultural studies.

As a concept that designates a fundamental indeterminacy and plurality of meaning, polysemy is related to Bakhtin's notions of heteroglossia and dialogism (1984 [1929]). Heteroglossia, in Bakhtin's account, exists in literary texts as well as in society at large. The notion of dialogism implies that any use of language inevitably involves a plurality of socially contingent voices.

In the work of Roland Barthes (1974 [1970]), polysemy is the conceptual tool that helps us distinguish between open (readerly) and closed (writerly) texts: an open text is one that encourages the reader to appreciate and actively exploit its polysemic potential; while a closed text tends to minimize the possibility of ambiguity. The degree of openness, however, is not an integral quality of a given text, but rather depends on the context of its reading and the audience.

John Fiske considers polysemy to be an essential feature of television as a medium, which is 'necessary if [a television text] is to be popular amongst viewers who occupy a variety of situations within the social structure' (1987: 16). He argues that television texts always possess an excess of meaning, which, although bounded by the social structure in which the viewers partake, is never entirely controllable by the dominant ideology.

The concept of polysemy also underlies the account of hegemony developed by post-Marxist theorists Ernesto Laclau and Chantal Mouffe (1985). According to Laclau and Mouffe, the excess of signification is instrumental in disarticulating a discursive structure. A discourse, they argue, is never fully self-contained: rather, there is always an overflow

P

that sifts into other discourses, where meaning can be contested and overturned.

See also: **Dialogism; Discourse; Heteroglossia; Intertextuality; Popular culture, folk culture; Text**

Further reading: Fiske (1987).

Popular culture, folk culture

Critics within the field of cultural studies have claimed that popular culture, despite being produced and disseminated by profit-making industries, cannot be adequately explained in terms of passive consumption. Popular culture, they maintain, belongs to the people, not to the culture industry. It is generated from within, rather than imposed from above. The role of the culture industries is simply to provide a reservoir of cultural resources that people can use in producing their specific versions of popular culture. Popular culture, in this view, represents a site of struggle over meaning. Its semiosis always exceeds the dominant norm and opens up possibilities of evasion and resistance. The view of popular culture as a site of contestation has been condemned by several critics for ostensibly collapsing the distinction between culture generated by the people, or 'popular classes', and mass-produced media culture.

Popular culture is ephemeral, repetitive and 'obvious', because it needs to be easily 'mapped onto the routines of everyday life' (Fiske 1991 [1989]: 65). Another distinctive feature of popular culture is its manifest intertextuality. The meanings of popular culture, it has been argued, 'exist only in their circulation, not in their texts; the texts, which are crucial in this process, need to be understood not for and by themselves, but in their interrelationships – with other texts – and with social life, for that is how their circulation is ensured' (Fiske 1991 [1989]: 4).

Popular culture should not be confused with folk culture, which is the product of relatively stable traditional societies. Folk cultures are more homogeneous than popular culture, since they 'do not have to encompass the variety of social allegiances formed by members of elaborated societies' (Fiske 1991 [1989]: 170). They are also more specific to the community that produces them. Outside this community, folk culture always appears exotic and alien. It is always 'theirs', while 'popular culture is ours, despite its alienated origins as industrial commodity' (p. 171).

See also: **Authentic culture; Hegemony; Intertextuality; Mass culture, culture industry; Polysemy; Populism**

Further reading: Fiske (1991 [1989]).

Populism

In contemporary usage, the word is commonly deployed to designate a political stance or rhetoric that upholds, or pragmatically claims to uphold, the majority interests of ordinary people. Populist rhetoric has been used to promote a variety of political ideologies, both on the right and on the left of the political spectrum. The semantic opposite of elitism, populism can be taken to represent a positive and egalitarian force in society. In political discourse, however, the word often has negative connotations, and implies suspect demagogy and the mobilization of the body politic by appealing to the lowest common denominator (McGuigan 1992: 1). Politicians such as Margaret Thatcher, Ronald Reagan or Silvio Berlusconi, for example, are typically considered to be populist leaders.

In his book *On Populist Reason* (2005), Ernesto Laclau has argued that populism needs to be explained in terms of its form, rather than its content. For Laclau, populist rhetoric is not a mere skill of manipulation, but rather a constitutive element of politics as such. The very notion of the 'people' is produced through a chain of demands for equivalence, among different segments of society, in terms of a perceived common antagonism in relation to a form of political power or authority. Populism thus has a tendency to polarize the social field into two distinct factions. The heterogeneous demands that motivate any specific populist mobilization are brought together not merely by their shared opposition to the status quo, but also by the emergence of an 'empty signifier': a term (for example, the name of the leader) that becomes devoid of its own specificity and comes to represent the 'people' as a whole. This process, whereby particularity assumes universal significance, lies at the heart of hegemony itself.

The term 'cultural populism' was used by Jim McGuigan (1992) to refer to the tradition within British cultural studies which privileges the symbolic experiences and practices of ordinary people over those of cultural elites, and emphasizes their productivity and subversive potential. This brand of cultural populism, McGuigan argues, does not take into account the social, political and economic structures within which popular culture is produced and thus over-rates the extent of agency in the act of consumption.

See also: **Agency; Consumption; Hegemony; National-popular; Popular culture, folk culture; Thatcherism**

Further reading: Laclau (2005).

Positivism

The term 'positivism' refers to a range of theoretical positions in the philosophy of science, based on an approach to knowledge elaborated most famously by nineteenth-century French philosopher Auguste Comte (1798–1857). Comte introduced the notion of 'positive philosophy', which would harmonize the theoretical positions and methods of the core scientific disciplines of mathematics, physics, astronomy, biology, chemistry and sociology. He distinguished three stages of thought in the history of humanity: the earliest, theological stage, in which phenomena were explained as expressions of supernatural forces; the metaphysical stage, in which occurrences were seen as products of abstract forces; and finally the positive stage, in which the laws that govern different phenomena are explained through observation and reasoning. Observation, in the positive stage, is envisaged as guided by scientific hypothesis. Comte regarded mathematics as the foundation stone of positive philosophy. He argued that both natural and social phenomena could be explained in terms of certain immutable laws of co-existence and succession.

Positivists contend that theories should be based upon generalizations drawn from direct observation. Any disagreement among theories, they argue, needs to be resolved by empirical examination. If this is not possible, the conflicting theories are considered meaningless, or irrelevant to scientific discourse.

Contemporary social and cultural theory is decidedly anti-positivist in both orientation and practice. By and large, it recognizes the contingent nature of social and cultural phenomena, and acknowledges its own intellectual position as a fundamental determinant of its interpretive practices.

See also: **Determinism; Discourse; Poststructuralism**

P

Postcolonialism, neo-colonialism

In the strictest sense, the term 'postcolonial' describes societies that emerged in the wake of colonial rule. It may be understood to encompass not only the former colonized countries, but also the ex-colonizers, still affected by the experience of colonialism. This definition is considered contentious by some critics, as it erases the difference between colonized and colonizer. Postcolonialism may also be understood to stretch back to the establishment of colonial rule, as a formative moment of crucial significance to future discourses of culture and identity in colonized and colonizing countries. Most commonly, however, the term postcolonial does not refer to a specific historical period, but rather to a theoretical stance that opposes the ideological legacy of colonial domination. Some critics object to the use of the word 'postcolonial' altogether, arguing that it classifies the world by reference to a minority of powerful countries. Another objection to the use of the term is that it elides the specificities of colonial experience in different parts of the former colonial world.

Despite the fact that the wars of liberation from European colonial rule occurred mainly in the 1950s and 1960s, postcolonial theory did not emerge as a distinct academic field until the early 1970s. Its consolidation as a discipline is commonly associated with the publication of Edward Said's book *Orientalism* in 1978. Primarily concerned with textual and literary analysis, and to a large extent poststructuralist in orientation, postcolonial theory engages in the study and critique of colonial discourses, with a focus on issues of subjectivity, nationhood, race, subalternity and hybridity, among others.

The term 'neo-colonialism' signals the way in which powerful Western nations retain considerable indirect control over former colonies by economic, political and cultural means.

See also: **Alterity; Colonialism; Discourse; Hybridity; Identity, identification, identity politics; Nation, nationality, nationalism; Orientalism; Subaltern, subaltern studies; Subject, subjectivity**

Further reading: Schwarz and Ray (eds) (2000).

Posthumanism

In social and cultural theory, the term 'posthumanism' refers to a range of twentieth-century approaches that seek to destabilize the ontological primacy of the liberal humanist subject. The birth of contemporary posthumanism is typically associated with the coming to prominence of structuralism, which dissolved the notion of the unified human self by ascribing its various functions to 'impersonal systems that operate through it' (Culler 1981: 37). Derrida's theory of deconstruction, which 'affirms play and tries to pass beyond man and humanism' (2001 [1967]: 292), takes this insight a step further and posits that there is no full presence which could guarantee a stability of meaning. Lacanian psychoanalysis, which interprets human subjectivity as constituted in language, is also posthumanist in orientation. Similarly, Michel Foucault and Marxist critics such as Louis Althusser argue that human agency is only possible within the confines of specific discourses or ideological systems. Postmodern theorists such as Gilles Deleuze and Félix Guattari associate the idea of a unified human subject with the logic of capitalism, and celebrate the liberatory potential of an interstitial subjectivity dispersed among diverse social, cultural, environmental and technological assemblages. In the work of feminist scholar Donna Haraway, the posthuman figure of the cyborg, a hybrid between organism and machine, represents a 'kind of disassembled and reassembled, postmodern collective and personal self' (1990 [1984]: 205).

See also: **Deconstruction; Postmodern, postmodernity, postmodernism; Post-structuralism; Psychoanalysis; Structuralism**

Further reading: Hayles (1999).

Post-Marxism

'Post-Marxism' is a portmanteau term for a heterogeneous range of approaches in social theory developed in the 1980s and 1990s, which claim to go beyond classical or conventional Marxism rather than emphatically opposing it. Post-Marxist theories may be understood as a consequence of a 'crisis of Marxism', prompted primarily by the declining role of communist parties in Europe since the 1970s and the disintegration of the Soviet Union and the former Eastern bloc in the late 1980s and early 1990s. In terms of ideas, post-Marxism is associated with the emergence of a postmodern sensibility, which is ostensibly wary of grand narratives of any kind. Drawing on the poststructuralist and postmodern approaches of theorists such as Foucault, Lacan, Derrida and Baudrillard, post-Marxists are critical of traditional Marxism for its totalizing discourse, its economic determinism and its class reductionism.

Post-Marxists such as Ernesto Laclau and Chantal Mouffe (1985) reject the traditional Marxist understanding of concepts such as class, society or history as essential and universal. In contrast, they argue that these categories should rather be seen as discursive or ideological constructs, upheld by an endless play of social and cultural signifiers. Inspired by the work of Antonio Gramsci, post-Marxists explain social relations in terms of hegemony, and theorize popular struggles as mobilized around a multiplicity of subject positions that cut across the boundaries of class, gender, race and nationality. Laclau and Mouffe have advocated a post-Marxist 'discursive democracy', based on a pluralist politics of social movements.

See also: **Base and superstructure; Class; Hegemony; Marxism, Leninism, Western Marxism; Poststructuralism**

Further reading: Docherty (1990).

Postmodern, postmodernity, postmodernism

The term 'postmodern' was originally used in architecture and art criticism, to signal a decisive break from modern architectural styles and the coming into vogue of eclectic blends of older stylistic varieties, which often involved a purposeful manipulation of kitsch aesthetics. In the humanities and social sciences, the term 'postmodern' is variously used to describe the social and cultural conditions, worldviews, texts and practices prevalent in post-industrial societies.

'Postmodernity' is a term that refers to the current historical period, the emergence of which is typically dated to the 1970s. Some critics prefer to use the term 'high' or 'late' modernity, arguing that there is no radical break between the modern and the postmodern periods, and describing the latter as one in which the 'consequences of modernity are becoming more radicalised and universalised than ever before' (Giddens 1990: 3).

The key developments associated with postmodernity are the escalation of multinational corporate power, the decline of the nation-state, the growth of consumption, the advancement of new media technologies and the concurrent weakening of traditional patterns of social legitimation. In a seminal analysis of the decline of modernity, the Italian philosopher Gianni Vattimo has attributed the emergence of postmodernity to the waning of Western hegemony and the fragmentation of political voices within Western societies (1988).

'Postmodernism' refers to a mode of thought or style of representation that contravenes the Enlightenment worldview and modernist aesthetics. According to its major proponents, postmodernism is reflected in a growing scepticism towards modernism's totalizing paradigms. In contrast to the modern emphasis on scientific or rational knowledge, universalism, holism, coherence, linear progress and symbolic meaning, postmodernism is characterized by its investment in culturally situated knowledges, libidinal economy, fragmentation, dispersion, co-presence and empty simulation.

The two key theorists of postmodernity are Jean-François Lyotard and Jean Baudrillard. In *The Postmodern Condition* (1984 [1979]), Lyotard argues that in a post-industrial, postmodern society, metanarratives can no longer serve to validate knowledge. Rather, contemporary legitimation should rest upon a proliferation of heterogeneous 'little narratives'. Baudrillard (1998 [1970], 1981 [1972]) interprets postmodernity as characterized by extensive commodification and consumerism and a disappearance of symbolic meaning. In Baudrillard's pessimistic account, social reality has now lost its ontological essence and given way to hyperreality and simulacra.

See also: **Enlightenment, the; Hyperreality; Modernity, modernization, modernism; Narrative; Parody, pastiche; Simulacrum**

Further reading: Hutcheon (1988), Lyotard (1984 [1979]).

Poststructuralism

The word 'poststructuralism' designates a range of theoretical approaches which have dominated the humanities and social sciences since the late 1960s. Poststructuralist theories are characterized by a degree of commonality with, as well as critical distance from, an earlier critical paradigm, namely structuralism. Although mostly associated with French theorists, such as Jacques Derrida, Michel Foucault, Jacques Lacan and Roland Barthes, among others, the term itself was coined retroactively in the English-speaking world and is rarely used in the French language as such.

Poststructuralist theories call into question the stability of meaning and the sovereignty of the human subject. They focus on difference and heterogeneity rather than identity; the process of signification rather than systems of meaning; representation rather than truth; discontinuity rather than linearity and causal progress; the process of subject formation rather than the supposedly unified knowing subject; and the discursive effects of power rather than power structures in themselves.

While structuralism had interpreted meaning as produced through the differential relationship of arbitrary signs within a system, poststructuralism emphasized the ultimate indeterminacy and socio-cultural contingency of meaning.

Derrida criticized the 'metaphysics of presence' within the Western philosophical tradition, and called attention to the logo-/phonocentrism of structuralist theory, which privileged speech over writing. He explained meaning as subject to the possibility of repetition and always only provisionally enacted through a perpetual play of deferral and difference. He introduced the concept of deconstruction, a reading strategy that does not seek to uncover the meaning supposedly embedded within a text, but rather endeavours to expose and subvert its binary oppositions. Foucault emphasized the historically contingent and essentially discursive production of subjectivity. His aim was to describe how specific 'regimes of truth' work to define and produce knowledge, and thereby ensure the continuity of an institution or a social system. Although opinion varies as to whether it is legitimate to consider Jacques Lacan a poststructuralist critic, his distinctive blend of psychoanalytic theory and structuralist linguistics, which describes human subjectivity in terms of lack and a continuous displacement of the object of desire, is in tune with poststructuralist anti-essentialism and anti-foundationalism. Roland Barthes is another thinker whose poststructuralist credentials are sometimes disputed. His key contribution to contemporary literary and cultural theory is his emphasis on meaning as inscribed in the practices of reading and writing, rather than being simply embedded within a specific text.

See also: **Deconstruction; Desire;** *Différance*; **Discourse; Imaginary, symbolic, real; Iterability; Logocentrism, phonocentrism,** *écriture*; **Phallus, phallocentrism, phallogocentrism; Structuralism; Text**

Further reading: Poster (1989).

Power

Derived from the Medieval Latin verb *potere*, which means 'can' or 'may', the term 'power' can refer to the 'ability to do something or act in a particular way', the 'capacity to influence the behaviour of others, the emotions, or the course of events', a 'right or authority given or delegated to a person or body' or 'political authority or control' (*COED*). The concept of power is of central significance for cultural studies, a discipline that defines itself as crucially concerned with the relations between 'culture and power, and the values and commitments which flow from that' (Couldry 2000: 6).

In social and cultural theory, power is a notoriously contested concept. Some theorists distinguish between the approaches that see power as essentially antagonistic ('power over', i.e. power of one social actor over another) and those that interpret it as a positive capacity to act ('power to', i.e. power to achieve goals in a context of social collaboration rather than opposition).

Perhaps the most influential definition of 'power over' is that offered by Max Weber. According to Weber, power is the 'probability that one actor within a social relationship will be in a position to carry out his will despite resistance' (1968 [1925]: 58). Weber considered class (economic power), status (normative social power) and command or domination (political power) as the three principal dimensions of power, and argued that they were unevenly distributed across the social spectrum. He made a clear distinction between power, authority and coercion. Within the Weberian paradigm, 'authority' refers to the exercise of power that is regarded by people as legitimate; and 'coercion' designates the use of force to overcome resistance. He emphasized the role of the state, as the exclusive holder of a legitimate right to use force. A notable account of 'power to' is that developed by the German political theorist Hannah Arendt. Arendt defined power as the 'human ability to act in concert', an

P

essentially positive force that 'belongs to a group and remains in existence only so long as the group holds together' (1970: 44, 40).

In Marxist theory, power is interpreted as dependent on the relations of production of a given society. Nicos Poulantzas (1973), for example, defined power as the ability of one class to achieve its own interests in opposition to other classes. Marxist accounts generally assume that power, in capitalist societies, is concentrated in the hands of the capitalist class, which owns and controls the means of production. Antonio Gramsci emphasized the role of cultural hegemony in sustaining the power of capitalism and of the nation-state.

Feminist theorists have argued that the notion of power in Western societies has strong masculine connotations, and primarily reflects male experience (French 1985).

Perhaps the most influential account of power in contemporary social and cultural theory is that developed by Michel Foucault. Foucault challenges the view of power as a discrete entity that can unproblematically belong to any specific individual or social group. In modern societies, he argues, the effects of power 'circulate through progressively finer channels, gaining access to individuals themselves, to their bodies, their gestures, and all their daily actions' (1980: 151–2). Power, in Foucauldian terms, is fundamentally concerned with the production of self-policing disciplined subjects. According to Foucault, there can be 'no possible exercise of power without a certain economy of discourses of truth which operate through and on the basis of this association. We are subject to the production of truth through power and we cannot exercise power except through the production of truth' (1980: 93). For Foucault, power and knowledge are always mutually constitutive, and one cannot exist without the other. The terms 'capillary', 'disciplinary', 'micro-' or 'bio-power' are variously used to denote the power from below, which is inherent in all social relationships.

See also: **Agency; Discourse; Feminism; Governmentality; Hegemony; Knowledge; Marxism, Leninism, Western Marxism; Post-Marxism**

Further reading: Wartenberg (1990).

Practice, theory, praxis

Prâxis is a Greek word for practice, action, or doing. Theōria, in contrast, refers to contemplation or speculation. The distinction between practice and theory, as two principal modes of human accomplishment, was articulated most influentially by Aristotle in the fourth century BCE. Aristotle distinguished among three types of disciplines or 'epistemes': theoretical disciplines (theōria), such as mathematics, physics and the natural sciences, the aim of which is to obtain knowledge through contemplation; productive disciplines (*poíēsis*), such as rhetoric and the arts, the purpose of which is to produce outcomes beyond knowledge; and practical disciplines (*prâxis*), such as ethics and politics, which have the aim of generating practical wisdom. The difference between *theōria* and *prâxis*, then, can be explained in terms of their respective aims, the principal aim of the former being to pursue knowledge for its own sake, and of the latter, to do what is right, or to live well.

In Marxism, 'praxis' designates a dialectical unity between theory and practice. Marxist theory notably seeks to produce a significant social and political impact, while at the same time being informed by social and political practices. This is why, in his *Prison Notebooks* (1971 [1929–35]), Gramsci referred to Marxist theory as the 'philosophy of praxis'. Moreover, the philosophy of praxis or critical philosophy can be interpreted more broadly as any counter-hegemonic intellectual engagement.

Cultural studies, especially in their Gramscian inflection, foreground the counter-hegemonic struggles in their many different forms, and advocate a fundamentally practice-oriented approach to knowledge.

See also: **Episteme; Hegemony; Intellectuals; Marxism, Leninism, Western Marxism**

Pragmatism

Deriving from the Greek noun *prâgma*, which means act, deed or affair, the word 'pragmatism' refers to a philosophical strand that postulates that the truth of a proposition is determined by its practical outcome. Pragmatism stands opposed to foundationalist theories, which hold that truth has verifiable *a priori* grounds. Pragmatism, in contrast, holds that truth can never be final, and that knowledge should always be subject to further scrutiny. Pragmatism was developed as a formal doctrine by American philosopher Charles Sanders Peirce (1839–1914). Other notable early pragmatists include William James (1842–1910), John Dewey (1859–1952) and Clarence Irving Lewis (1883–1964). The most prominent contemporary pragmatist is Richard Rorty.

P

Pragmatism re-emerged as an important theoretical approach in contemporary philosophy in the early 1980s, partly as a consequence of the growing fortunes of poststructuralism and postmodernism. It shares an 'anti-foundationalist, anti-representationalist, anti-realist view of truth' with the former, and an 'incredulity towards metanarratives' with the latter (Barker and Galasinski 2001: 16–17). Rorty (1983) describes his neo-pragmatic stance as 'postmodernist liberal bourgeois': postmodernist, because of its scepticism towards grand theory; liberal, because it relies on democracy and freedom of expression; and bourgeois, because, according to Rorty, liberalism has so far only been achieved in capitalist societies. His pragmatism is also ironic, because for the conversation to continue we need to affirm certain principles, such as justice, freedom, humanity or democracy, even though we know that they have no intrinsic meaning.

See also: **Irony; Liberalism, neoliberalism; Postmodern, postmodernity, postmodernism**

Further reading: Depew and Hollinger (eds) (1999).

Psychoanalysis

The word refers to a theory that seeks to explain both the development and nature of subjectivity, principally in terms of the concepts of the unconscious and of the Oedipus complex. Moreover, the term is used to designate a set of methods in psychotherapeutic practice which seek to resolve neurotic conflicts by means of remedial emotional experiences prompted by techniques such as hypnosis and free association. Inaugurated by the Austrian neurologist Sigmund Freud in the late nineteenth century, psychoanalytic theory has had a profound impact on a number of academic disciplines, including literary criticism, social and political theory, feminism, gender studies and cultural studies. The principal contribution of psychoanalysis to these fields of inquiry has been its insight that the human subject is neither unitary nor centred, but rather, fragmented and fraught with tension and internal conflict. A major criticism of psychoanalytic theory has been that it interprets the construction of subjectivity as a universal, rather than historically contingent process.

As a result of his treatment of patients suffering from neurotic symptoms, Freud gained a number of penetrating insights related to personality development (for his entire opus, see Freud 1953–74). He understood neurotic disorders such as depression, phobias and anxiety, among others, as resulting from early childhood experiences and unresolved conflicts between different registers within the human psyche. Moreover, he believed that sexuality was a determining factor in the formation of neurotic disorders, as well as in personality development overall.

Combining the tenets of Freudian psychoanalysis with insights from the structuralist linguistics of Ferdinand de Saussure and others, the French theorist Jacques Lacan emphasized the role of language in the structuring of subjective identity (1977). According to Lacan, the Oedipal child enters the symbolic order, in which meanings of self, gender and the body are crystallized. The entry into the symbolic, for Lacan, is predicated on a loss of the pre-symbolic sense of non-differentiation and unity with others, above all with the mother.

Bulgarian-born French theorist Julia Kristeva took Lacan's account of language and subjectivity a step further. She introduced the notion of the 'semiotic', a pre-imaginary realm of signification generated within the body of the mother – a space that Kristeva, drawing on Plato, names the *chora* (1980 [1970]). The *chora* continues to function in adult life, as an imaginary site of perfect communication, to which a subject may desire to return. The semiotic, however, is only intelligible through language and thus cannot function independently of the symbolic.

Marxist philosopher Louis Althusser used Lacanian psychoanalysis to explain how ideology works (2001 [1970]). More specifically, he focused on the way the symbolic summoned individuals into their subject positions to maintain social order. Slovene cultural analyst Slavoj Žižek also inflects Lacanian psychoanalysis with Marxist theory, albeit in a somewhat different way. He rejects Althusser's account, according to which an individual is always entirely interpellated by a dominant ideology. In contrast, he argues that ideology always allows some degree of 'ideological disidentification' or critical distance. Marxism, for Žižek, is similar to psychoanalysis, as it seeks to explain the processes of becoming rather than a hypothetical essence of being. Capitalism, he contends, is built around a lack that cannot be filled, and its subjects experience this lack and seek to find something that would make them feel whole. For Žižek, capitalism is characterized by the 'crippling contradiction, discord, by an immanent want of balance', and is therefore engaged in a 'permanent revolutionizing of its own conditions of existence' (1989: 52).

Michel Foucault (1980 [1976]) interpreted psychoanalysis as a key technology of the self in modernity, arguing that it represented the culmination of a tradition, which grew out of the confessional practices introduced by the early Catholic Church. Philosopher Gilles Deleuze and psychoanalyst Félix Guattari (1977 [1972]) also understood psychoanalysis as a symptom of modernity, and challenged its interpretation of desire as rooted in lack. In its place, they proposed a 'schizoanalysis' based on the notion of a fluid desire, free from oedipal constraints.

P

See also: **Desire; Deterritorialization/reterritorialization; Id, superego, ego; Ideology; Imaginary, symbolic, real; Interpellation; Oedipus complex; Schizoanalysis; Subject, subjectivity; Uncanny; Unconscious, collective unconscious**

Further reading: Milner (1994).

Public/private

The word 'public' derives from Latin *pūblicus*, which means pertaining to the people, and ultimately from *pūbēs*, adult. Private, on the other hand, derives from Latin *prīvātus*, meaning 'deprived (of public life)'. The public/private distinction has a long, complex and in many ways controversial history in Western thought. The association of the public with freedom and the political state, and of the private with privation and material necessities, can be traced back to the distinction, in classical Greek tradition, between *pólis* (city, city-state: the domain of free citizens and political activity) and *oîkos* (house, household: the domain of women, slaves, biological reproduction and material production).

The nature and makeup of what is considered 'public' and 'private' have been theorized in many different ways, depending on the specific sets of power relations under scrutiny. In contemporary liberal theory, the public/private dichotomy is variously interpreted as a distinction between the state and the market, between the state and civil society, or between the social and the personal realms more broadly (Kymlicka 2001).

Numerous feminist theorists have argued that the public/private discourse has been instrumental in the exclusion of women from political rights and other rights commonly associated with citizenship. According to Carole Pateman, the strong separation between public and private spheres in liberalism meant that domestic power relations were seen as a matter of personal 'choice', not to be incorporated in the scope of democracy. The issue for women then was to apply democratic ideals 'in the kitchen, the nursery and the bedroom' (Pateman 1988: 216). More generally, feminists have emphasized the ways in which women's chances of becoming political equals are in fact influenced and often determined by power relations within the household and work force. It has been recognized that the 'boundary between the public and the private is a political act in itself' and that 'political power relations with their own dynamics exist in each social sphere' (Yuval-Davis 1997: 80).

Some feminists have endeavoured to reconceptualize the notions of the public and the private, interpreting the former as being more heterogeneous and all-encompassing, and the latter as simply representing those aspects of someone's life and activity 'that any person has the right to exclude from others' (Young 1990: 119). If public spaces are to be truly inclusive, they have argued, they have to promote a positive acknowledgment of difference at all levels.

More generally, poststructuralist and postmodern theories have rejected the logic of dichotomous thinking and disputed the notion of stable gender categories, defined in terms of the public/private binary. It is now widely recognized that any distinction between the public and the private has to be historically contingent and subject to different discursive articulations.

P

See also: **Binary opposition; Poststructuralism; Postmodern, postmodernity, postmodernism; Public sphere**

Further reading: Landes (1998).

Public sphere

The concept of the public sphere, as the domain in which political and social debate takes place, was most influentially elaborated by the German social theorist Jürgen Habermas (1991 [1962]). Habermas outlined the history of the public sphere (German, *Öffentlichkeit*) from ancient Greece to the twentieth century. He was particularly interested in the bourgeois public sphere, which began to emerge in Europe in the late seventeenth and eighteenth centuries. This public sphere was comprised of scholars, teachers, lawyers, diplomats, doctors, clergymen, artists, creative writers, merchants and manufacturers, who congregated in public places such as clubs, salons and coffee houses, to discuss the most significant social and political developments of the time. These debates were encouraged by a new kind of political journal, which were then becoming exceptionally popular in England and other European countries. The bourgeois public sphere was independent of the mechanisms of the state and often highly critical of state policies. It had a significant impact on the development of modern state institutions, by exposing them to public scrutiny. For Habermas, the public sphere represents a normative ideal and the privileged site where 'communicative action' can take place. He argues, however, that the public sphere, with all its moral and political implications, has all but disappeared with the increasing power of the state, and the commodification of the mass media and everyday life. He refers to this dual process as the colonization of the lifeworld (the public and the private spheres) by the system (the state and the economy).

Critics have argued that Habermas unduly glorifies the bourgeois public sphere and fails to theorize its exclusive character, especially in terms of class and gender. They have also rejected the notion of a singular homogeneous public sphere in favour of a multiplicity of articulated publics and counterpublics, which characterize today's complex societies (Benhabib 1996, Fraser 1992).

See also: **Lifeworld and system; Patriarchy; Public/private**

Further reading: McGuigan (1996).

P

Queer, queer theory

Originally denoting strangeness or otherness, the word 'queer' was first used as a derogatory label for male homosexuality in the early twentieth century. Since the late 1980s, gay and lesbian activist groups such as Queer Nation, ACTUP and OutRage, in the US and the UK, have reappropriated the word as a positive term of self-identification. Queer Nation sought to revitalize gay activism by combining guerrilla politics, street performance and strong media exposure. Although the original group no longer exists, it has inspired other gay activist groups in many countries worldwide, most notably in Great Britain and the US. The term 'queer', however, has not been universally accepted within the gay and lesbian movement. Some radical lesbian feminists, for example, argue that it blurs the boundaries between male and female sexualities, and thus obfuscates the origins of women's subordination to men (Jeffreys 2003).

As a critical concept, 'queer' has gained wide currency across a range of discourses, as a portmanteau term for a meta-identity that encompasses a range of non-normative and resistant sexualities, or, to quote Annamarie Jagose, for 'those gestures and analytical modes which dramatize incoherence in the allegedly stable relations between chromosomal sex, gender and sexual desire' (1996: 2–3).

Queer theory deconstructs and defies discourses of heteronormative sexuality, bringing together and extending perspectives from gay and lesbian studies, feminism and women's studies, gender studies, history, literary criticism, and social and cultural theory more generally. It is a heterogeneous and interdisciplinary body of thought, which emerged in the early 1990s and has particular resonances with psychoanalysis, poststructuralism and postmodernism. Foucault's work on sexuality and his understanding of the body as constituted by discourse have made a significant impact on the development of queer theory. A distinguishing feature of queer theory is that it foregrounds sexuality as the 'key category through which other social, political, and cultural phenomena are to be understood' (Edgar and Sedgwick 1999: 321).

Eve Kosofsky Sedgwick's *Between Men: English Literature and Male Homosocial Desire* (1985) and Judith Butler's *Gender Trouble: Feminism and the Subversion of Identity*. (1990) are typically quoted as the founding texts of queer theory. In *Between Men*, Sedgwick analysed a range of canonical English literary texts to uncover their underlying homosexuality or homosociality (male bonding premised on the sublimation of homosexual desire) and to reveal how the two often converge or blend together. Her work has since become a blueprint for the 'queering' of representations of gender and sexuality in a variety of cultural and media texts. In *Gender Trouble*, Butler introduced the idea of performativity, to argue that gender roles are the result of social norms we actively enact or reject.

Criticisms levelled against queer theory have emphasized its roots in and affinities with the privileged middle class of affluent Western societies (Altman 2000). Murray Pratt, for example, has criticized the exclusive nature of queer acts, which are, according to him, available only to the privileged few, while 'for ordinary gay men and lesbians, open to entrapment, discrimination and abuses, the chance of enjoying forms of relationships and identities which value trust, sincerity and security is a much more urgent need' (Pratt 2002: 194).

See also: **Body; Discourse; Gender; Performativity, perverformative, performance; Postmodern, postmodernity, postmodernism; Poststructuralism; Sexuality**

Further reading: Jagose (1996).

Questionnaire

Questionnaires are instruments for quantitative data collection in a variety of disciplines. It needs to be noted, however, that qualitative analysis is typically applied in examining the responses to open-ended questions.

Relatively inexpensive to design and manage, questionnaires are particularly useful for collecting data from a large number of respondents. The most common ways of administering questionnaires are by mail, household drop off and pick-up, hand distribution, telephone, email or online. Group-administered questionnaires can be used for gathering data from a sample of respondents brought together in a particular location, for example when conducting a focus group. The main advantage of group-administered questionnaires is that they commonly attract higher response rates than other questionnaire types.

An important step in preparing a questionnaire is to determine a suitable size and composition of the respondent sample. Stratified sampling involves an analysis of the population under scrutiny, and devising a sample that adequately represents the whole. For example, if 50 per cent of the target population is female, then 50 per cent of the respondents should also be female.

Q

Once a questionnaire has been designed, it can be 'piloted' among colleagues or a small sample of future respondents. This practice is useful for identifying weaknesses and inconsistencies in the original design.

When administering a questionnaire, it is a common practice to use a covering letter that explains the topic, objectives, expected outcomes and the institutional context of the research project. The letter should also clearly indicate whether data are to be used anonymously.

There is a common understanding among researchers that questionnaires should not take more than fifteen to twenty minutes to complete. Clear instructions to the respondent are usually provided at the beginning, and at other relevant points of the questionnaire. Routing instructions (for example, 'if your answer is "no", please go to question x') are sometimes used to direct the respondent to relevant areas of the questionnaire. Response rates can be maximized by including a pre-paid return envelope (in the case of a mail questionnaire), or by offering a 'reward' to the respondent, such as access to the publication in which the findings of the research will be presented.

Questionnaires usually include several different types of questions. Examples of closed questions are yes/no questions, multiple-choice and scale or ranking questions. Open-ended questions are those that give the respondent the freedom of a creative response.

For the ease of data analysis, most researchers code the replies to the questions, by assigning them a numerical value. Numerical coding is also useful in calculating an average score in ranking questions. Coding frames provide instructions on how to use the numerical codes. Also, computer software can be used for entering questionnaire data into a project-related database.

See also: **Focus groups; Interview; Method, methodology**

Further reading: Denzin and Lincoln (eds) (2000 and 2003).

Q

Rr

Race

The word 'race' is used to designate a group or category of persons assumed to share a range of identifiable characteristics, such as skin pigmentation, type of hair, certain facial features, and even personality disposition, as a result of common biological descent. Although the concept of race, as an ostensibly discrete category of human variation, emerged in the Renaissance period, the height of racialist thought is usually associated with the Enlightenment worldview, as expressed in late eighteenth- and nineteenth-century natural sciences and anthropology. The Swedish naturalist Carl von Linné (1707–78), for example, classified the human species into four groups: *homo sapiens afer* (African), *homo sapiens americanus* (Native American), *homo sapiens asiaticus* (Asian), and *homo sapiens europaeus* (European). To each group, he attributed a distinct physical appearance and temperament, describing *homo sapiens afer* as 'black, slow, foolish, relaxed, crafty, indolent, negligent, [and anointed] with grease'; *homo sapiens americanus* as 'obstinate, merry, free, and painted with fine red lines'; *homo sapiens asiaticus* as 'pale, yellow, melancholy, stiff, severe, haughty, greedy, and covered with loose garments'; and *homo sapiens eurapaeus* as 'white, optimistic, and muscular, gentle, active, very smart, inventive, and covered with close vestments' (Smedley 1993). In the nineteenth century, physical anthropology typically employed a tripartite classification of humankind into Negroid, Mongoloid, and Caucasoid subspecies.

In the twentieth century, genetic research has revealed that racial classifications are of limited value, as it is by no means certain whether the visible differences between groups which are conventionally labelled as races, are typical of any identified genetic variation.

From the earliest racial taxonomies, however, it is evident that the concept of race may be used to articulate value judgements and ideological bias. Specific racial discourses, such as those that were at work in different colonial contexts and under fascism, were used to justify slavery, genocide, and other forms of oppression and exploitation.

Cultural studies understands race as a social construct, subject to context-specific encodings and decodings. In a volume entitled *The*

Empire Strikes Back (1982), the Birmingham Centre for Contemporary Cultural Studies examined the complex processes by which our understanding of race is socially structured, negotiated and contested. The arguments to be found in that volume sought to generate a critical debate about race and racism in contemporary British society, promoting an inclusive notion of 'black identity', which would simultaneously allow heterogeneity of national and cultural identifications. More recently, Stuart Hall (1991) and others have argued that, in contemporary societies, we are witnessing an ever-increasing multiplicity and fluidity of identifications, subject positions and social experiences, which cannot be explained in terms of stable identity categories.

'Critical Race Theory' (CRT) is the umbrella term for a number of related strands of inquiry that 'focus on the discursive relations between race, racism and power, and that seek to dismantle those relations' (Allatson 2007).

See also: **Centre for Contemporary Cultural Studies (CCCS); Colonialism; Ethnicity; Hybridity; Identity, identification, identity politics; Postcolonialism, neo-colonialism; Whiteness**

Further reading: Solomos (1999).

Reader-response criticism, reception theory

The term 'reader-response criticism' refers to an array of approaches in literary analysis that emerged in the US in the 1960s. The common feature of these approaches is their focus on the reader and the reading process, rather than on the text itself. Originally articulated as a critical response to New Criticism, this paradigm rests on an assumption that reading generates meaning, rather than simply discovering it. Some of the scholars commonly associated with reader-response criticism are Stanley Fish, Norman Holland and David Bleich, among others. While Holland (1975) and Bleich (1975) share an interest in the psychological processes that influence the reader's response, Stanley Fish emphasizes the social context in which reading takes place.

R

A reader-oriented school of literary analysis, which developed at the University of Constance in West Germany around the same time, is known as 'reception theory' (German, *Rezeptionsästhetik*). The most prominent reception theorists are Hans Robert Jauss and Wolfgang Iser. Jauss (1982) in particular sought to reconcile the demand for historicity in Marxist literary analysis, and the purely aesthetic approach advocated by formalist critics. He argued that literary interpretation should situate a text in a historical continuum that has to include readers' reception of it across time. He introduced the notion of the reader's 'horizon of expectations' (German, *Erwartunghorizont*), to describe the set of cultural and literary expectations with which a reader approaches a work of literature. The horizon of expectations changes over time, and so does the meaning of specific texts, as constructed by different audiences in different historical contexts. According to Jauss, the aesthetic value of a text and its historical significance are intimately related.

Iser emphasized the relation between what is explicit and implicit in the text, arguing that the reader's position is 'marked by the gaps in the text' and that 'whenever the reader bridges the gaps, communication begins. The gaps function as a kind of pivot on which the whole text–reader relationship revolves' (1978: 169).

See also: **Audience; Encoding/decoding; Hermeneutics; New Criticism**

Further reading: Holub (1984).

Real

See **Imaginary, symbolic, real**.

Register

The term 'register' has particular currency in linguistics, sociolinguistics and communication studies. It can be defined narrowly as a set of vocabulary, syntactic structures and rhetorical devices, used by particular social and occupational groups for specific purposes. We can thus talk about the register of law, the register of medicine or the register of engineering. More generally, however, 'register' can refer to varieties of language use that are determined by three principal aspects of a communicative event: the field, or the social context and purpose of the interaction; the tenor, or the relationship between the participants in the event; and the mode of communication, such as 'spoken' or 'written'.

Representation

R

The term derives the Latin verb *repraesentare*, which means 'to make present or manifest', either literally, in the sense of physical presence, or by means of a symbolic substitution of one object for another. Representation has been defined as an 'essential part of the process by which meaning is produced and exchanged between members of a culture', which involves the 'use of language, of signs and images which stand for or represent things' (Hall 1997: 15).

As a concept that links meaning and language to culture, representation is of particular relevance to cultural studies. We can distinguish three broad theoretical models that seek to explain how representation works: the reflective, the intentional and the constructionist models (see Hall 1997). According to the reflective or mimetic approaches, meaning resides in the real world of objects, persons and ideas, while language simply mirrors or imitates the true meaning that is already present 'out there'. The intentional approaches posit that the person who produces an utterance, the subject or the author, imparts a distinctive meaning to reality through language use. Finally, the constructionist approaches build on an assumption that meaning cannot be explained either in terms of the 'real' world, or in relation to individual speakers. Rather, they argue that it is 'social actors who use the conceptual systems of their culture and the linguistic and other representational systems to construct meaning, to make the world meaningful and to communicate about that world meaningfully to others' (Hall 1997: 25).

Constructionism is the privileged paradigm in cultural studies, to the extent that its underlying assumptions are currently by and large taken for granted. These include the notion that social and cultural meanings are constructed in and by language; that subjectivities and power relations are formed and contested through signifying practices; and that the politics of representation has the power to produce social change.

See also: **Deconstruction; Discourse; Encoding/decoding; Performativity, perverformativity, performance; Poststructuralism; Semiotics; Structuralism**

Rhetoric

The term refers to the art of speaking and writing in such a way as to persuade, or, more generally, to produce certain effects. As a systematic study of oratorical techniques, rhetoric emerged in the Greek cities of Sicily in the fifth century BCE, and was theorized, most famously, in Aristotle's *Rhetoric* (about 330 BCE). Aristotle distinguished between three types of oratory, each associated with one of three respective institutions: forensic with the law courts, deliberative with the public assembly, and epideictic with the public ceremony. In the Middle Ages, rhetoric was included among the seven liberal arts, which represented the core of the educational curriculum at European universities. Along with grammar and dialectic, rhetoric was part of the set of disciplines called the Trivium, while arithmetic, geometry, music and astronomy constituted the Quadrivium. Rhetoric remained an important component of Western education until the late nineteenth century.

'The new rhetoric' is an umbrella term that designates a range of approaches to rhetoric that have emerged in the latter half of the twentieth century. Rather than interpreting the speaker as a measure of truth, the new rhetoric understands truth as malleable and conditioned by the rhetorical process. Since at least the 1970s, the resurgence of critical appreciation of rhetoric in the humanities and social sciences coincides with the rise of poststructuralism, which emphasizes the constructed nature of all representation.

Recent studies in the rhetoric of inquiry have argued that scientific discourses are not neutral accounts of reality, but rather, rhetorical constructs, aimed at achieving certain effects. In this respect, rhetorical studies share a number of theoretical concerns with cultural studies. More specifically, both of these strands of inquiry aim to reveal the relationship between expressive forms and the social order; they both operate within the field of discursive practices; they are both concerned with the production of meaning at the point of consumption; and they both interpret textual practices as forms of power and performance (Rosteck 1999).

See also: **Discourse; Episteme; Knowledge; Poststructuralism**

Further reading: Rosteck (1999).

Rhizome, rhizomatics

'Rhizome' is a botanical term that designates stems that propagate horizontally across the ground, and grow from multiple nodes rather than from a single root. Bamboo and fern are plants that spread via rhizomes.

Deleuze and Guattari used the notion of the rhizome as a metaphor for a model of knowledge and power opposed to the 'arborescent' (tree-like) paradigm, prevalent in Western metaphysics (1987 [1980]). The metaphor of the tree illustrates the notion of a point of origin from a single root, out of which other structures grow uni-directionally through binary division. In contrast, the rhizome has no centre. Rather, it is constituted by lines of intensity and flight, which enable a continuous play of deterritorialization and reterritorialization. The model of rhizomatic spatiality is the map, which can be 'torn, reversed, adapted to any kind of mounting, reworked by an individual, group or social formation' (ibid.: 12).

R

The key significance of the concept of the rhizome in cultural studies is that it emphasizes that cultural hegemony operates rhizomatically, rather than from a unified centre. The rhizome has been used as a metaphor that describes the technical, social and cultural functioning of the Internet (see, for example, Moulthrop 1994). In postcolonial studies, the metaphor of the rhizome has been deployed to challenge the binary logic of colonial discourse, based on the margin/centre dichotomy (Ashcroft 2001).

Rhizomatics is a critical practice that rejects the hierarchical binary nexus between ground and consequent, cause and effect, reality and representation. Rather, it is primarily concerned with the proliferation of articulations and disarticulations between diverse objects, aims, functions and effects. According to Lawrence Grossberg, rhizomatics is entirely a 'philosophy of the other: there are only others, only the real. A particular point – a "partial object" – is defined by its externality, by the connections it has with other points, by its field of effects' (1997a: 84).

See also: **Deterritorialization/reterritorialization; Nomad**

Further reading: Deleuze and Guattari (1987 [1980]).

Right, New Right

Commonly used to designate the conservative parties, movements and ideas in modern politics, the term 'right' derives from the seating arrangement in the National Constituent Assembly in the early years of the French Revolution. In contemporary liberal democracies, the right is often defined in opposition to social democracy or socialism. Proponents of the right typically support traditional institutions, social hierarchies and modes of behaviour. Parties such as the Conservatives in the UK, Republicans in the US, and a range of European Christian Democratic parties are commonly seen as representing right-wing politics. These should be distinguished from extreme or far-right parties and ideas, which actively seek to effect radical social change and characteristically promote authoritarianism, extreme nationalism and xenophobia.

The term 'New Right' refers to a spectrum of conservative and liberal political positions that took hold in a number of advanced industrial democracies in the wake of the 1973–74 economic crisis. It is associated, in particular, with the Reagan administration in the US (1981–89) and the Thatcher era in Britain (1979–90). The New Right is characterized by a commitment to individualism, minimal government and the free market. Some of the policies typically advanced by New Right governments are the increasing privatization of the public sector, deregulation and the dismantling of the welfare state. Since the early 1980s, this orientation has made a significant impact on state policies worldwide, and New Right movements have gained prominence in a number of advanced industrial democracies, including France, Germany, the Netherlands, Belgium, Italy, Australia and New Zealand, among others.

See also: **Left, New Left; Thatcherism**

Russian Formalism

The term refers to a school of literary and linguistic analysis that flour-ished in Moscow and Petrograd (St Petersburg) in the early decades of the twentieth century. The Formalists shared a critical approach based on the idea that literature constituted a unique aesthetic realm governed by its own internal laws and principles, rather than being a simple reflection of social reality or the author's psyche. The Moscow Linguistic Circle, founded in 1915 by Roman Jakobson and others, elaborated a new approach to the study of language, which involved a systematic comparison between poetic and everyday language. The Petrograd Society for the Study of Poetic Language, established in 1916 by Viktor Shklovsky and others, studied the underlying principles of literary form.

The Formalists challenged the traditional dichotomy between form and content, arguing that content in literature exists only through form, and thus does not require autonomous study. They defined the object of literary analysis as 'literariness', that is, 'that which makes a given work a literary work' (Jakobson, in O'Toole and Shukman 1977, vol. ?: 17). They introduced the concepts of material (*mater'ial*) and device (*priem*), to refer, respectively, to the pre-aesthetic and aesthetic stages of the creative process. A parallel distinction, in the study of the narrative, was made between story (*fabula*) and plot (*sjuzhet*). The term 'defamiliariza-tion' (*ostranenie*), which retains considerable currency in contemporary criticism, refers to the literary device of making objects unfamiliar or strange, and thus disrupting the reader's habitual perception of reality.

Russian Formalism had a significant impact on structuralist literary analysis, as well as on twentieth-century literary theory more broadly.

See also: **Narrative; Structuralism**

Further reading: Bennett (2003).

R

Scape

Indian-born US anthropologist Arjun Appadurai has outlined five dimensions or 'scapes' of what he calls a disjunctured 'global cultural economy':

- Ethnoscapes – the people who move, such as tourists, immigrants, refugees, exiles and guestworkers.
- Mediascapes – newspapers, magazines, television stations, film production studios etc.
- Technoscapes – mechanical and information technology.
- Finanscapes – currency markets, national stock exchanges.
- Ideoscapes – ideological terms and images, such as democracy, freedom and welfare.

The term 'scape' is intended to convey the asymmetric flows of ideas, information, people and capital. Scapes are 'navigated' by individual social actors, who use them to construct 'multiple worlds which are constituted by the historically situated imaginations of persons and groups spread around the globe' (1990: 296–7).

See also: **Cultural flow; Globalization; Ideology; Mass communication and mass media; Transnational, transnationalism**

Further reading: Appadurai (1990).

Schizoanalysis

Schizoanalysis is a theoretical concept developed by Deleuze and Guattari in *Anti-Oedipus* (1977 [1972]), as a parody and, at the same time, radical critique of psychoanalytic theories of subjectivity and capitalist society more broadly. According to Deleuze and Guattari, most of Western thought is constructed around a paranoid structure. Paranoia is a mental disorder that involves excessive anxiety and delusions of persecution from the outside world. In modern society, this outside world is represented by society, law, conscience or the father. Paranoia impels modern subjects on a quest to find the authority that endows signs with meaning. Deleuze and Guattari see psychoanalysis – with its understanding of subjectivity as a knowable structure, built around the libidinal economy of Oedipal desire and lack – as a prime example of this paradigm. In contrast, they claim that the Oedipal pattern is not universal, but rather representative of the conditions of the modern subject under capitalism. This is because, they argue, the 'supreme goal' of capitalism is 'to produce lack in the large aggregates, to introduce lack where there is always too much, by effecting the absorption of overabundant resources' (p. 235).

Rather than examining subjectivity from the perspective of the universal Oedipal subject, as psychoanalysis does, schizoanalysis approaches it from the point of view of the schizophrenic. The schizophrenic, who experiences a range of symptoms that affect her or his relations with the surrounding world, is seen by Deleuze and Guattari as existing beyond the process of Oedipal normalization that underlies capitalist relations. Rather than interpreting subjectivity as a stable structure constituted by lack, schizoanalysis sees it as a dynamic mechanism for an endless production of new desires. The subject, for Deleuze and Guattari, is a desiring machine continuously engaged in seeking out new, multiple and conflicting possibilities of production, contact and relationship.

See also: **Capitalism; Desire; Deterritorialization/reterritorialization; Nomad; Oedipus complex; Psychonalysis; Subject, subjectivity**

Further reading: Deleuze and Guattari (1983 [1977]).

Selective tradition

The concept of the selective tradition derives from the early work of Raymond Williams. Contrary to the Leavisite notion of the 'great tradition' in literature, interpreted as a reflection of the organic properties of a community, Williams argued that traditions are always selective, and governed by contemporary values and interests. Selection, Williams argued, is a retroactive process of a 'continual selection and re-selection of ancestors' (1965 [1961]: 69). Culture, for Williams, is articulated at three levels: first, the level of the 'lived culture of a particular time and place', which is only fully available to those who participate in it; secondly, the documentary or recorded culture of existing texts and artefacts; and thirdly, the selection of texts, from the repository of recorded culture that constitutes what a given culture regards as its tradition.

See also: **Culturalism; Structure of feeling**

Semiology, semiotics

Both terms derive from the Greek word *sēmeîon*, which means sign, token or evidence. Sometimes used interchangeably, they refer to two distinct traditions in the study of signs: 'semiology' is commonly associated with the structuralist tradition, pioneered by the Swiss linguist Ferdinand de Saussure; while 'semiotics', in the narrow sense, refers to the cognitive–interpretive tradition, heralded by the US philosopher and logician Charles Sanders Peirce. The main difference between the two traditions is that the former focuses on arbitrary signs, especially those belonging to the language system, while the latter takes into account any signs, regardless of their level of conventionality or the signifying system they belong to. The most prominent scholars in the structuralist tradition have been the Danish Louis Hjelmslev (1899–1966), the Lithuanian-born Algirdas Greimas (1917–92), and the French Roland Barthes (1915–80). The cognitive-interpretive tradition is typically associated with the American Charles William Morris (1901–79), Hungarian-born American Thomas Sebeok (1920–2001), and the British Ivor A. Richards (1893–1979) and Charles K. Ogden (1989–1957). Some scholars, such as the Italian Umberto Eco (b. 1932), have fruitfully combined insights from both traditions.

Saussure used the term 'semiology' (French *sémiologie*) to designate a discipline, not existent at the time, which would be dedicated to studying signs and their use in social life. He conceived of the new discipline as a subdivision of social psychology, which would be concerned primarily with arbitrary or socially constructed signs, such as those that operate within the language system, social rites and customs, or military and nautical signalling codes. He argued that linguistics was best suited to serve as a 'model for the whole of semiology, even though languages represent only one type of semiological system' (1983 [1915]: 68). In contrast, Roland Barthes interpreted semiology as a branch of linguistics, arguing that signs in any signifying system can only be understood by means of language (1968 [1964]). Barthes developed a theoretical framework for the practice of examining cultural signs and reading their meaning within larger structures of myth. By shifting his emphasis from language as a system to specific instances of language use, or texts, Barthes inaugurated a poststructuralist turn in the study of signs. His writings had a significant impact on the work of the Centre for Contemporary Cultural Studies (CCCS) at the University of Birmingham, especially under the directorship of Stuart Hall (1969–79).

Peirce used the term 'semiotic' to describe his own 'formal doctrine of signs', which he saw as closely related to logic (1931–58, vol. 2: 227). His emphasis on the ways in which sign systems operate in communicative acts gave rise to the British and American speech-act and communications theories, and to a broader philosophical strand known as 'pragmatism'. Rather than focusing on signs in themselves, Peirce was interested in signification as a process. He used the word 'semeosis', or 'semiosis', to refer to the 'activity' of signs in communicative acts. He argued that signs do not engender a single meaning, but rather produce a potentially never-ending series of meanings, thus participating in what has become known as 'infinite semiosis' (1931–58, vol. 1: 339).

The principle of infinite semiosis was further elaborated by Umberto Eco in his book *A Theory of Semiotics* (1976). Arguing that 'semiotics is concerned with everything that can be taken as a sign' (1976: 7), Eco developed a semiotic theory of culture based on a dialectic between codes (signification) and modes of sign production (communication).

Semiotics has extended to a wide range of areas of inquiry beyond literary, media and cultural studies. These areas include, for example, anthropological, social and psychological semiotics (social, cultural and behavioural codes); medical semiotics (medical symptoms); zoosemiotics (animal communication); paralinguistics (voice qualities); kinesics and proxemics (physical postures or gestures); musical semiotics; film semiotics; semiotics of visual, tactile and olfactory communication; semiotics of scientific and natural languages; semiotics of architecture and urban space; and semiotics of material objects.

See also: **Code; Poststructuralism; Sign; Structuralism**

Further reading: Chandler (2002).

Semiotic analysis

Semiotic analysis is a qualitative research method aimed at interpreting the structures and processes of signification in cultural texts and practices. In structuralist semiotics, the focus is on synchronic analysis and on formal signifying systems, rather than on historically situated social and cultural practices of signification. Social semiotics, in contrast, takes a poststructuralist approach in emphasizing the social dimension of representation and consumption. Its aim is to uncover how meaning is generated, maintained, challenged or subverted. Social semiotics assumes that the relationships between signifiers and their signifieds, albeit being ontologically arbitrary, are both socially motivated and dependent on certain media-specific and genre-specific conventions.

In sociology and cultural studies, semiotic analysis is usually deployed in conjunction with other methods of text analysis and ethnographic fieldwork, and within different theoretical frameworks, such as

Marxism, psychoanalysis, or Foucault's theory of discourse. Based primarily on personal interpretations of the researcher, semiotic analysis provides a 'powerful framework for analysis and very few practical guidelines for rigorously employing it' (Slater 1998: 238).

Despite the absence of a definite set of rules for semiotic analysis, it is possible to identify some steps that semioticians typically follow when conducting their investigation. These steps are as follows:

- Selecting a number of texts and/or practices that lend themselves to addressing the hypothesis of the research project. Depending on the topic and the hypothesis, these texts may be in a variety of different media.
- Gathering the texts and/or recording the practices. Cultural practices can be recorded by note taking, or in audio or video formats.
- Identifying the key signs or signifying resources and explaining their denotative and connotative meanings, in the specific social and cultural context under scrutiny.
- Synchronic analysis. This entails describing the paradigmatic structure of the text, or the interrelationship between signifying resources. Researchers typically consider the cultural codes within which meaning is established, maintained or challenged. This may involve identifying and explaining instances of intertextuality and the specific conventions of the medium and the genre.
- Diachronic analysis. This involves describing the syntagmatic structure of the text, or the sequential arrangement of elements that forms the narrative. The syntagmatic structure is also examined in terms of the underlying cultural codes and conventions.
- Making conclusions about the shared structures of understanding, or discourses, in the social and cultural context within which the signs and codes that have been identified operate.
- Testing the findings. This can be done, for example, through interviews, surveys or focus groups. Respondents are typically drawn from the audiences of the cultural texts or the participants in the cultural practices examined in a specific research project.

See also: **Diachronic/synchronic; Method, methodology; Semiology, semiotics**

Further reading: Slater (1998).

Senses

The word 'sense' refers to a faculty by which our bodies perceive external stimuli. Vision, hearing, smell, taste and touch are commonly considered to be the five core senses, and balance is sometimes added as the sixth sense. The word 'sensorium' is used to denote the entire sensory apparatus of the body. Over the past few decades, we have witnessed a growing interest in the study of our sensory experience across a range of disciplines, most notably in anthropology, sociology and cultural studies. In all these disciplines, it is generally acknowledged that our experience of the senses, although dependent on our physiological capacities, is also substantially mediated by our previous experience and socio-cultural conditioning.

The tendency to privilege vision over any other sense, deeply rooted in Western metaphysical tradition, is commonly referred to as ocularcentrism. Both Plato and Aristotle posited a hierarchy of the senses, in which sight was considered to be highest, and closely related with reason. For Aristotle, touch and taste were the least 'honourable' of all the senses. In his view, these two senses were conducive to lust and gluttony, and thus more consonant with animal nature than with human nature. The vision-centred perspective also figures prominently in medieval religious writing, most notably in the scholastic theology of Thomas Aquinas.

Aristotle's account of the sensorium exerted a considerable influence on the work of German idealist philosopher Hegel. Contrary to Hegel's perspectives, the young Marx argued that human beings were affirmed in the objective world precisely through the entire range of their sensory experience, and he denounced the sensory deprivation of the proletariat in nineteenth-century capitalism.

In his account of Western history as tied to the revolutions in media technologies, Marshall McLuhan (1962) saw modernity as emerging alongside the specific type of visuality at the heart of the print culture. The extreme opposite of Western visuality was, for McLuhan, the 'ear culture' of tribal societies, in which spoken words had a magical quality. It was the 'interiorization of the technology of the phonetic alphabet', he argued, that 'translated man [sic!] from the magical world of the ear to the neutral visual world' (1962: 18).

A novel perspective in the study of the sensorium was introduced by McLuhan's former student Walter Ong, who emphasized the importance of studying the relations between the senses, rather than the senses *per se*. He argued that cultures differ in their exploitation of the various senses, to the extent that culture can be defined 'in terms of the organization of the sensorium' (1967: 6). Ocularcentrism is considered to have reached its popular-cultural high point in the postmodern society of spectacle.

The flip side of ocularcentrism, in Western modernity, has been the neglect and even denigration of the other senses. Furthermore, Western

S

hierarchies of the senses have been decidedly gender-biased, in that the so-called 'higher' senses, such as vision and hearing, have typically been considered more 'masculine' in nature (Classen 1998).

See also: **Aesthetics; Affect, emotion, feeling; Phenomenology**

Further reading: Classen (1993 and 1998); Howes (ed.) (1991); McLuhan (1962); Ong (1967).

Sexuality

A derivative of the word 'sex', 'sexuality' is a relatively new term, which gained currency in the English language in the late nineteenth century. In contemporary popular usage, the word 'sexuality' brings together connotations of gendered identities and subjectivities; of eroticism and sexual desire; and those of anatomy and sexual reproduction.

Nineteenth-century European sexology, or systematic study of human sexuality, was largely based on an assumption that sexuality is fundamentally biological, and thus beyond social control. Combined with prefixes such as bi-, hetero- or homo-, the word 'sexuality' was used to classify people into 'types', taken as embodiments of diverse sexual behaviours and desires. Relying heavily on medical science, early sexology was primarily interested in documenting those sexual desires and behaviours that were seen as deviating from the norm. It interpreted sexual otherness as a type of disease caused, in most cases, by hereditary factors.

In the early decades of the twentieth century, the discipline of anthropology heralded a shift away from biological approaches to sexuality, towards perspectives focusing on social and cultural aspects of sexual behaviour. The diversity of socially sanctioned manifestations of sexuality recorded by anthropologists in cultures outside the European sphere of influence suggested that sexuality was in many ways influenced by the social and cultural context. A pioneering example of such ethnographic work is Bronisław Malinowski's seminal study of the Trobriand Islanders, *The Sexual Life of Savages* (1987 [1929]). Although Malinowski and other early twentieth-century anthropologists never questioned the universal nature of the sexual 'drive', they began to carve out intellectual space in which it was possible to consider the complex interplay between sexuality and the broader society.

Freudian psychoanalysis was perhaps the leading influence that shaped modern approaches to sexuality, by interpreting it as the paramount force behind the development of the human psyche. Freud was also instrumental in shifting the focus of attention from the reproductive aspects of sexuality, to the realm of erotic pleasure and desire. A further

S

step was taken by Jacques Lacan, who argued that sexuality was structured around the quintessential symbol of social authority, the phallus.

Within contemporary cultural studies, the most influential framework
for understanding human sexuality has been the one articulated by
Michel Foucault. For Foucault, sexuality is a historical construct, which
became prominent in the nineteenth century as a desirable object of
knowledge and, at the same time, a tool for regulating the social order
in Western societies (1980 [1976]). Drawing on Foucault's work, queer
theorists such as Judith Butler (1990) and Eve Kosofsky Sedgwick (1995)
have challenged the essentialist notions of sexual desire, which have
dominated modern approaches to sexual identities, orientations and
practices.

See also: **Discourse; Feminism; Gender; Performativity, perverformative, performance;
Psychoanalysis; Queer, queer theory**

Further reading: Weeks (2003).

Sign

Deriving from the Latin noun *signum*, which means mark or token, the
word 'sign', in common usage, designates an object, quality, or event
whose presence or occurrence indicates the probable presence, occurrence, or advent of something else (*COED*). It is possible to distinguish
between two kinds of signs: natural signs, where the connection
between the two objects, qualities or events appears to be a natural fact
(for example, medical symptoms); and conventional signs, where the
connection is clearly artificial (for example, Morse code). In structuralist
linguistics and semiotics, the term 'sign' refers to the basic unit of
meaning production. Signs are typically organized into codes, and
largely determined by social and cultural conventions.

In the work of the Swiss linguist Ferdinand de Saussure, the linguistic
sign is described as consisting of two distinct elements: the signifier
(French *signifiant*, the form that signifies, such as a sound pattern), and
the signified (French *signifié*, the conceptual meaning). According to
Saussure, the signifier and the signified are as indivisible as the two
sides of a piece of paper (1983 [1915]: 111). Their relationship, however,
is always a matter of arbitrary convention, as 'there is nothing at all to
prevent the association of any idea whatsoever with any sequence of
sounds whatsoever' (p. 76).

Saussure's insight into the arbitrary nature of the sign represented a
breakthrough in the Western philological and philosophical tradition, as
it asserted the autonomy of language with respect to reality. Saussure
argued that signs have no intrinsic meaning: rather, their meaning

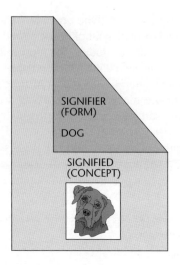

Figure 7 Saussure's model of the linguistic sign

derives entirely from their relation to, or difference from, other signs within the language system. He illustrated this by analogy with the game of chess, where the value of each piece depends on its position on the chessboard (Chandler 2002: 23–4).

The US philosopher and logician Charles Sanders Peirce (1839–1914) developed an alternative model of the sign, which consists of three interconnected elements: the representamen (the form a sign takes, roughly equivalent to Saussure's signifier), the interpretant (the sense attributed to a sign, similar, to some extent, to Saussure's signified, but understood here as itself constituting a sign in the mind of the interpreter), and the object to which the sign refers (1931–58). Peirce's model, which foregrounds the importance of the process of interpretation, is of particular interest for communication and media studies.

Peirce also distinguished between three different modes of relationship between the signifier and the signified: the symbolic mode, in which the relationship is entirely arbitrary or conventional; the iconic mode, in which the signifier can be understood as being similar to the signified (for example, a metaphor); and the indexical mode, in which the signifier and the signified are seen as directly related, in a physical or causal sense (for example, a photograph, or a directional sign). These three modes are not always mutually exclusive, and the same sign can be an icon, a symbol or an index, or any combination of these, depending on the context in which it is used.

While structuralists privileged speech over writing, the signified over the signifier and the synchronic study of language over the diachronic one, poststructuralist critics endeavoured to revalorize writing, temporality and the materiality of the linguistic form (Derrida 1974 [1967]).

In contemporary communication and media studies, it is generally acknowledged that different media in which signs are anchored have their own principles of structure, which may affect the sense the audience makes of a specific mediated text.

See also: **Code; Diachronic/synchronic;** *Différance*; **Logocentrism, phonocentrism,** *écriture*; **Poststructuralism; Semiology, semiotics; Semiotic analysis; Structuralism**

Further reading: Chandler (2002).

Simulacrum

In Latin, the word 'simulacrum' refers to a likeness, image or representation. In the Platonic theory of form, a distinction is made between *eidos*, the primary essence or idea; *eikôn*, a likeness or copy that resembles the original; and *eidôlon*, a semblance or phantasm that falsifies reality, rather than faithfully representing it. In the Judeo-Christian tradition, the notion of a copy that bears no resemblance to the original is exemplified by the story in the book of Genesis. According to this account, God made humans in his image and likeness. Through sin, however, humans lost their resemblance to God and became simulacra. In other words, they have 'forsaken moral existence in order to enter into aesthetic existence' (Deleuze 1990 [1967]: 257). Throughout the Middle Ages, the word 'simulacrum' carried negative connotations, as a copy so far removed from the original that it becomes an entity in itself, an image without a model.

It was not before the latter half of the twentieth century that the pervasive diffusion of new media technologies profoundly undermined the primacy of the real. In his essay 'The Simulacrum and Ancient Philosophy' (1990 [1967]), Gilles Deleuze sought to contest the Platonic tradition and reinstate the simulacrum as a crucial critical term for contemporary society, capable of subverting the traditional dichotomy between reality and representation. The simulacrum, according to Deleuze, is not a degenerate copy. Rather, it possesses a positive power to challenge the possibility of a privileged point of view.

In Jean Baudrillard's account of postmodern hyperreality, simulacra have entirely supplanted reality in today's mediated society. For Baudrillard (1983 [1981]), the simulacrum represents the key metaphor of society because 'authentic' social life can no longer be separated from its representations. Baudrillard argues that this displacement happened

Key Concepts in Cultural Studies

gradually, with the media first reflecting reality, then masking its absence, and finally superseding reality altogether.

See also: **Authentic culture; Hyperreality; Postmodern, postmodernity, postmodernism; Representation; Spectacle**

Further reading: Baudrillard (1983 [1981]).

Space, place

Defined respectively as a 'continuous area or expanse which is free or unoccupied', and a 'particular position or point in space, a location' (*COED*), the terms 'space' and 'place' are intimately related. In the humanities and social sciences, space and place represent two distinct but interconnected concepts, which have been theorized in a number of different and not always mutually compatible ways.

Scholarly interest in space and place grew in the 1970s, most notably in the field of human geography. In a seminal book entitled *Space and Place* (1977), Chinese-born American geographer Yi-Fu Tuan argued that place is produced and maintained through the 'fields of care', or the emotional investment people make in a particular setting. Places, according to Tuan, provide a sense of security, identity and belonging, while space suggests openness and freedom. Furthermore, he contended, 'if we think of space as that which allows movement, then place is pause; each pause in movement makes it possible for location to be transformed into place' (Tuan 1977: 6). He introduced the notions of topophilia and topophobia to describe the affection and fears that people feel in relation to specific places.

Others have theorized space and place through a Marxist lens, interpreting them as deeply embedded in social relations. The French Marxist sociologist Henri Lefebvre (1991 [1974]) has argued that space is always historically contingent, as each mode of production engenders its own understanding of it. According to Lefebvre, each historically produced type of space contains within it both traces of its forerunners and the portents of the ones yet to come. He explains space as produced through a three-way dialectic between cultural practices, representations and imaginations. Lefebvre distinguishes between two different types of space: dominated space, which is hegemonic or controlled, and appropriated space, which is space transformed through everyday practices, to meet specific needs.

Drawing on Lefebvre, de Certeau interprets place as a 'dominated' or institutional space. Place, for de Certeau, is the domain of strategy, and is characterized by closure and internal administration. In contrast, space is understood as pertaining to tactics. Space, in other words, is an 'appropriated' or practised place, in the sense that the 'street geometri-cally defined by urban planning is transformed into a space by walkers' (1984 [1980]: 117).

In cultural studies, it is now widely acknowledged that both space and place are culturally produced, while at the same time themselves partic-ipating in the making of culture.

See also: **Everyday; Hegemony**

Further reading: de Certeau (1984 [1980]).

Spectacle

Deriving from the Latin noun *spectaculum*, which means public show (from *specere*, to look at), the word 'spectacle' refers to a visually strik-ing performance or display (*COED*). In today's popular usage, it commonly designates heavily marketed performances targeted at mass audiences, such as major sports events, concerts or cultural festivals. The key feature of contemporary spectacle is that it attracts significant media attention.

The concept of the 'society of the spectacle', elaborated by French thinker Guy Debord in the 1960s, has had a significant impact on contem-porary social and cultural theory. For Debord, spectacle is not just a phenomenon related to performance and the media. Rather, it brings together the market relations of late capitalism and the regimes of the senses, particularly the visual. The spectacle, Debord argued, is an '*affir-mation of appearances* and an identification of all human social life with appearances' (2005 [1967]: 12). According to him, advanced capitalism has become a society of the spectacle and the image. Exchange value of commodities has eclipsed use value, and authentic human needs have given way to pseudo-needs manufactured by the media. The alienated 'spectator' is utterly deprived of agency, reduced to being a passive viewer and consumer. For Debord, the relentless consumption of the spectacle gets in the way of authentic human experience, since authen-ticity needs to be based on a close engagement with the material world.

See also: **Consumption; Hyperreality; Postmodern, postmodernity, postmodernism; Simulacrum**

Further reading: Kellner (2003).

Structuralism

The word structuralism was coined by the Russian-born linguist Roman Jakobson, to designate the 'leading idea' underpinning various scholarly discourses in the early decades of the twentieth century. That idea, according to Jakobson, was that any set of phenomena under scientific scrutiny needs to be 'treated not as a mechanical agglomeration but as a structural whole', and that the basic task of analysis was 'to reveal the inner laws of the system' (1971 [1929]: 711). With a focus on the functioning of society as a system, structuralism takes an ahistorical and anti-humanist approach to the study of culture and society.

A major twentieth-century theoretical and methodological strand in the humanities and social sciences, structuralism owes a great deal of its insights to the work of the Swiss linguist Ferdinand de Saussure. Between 1907 and 1911, Saussure delivered a course in linguistics at the University of Geneva, which was published after his death from the lecture notes taken by two of his students (1983 [1915]). In this book, Saussure developed a framework for synchronic linguistics, the study of the relations among language elements at a particular point in time. He distinguished between specific instances of language use (*la parole*) and the underlying system that governs these concrete linguistic events (*la langue*). Linguistics, he believed, should be concerned with studying the language system, rather than its specific manifestations.

Structuralism became prominent in France in the 1960s, principally through the anthropological work of Claude Lévi-Strauss. Lévi-Strauss developed a structuralist method of anthropological investigation, which he employed in his analysis of kinship and marriage relations, systems of classification, and myth. In each case, he looked for an underlying deep structure that governed the relationships within the system. He argued that certain binary oppositions derived from everyday experience, such as 'raw' and 'cooked', 'fresh' and 'rotten', 'moist' and 'parched' and others, could serve as the basis for the formation of abstract notions and propositions within complex social and cultural formations. Roland Barthes extended the methods of structural linguistics to the study of texts and socio-cultural practices.

With its focus on the stability of relations within synchronic systems, structuralism does not provide the conceptual tools necessary for examining social and cultural change. While retaining the structuralist anti-humanism and its commitment to foregrounding language in the analysis of socio-cultural phenomena, poststructuralism emphasizes the malleability and historical contingency of discursive formations.

See also: **Binary opposition; Diachronic/synchronic; Poststructuralism; Semiology, semiotics; Sign**

Further reading: Hawkes (2003).

Structure of feeling

In the work of Raymond Williams (1965 [1961]; 1977), the notion of a structure of feeling designates the particular spirit or mood of a given culture, as actively experienced by people at a specific time in history. Like the Hegelian concept of *Zeitgeist*, or spirit of time, Williams' structure of feeling blends the subjective and the objective levels of experience, assuming a dynamic relationship between people's feelings and impulses and social structures. A structure of feeling is experienced in the present as something 'in solution', or a 'complex whole', which cannot be reduced to the 'fixed explicit forms' of the dominant ideology. It thus signals those aspects of feeling that have not yet been completely articulated, as they still exist at the 'very edge of semantic availability' (1977: 134). In this sense, a structure of feeling can be a sign of the emergent forces which have the potential to generate social change. For Williams, a structure of feeling is not an attribute of any individual in isolation, but rather a horizon shared by a community defined in generational terms. Historians, Williams believed, can to some extent recapture a structure of feeling by studying material culture and documentary evidence, which expresses life in direct terms.

Fredric Jameson (1991 [1984]) has deployed the concept of a structure of feeling to describe postmodernism not as ideology, but rather as a dynamic fusion between 'new forms of practice and social and mental habits' and the 'new forms of economic production and organization thrown up by the modification of capitalism – the new global division of labor – in recent years' (1991 [1984]: xiv).

See also: **Dominant, residual, emergent; Generation; Postmodern, postmodernity, postmodernism**

Further reading: Jameson (1991 [1984]), Williams (1977).

Style, lifestyle

S

Deriving from Latin *stilus*, an ancient implement for writing on wax tablets, the word 'style' refers to a manner of self-expression, which always combines elements of similarity, identity and difference. Thus, someone's handwriting necessarily draws on pre-existing codes (alphabetic conventions), while also exhibiting a range of attributes specific to a particular individual or group.

According to German sociologist Georg Simmel (1858–1918), the notion of style pertains only to applied arts and crafts, while genuine art has to be individual and unique. Simmel (1991 [1908]) established a direct correspondence between the style of objects people use in their everyday lives, and people's lifestyles more generally. He argued that, although commodities and lifestyles are always fashioned in a stylized manner, members of a society are nevertheless able to express their full individuality by combining the variously stylized commodities and lifestyles in a particular manner.

The notion of style as *bricolage* was developed by media theorist and cultural critic Dick Hebdige, in his classic study of youth subcultures in 1970s Britain (1979). For Hebdige, subcultural style is a counter-hegemonic signifying practice that entails the continual appropriation and re-articulation of objects from various fields of signification. These objects or commodities are 'magically appropriated; stolen by subordinate groups and made to carry "secret" meanings: meanings, which express, in code, a form of resistance to the order, which guarantees their continued subordination' (p. 18). But this appropriation, Hebdige argues, is far from stable, since objects can always be recommodified and reintegrated into the hegemony.

The concept of lifestyle designates specific ways of living, usually defined in terms of cultural values and modes of consumption. According to French sociologist Pierre Bourdieu (1984), lifestyle is always conspicuous and distinctive. It pertains to the work of representation, through which social relations are articulated. Mike Featherstone has argued that, in contemporary consumer culture, people 'display their individuality and sense of style in the particularity of the assemblage of goods, clothes, practices, experiences, appearance and bodily dispositions they design together into a lifestyle' (1991: 86).

See also: **Bricolage; Consumption; Everyday; Habitus and field; Identity, identification, identity politics; Subculture**

Further reading: Bourdieu (1984), Featherstone (1991), Hebdige (1979).

Subaltern, subaltern studies

Deriving from late Latin *subalternus*, from *sub-*, under, and *alternus*, every other one, the word 'subaltern' refers to groups of people occupying a subordinate position in a social hierarchy, 'whether this is expressed in terms of class, caste, age, gender and office or in any other way' (Guha 1983: i). The term 'subaltern studies' designates a range of approaches in the fields of history, literary criticism and cultural studies, which focus on the disempowered and politically 'voiceless' populations as agents of social and political change.

The concept of the subaltern derives from the work of Italian political activist and Marxist Antonio Gramsci. In his *Prison Notebooks*, Gramsci argued that Italy's Risorgimento was not a genuine national revolution, because it failed to produce cohesion between the nation's subaltern classes (the peasantry and the proletariat), and the radical segments of its bourgeois elite.

Gramsci's work had a significant impact on the Subaltern Studies Group (SSG) or Subaltern Studies Collective, a group of historians and social critics based in Delhi, India. Calling into question both colonial and bourgeois-nationalist narratives of South Asian history, which interpret anti-colonialism and the making of the Indian nation as achievements of the elite minority, the subaltern historians seek to recover the collective agency of the poor and the outcast.

Literary critic and theorist Gayatri Chakravorty Spivak has described the subaltern as structurally excluded from dominant discourses. Subalternity, for Spivak, exists 'where social lines of mobility, being elsewhere, do not permit the formation of a recognisable basis of action' (2005: 476). It cannot be effectively represented by academic knowledge, because academic knowledge is itself a hegemonic discourse that generates subalternity in the process of representing it. Spivak focuses on the historical erasure of women as subaltern subjects, claiming that if, 'in the context of colonial production, the subaltern has no history and cannot speak, the subaltern as female is even more deeply in shadow' (1988a [1985]: 287). Her claim that the 'subaltern cannot speak' (p. 308) has spawned much controversy about the inadequacies of contemporary theoretical frameworks and political systems of representation.

Since the 1990s, two US-based subaltern studies collectives have applied the paradigm of subalternity to the Latin American context, one in the field of history, and the other in literary studies.

See also: **Agency; Colonialism; Discourse; Hegemony; National-popular; Postcolonialism, neo-colonialism**

Further reading: Spivak (2005).

Subculture

The term 'subculture' connotes value systems, beliefs, customs, practices, cultural preferences and lifestyles distinct from, but interconnected to, those widely held in mainstream culture. As the prefix *sub-* (Latin for 'under') indicates, subcultures are often perceived as existing 'beneath' the larger society or culture to which they belong, in terms of their social status, marginalization or, in the case of criminalized or criminal subcultures, their perceived or factual deviance. Contemporary societies encompass a great diversity of subcultures, especially in densely populated urban settings. In sociology and cultural studies, subcultures are commonly seen as more transient and less compliant to the dominant norm than communities. Youth subcultures, for example, tend to define their ethos against the normative values of the adult population. Subcultural groups that explicitly seek to destabilize aspects of the dominant culture are sometimes referred to as countercultures.

The origins of subcultural studies can be traced back to the work of the Chicago School of sociology in the early decades of the twentieth century (see, for example, Park, Burgess, Watson and McKenzie 1967 [1925]). In contemporary cultural studies, however, subcultural theory is largely associated with the research conducted at the Centre for Contemporary Cultural Studies at Birmingham University from the 1970s onwards. Drawing principally upon Marxist, structuralist and poststructuralist theories, Birmingham researchers were particularly attentive to the intersections between the formal and symbolic aspects of subcultural practices and lifestyles, ideology and class relations.

Perhaps the most influential study of subcultures has been Dick Hebdige's *Subculture: The Meaning of Style* (1979). Hebdige interpreted working-class youth subcultures in 1970s Britain as arising out of, and in response to, the specific political and material conditions at work in Britain at the time, including the increased immigration from former colonies and an overall economic decline. He argued that subcultures such as teddy boys, mods, skinheads, punks, and dreads, to name only a few, challenged mainstream society through style, rather than through explicitly ideological articulations. Furthermore, he explained the re-integration of subcultural elements into hegemonic frameworks in terms of either their economic conversion into commodities, or their ideological conversion into complete otherness or spectacle.

Subcultural theory has been challenged on several grounds. Some have lamented its almost exclusive focus on male subcultural practices (McRobbie and Garber 1993 [1975]). Others have criticized its tendency to conceptualize both mainstream culture and subcultures as overly homogeneous, especially in terms of age and social class.

See also: **Bricolage; Centre for Contemporary Cultural Studies (CCCS); Generation; Hegemony; Style, lifestyle**

Further reading: Gelder and Thornton (1997).

Subject, subjectivity

'The subject' and 'subjectivity' are central terms in social theory and cultural studies. Indeed, it has been argued that cultural studies, 'even at its most political and deconstructive, is the intellectual field that has remained most concerned with theorizing the subject' (Mansfield 2000: v).

The word 'subject' derives from Latin *subjectus*, the past participle of the verb *subicere* (*sub + jacere*), which means 'to throw or cast under'. In contemporary usage, the notion of the subject is liable to contradictory readings: on the one hand, it entails agency and authorship (the grammatical subject, traditionally defined as the 'doer' of an action); on the other, it implies subjection (subjects before the law, or subjects owing allegiance to a ruler or a state). The tension between independent agency and subjection to external forces is at the core of a range of approaches to subjectivity and the subject, variously derived from humanist, Marxist, psychoanalytic, feminist and poststructuralist traditions.

In common usage 'subjectivity' refers to personal experience, feelings and beliefs, as opposed to 'objectivity', which ostensibly transcends any individual point of view. In contemporary social and cultural theory, subjectivity is typically understood as a person's perception of the self, as constituted by and mediated through language, culture and society. Subjectivity, on this account, is closely related to identity, but not synonymous with it. The difference between the two is probably best understood by conceiving of identity as a 'limited and temporary fixing for the individual of a particular mode of subjectivity as apparently what one is'. Identity thus serves to 'restrict the multiple possibilities of subjectivity inherent in the wider discursive field and to give individuals a singular sense of who they are and where they belong' (Weedon 2004: 19).

The Cartesian dictum *cogito, ergo sum* (I think, therefore I am) succinctly epitomizes the humanist notion of the subject as a centred and autonomous individual, endowed with consciousness, reason and agency. Contemporary theories of subjectivity univocally reject this Enlightenment model of the humanist subject, understood as the prime purveyor of knowledge and meaning.

The humanist model of subjectivity was submitted to scrutiny as early as the nineteenth century, most notably in the classical Marxist tradition. In Marxism, subjectivity is seen as shaped by ideology, and ultimately by class relations in a given society. The relationship between ideology and subjectivity was further elaborated by Marxist philosopher Louis Althusser in the latter half of the twentieth century (2001 [1970]). According to Althusser, ideological state apparatuses (ISA), such as the family, the education system, the church and the mass media, play a key part in the reproduction of capitalist relations, by producing subjects through the process of interpellation. Individual subjects take in particular meanings and values and adopt the identity offered to them through interpellation, for example, that of worker or law-abiding citizen. For Althusser, subjectivity is socially produced and fundamentally malleable, because it can respond differently to different kinds of interpellation.

Another field of inquiry that is crucially concerned with issues of subjectivity is psychoanalysis. By emphasizing the role of the unconscious in shaping human thought and action, Freud destabilized the notion of the unified rational human self. Taking Freud's work a step further, Jacques Lacan interpreted the unconscious as a sign system which functions like a language (1977). He argued that humans obtain a 'subject position' when they enter into the symbolic order and that, therefore, the process of signification coincides with the process of subject formation. Subjectivity, for Lacan, is predicated on the loss of an unmediated consciousness of body or psyche and shaped by identifications through a pattern of misrecognition, foreshadowed in the mirror stage in early childhood.

Lacanian theory exercised profound influence on a range of feminist accounts of the sexed and gendered subject. Feminists largely agree that most Western theories of subjectivity focus on the male subject. Luce Irigaray (1985 [1977]), for example, has argued that female subjects have consistently been excluded from the symbolic order. According to Irigaray, women have an unmediated relation to their bodies, which makes them capable of subverting patriarchal norms. In Julia Kristeva's theory of female subjectivity, women are associated with the semiotic rather than the symbolic realm of signification (1980 [1970]). Other feminists have criticized the essentialist assumptions of French feminist theory, arguing that women's subjectivities are shaped through social and cultural mediation as much as men's (Butler 1990, Grosz, 1989).

Michel Foucault's work, which interprets the subject as the self constituted and mediated through discourse, has probably had the most widespread application in cultural studies. For Foucault (1979 [1975]), subjectivity is a product of the historically specific discourses of disciplinary power, used to manage social relations. Subject formation, on this account, necessarily entails subjection to power.

See also: **Discourse; Feminism; Ideology; Imaginary, symbolic, real; Interpellation; Marxism, Leninism, Western Marxism; Phenomenology; Poststructuralism; Power; Psychoanalysis**

Further reading: Blundell and Shepherd (eds) (1993).

Superego

See **Id, superego, ego**.

Symbolic

See **Imaginary, symbolic, real**.

Tactic/strategy

See **Everyday**.

Taste, taste culture

In addition to designating one of the five senses, the word 'taste' can refer to a person's aesthetic and lifestyle choices, often expressed through her or his consumption practices. It is commonly acknowledged today that taste is neither universal nor innate, but rather, ephemeral, consensual and culturally constructed.

In *The Critique of Judgment* (2000 [1790]), German Enlightenment philosopher Immanuel Kant (1724–1804) argued that aesthetic judgements were not related to any intrinsic quality of the perceived object, but rather, based on the subjective feelings of pleasure or displeasure. Furthermore, he posited that judgements of taste were normative by nature, as they were always grounded in claims to universal validity.

American sociologist Herbert Gans (1974) introduced the notion of 'taste cultures' to explain why certain groups of people tended to exhibit preferences for certain types of cultural texts. In opposition to the then dominant mass culture theories, Gans argued that culture was an active process, in which the audience could freely choose those texts that were relevant to their experience in society. He conceptualized taste cultures as 'aggregates of similar people making similar choices, and aggregates of similar content chosen by the same people' (1966: 582). He believed, however, that individual taste was to some extent shaped by education and economic class.

Perhaps the most influential contemporary theory of taste has been formulated by French sociologist Pierre Bourdieu (1984). According to Bourdieu, taste is simultaneously structured and structuring: 'Taste classifies, and it classifies the classifier. Social subjects, classified by their classifications, distinguish themselves by the distinctions they make, between the beautiful and the ugly, the distinguished and the vulgar, in which their position in the objective classification is expressed or betrayed' (p. 6). Bourdieu uses the term 'habitus' to designate what constitutes and is in turn constituted by a person's taste, or the taste of a social group. His key interest is in explaining the power of the dominant class to define the distinction between what is considered good or legitimate taste, and what is regarded as vulgar or illegitimate. According to Bourdieu, competence in aesthetic judgements constitutes a form of cultural capital, which has the ability to maintain and reinforce class divisions.

See also: **Audience; Cultural capital; Consumption; Habitus and field; Mass culture, culture industry**

Further reading: Bourdieu (1984).

Text

Deriving ultimately from the Latin verb *texere*, to weave, the term 'text' is commonly used to denote a piece of writing. In the humanities and social sciences, the concept of text extends beyond the domain of written expression, to denote 'any ordered set of signs for which or through which people in a culture construct meaning' (Witte 1992: 269). In this sense, a text can be an image, a piece of music, an object of material culture, a ritual, or an event.

Prior to the emergence of structuralism in the first half of the twentieth century, literary texts had been understood as repositories of a fixed content, which could be grasped by gaining knowledge about the author and her or his original motivations and intentions. The structuralist theory challenged the notion of a text as a simple vehicle of communication between author and reader. Rather, the text was seen as a 'series of forms produced by the institution of literature and the discursive codes of a culture' (Culler 1983: 82). The text, the structuralists claimed, needs to be studied independently from its origins and context. Poststructuralism went a step further by arguing that texts have no inherent meaning, since meaning always resides in the specific encounter between the text and reader. According to poststructuralists, the reader constructs the text, and the text in turn regulates the interaction. This means that the outcome of every reading is unique, temporary and open-ended. The aim of reading, for poststructuralists, is not to uncover the truth or gain knowledge, but rather to derive pleasure from the experience.

The French semiotician Roland Barthes (1974 [1970]) differentiated between two types of texts: 'writerly' texts (French *scriptible*), which are sufficiently open-ended and plural in their meanings to encourage the reader to 'write' them in the process of reading; and 'readerly' texts (French *lisible*), which are simple and conventional and thus do not present any challenge to the reader. Umberto Eco has proposed a similar distinction between 'open' and 'closed' texts (1989 [1979]).

See also: *Jouissance*; **Poststructuralism; Structuralism**

Further reading: Barthes (1974 [1970]).

Thatcherism

The term 'Thatcherism' was coined by Stuart Hall, to designate the political rhetoric and policy orientation promoted, most notably, by the former British Prime Minister Margaret Thatcher in the 1980s. Thatcherism can be understood as an articulation that effectively blends the principles of the free market economy and a particular brand of 'authoritarian populism', which appeals to national interests above and beyond any interests related to social class, gender, sexuality, race or ethnicity.

Drawing principally on Gramsci's notions of hegemony and the national-popular, Hall attributed the success of Thatcherism to its capacity to mobilize broad-spectrum support (1988). This was achieved, according to Hall, by appealing to a social imaginary that privileged the family, order, and hard work; and by exploiting and effectively articulating the growing popular antagonism to the state-centred rhetoric and policies of the Labour Party. In opposition to the Thatcherist vision of a homogeneous 'Englishness', Hall emphasized the need to recognize the diversity and fundamental instability of specific subject positions.

See also: **Hegemony; National-popular; Populism; Right, New Right**

Thick description

The US anthropologist Clifford Geertz used the term 'thick description' to describe a particular style of interpretive writing that seeks to get beneath the surface of events, behaviours or practices by progressively uncovering deeper and deeper layers of their symbolic meaning. Thick description requires a qualitative rather than quantitative methodology, and is only possible in long-term participatory research. Writing thick description is a complex process, because the frameworks of meaning underlying any one event are multiple and intertwined. Furthermore, the anthropologist's description itself remains fluid and can be 'refuted by events, past and future', or 'superseded by interpretations more deeply grounded, more complexly conceptualized' (Overing and Rapport 2000: 352). The most widely cited example of thick description is Geertz's own essay 'Deep Play: Notes on the Balinese Cockfight' (1972).

T

See also: **Ethnography; Method, methodology**

Further reading: Geertz (1972).

Time

A fundamental category integral to human existence, time may be conceptualized in terms of sequence and duration. The measuring of time is now standardized worldwide. The Gregorian calendar, which is widely accepted as the international standard, was introduced in the sixteenth century. Other calendars, such as the Islamic, Persian, Chinese, Hebrew, Hindu, and Julian calendars, continue to be used in specific social and religious contexts. Time-zones separated by differences of one hour were introduced in the late eighteenth century.

Time, however, can also convey a wide variety of meanings, which extend far beyond the abstract calendar or clock measure. People experience time with reference to events, occurrences, social practices and relations. A time can be 'good' or 'bad', 'right' or 'wrong', 'adverse' or 'propitious', 'stressful', 'difficult' or 'exciting'. The way we experience time and endow it with meaning varies across cultures and is contingent to specific socio-historical circumstances. Anthropologists have distinguished between the perceptions of time in traditional and modern societies, describing the former as cyclical, reversible, biological/ecological, mythical, qualitative and conducive to stability; and the latter as linear, unidirectional, historical, quantitative-mathematical, commodified and transformative.

In classical Marxist theory, the exploitation and regulation of labour time is seen as the fundamental characteristic of capitalist societies. In capitalism, time itself is reified and commodified. According to Max Weber, the Protestant ethic that underpinned the development of capitalism relied heavily on precise time calculation and regarded waste of time as morally reprehensible (1992 [1905]).

Following Albert Einstein's (1879–1955) theory of relativity, scientists now recognize that there is no absolute time independent of the system of observation. Einstein also demonstrated that time and space do not exist separately, but rather in a four-dimensional 'space–time' continuum. These findings underpin a range of recent approaches to time and space in the humanities and social sciences.

In postmodern societies, the significance of past traditions and imagined futures has ostensibly been undermined by the sweeping changes in the conditions of life caused by technological progress, the influence of the mass media and globalization. Arguably, these changes have ushered in an 'instantaneous' culture, in which the nature of represen-

T

tation, of subjectivities and of lived experience are becoming increasingly fragmented, fluid and ephemeral.

See also: **Chronotope; Globalization; Marxism, Leninism, Western Marxism; Memory; Narrative**

Further reading: Frow (1997).

Totem and taboo

These two closely related concepts represent forms of credence that regulate moral laws and social order in pre-literate societies. The word 'totem' derives from the language of the Ojibwa Indian tribe originally inhabiting the area of the Great Lakes in eastern North America. In contemporary English usage, it refers to a natural object – usually an animal, bird or plant – that carries a spiritual meaning and often symbolically represents a particular social group. The word 'taboo' is of Polynesian origin, and signifies the prohibition of a practice, contact with a person, use of an object, consumption of a type of food, or access to a place, which may be considered sacred, dangerous or unclean by a specific society. A violation of the taboo is often believed to bring misfortune or punishment to the perpetrator. Just what is regarded as a totem, and what constitutes a taboo, varies from one culture to another.

In the collection of essays published under the title of *Totem and Taboo* (2001 [1913]), Freud sought to explain the origins of society by employing a theoretical model parallel to the one he had elaborated for the development of the individual psyche. He suggested that the totemic animal represented a symbol for the all-powerful father of the primeval patriarchal horde. This father, he speculated, had excluded his own sons from the group in which he himself had sole control over women. The brothers, resentful of their predicament, eventually came together to kill and devour their father. Remorseful for this act, they then undertook to atone for it by prohibiting the killing of the totemic animal and repudiating endogamous sexual relations. Totem and taboo thus provided, according to Freud, the two fundamental principles of the new fraternal society. Freud also argued that taboos arise where there exists a powerful desire to perform an act, usually of a sexual nature. The memory of the primeval parricide, in Freud's account, continues to exist in myths, religions, social rituals, arts and politics.

In cultural studies, totemic objects and taboo areas have been identified in a variety of cultural texts and practices. Heraldic animals and animal mascots of sports teams can be understood as traces of totemism in contemporary society. Sports fans sometimes engage in quasi-tribal rituals that involve 'totemic' identification with their team's mascot, which is regarded as a symbolic 'ancestor' (Voigt 1980). Rave parties are occasionally described as related to the Great Mother, Gaia, or womb, with the 'implication of a shared sibling status between ravers, which raises a symbolic "incest taboo", thus attenuating sexual tensions and replacing them with familiarity and friendliness' (Tramacchi 2004: 139). More generally, different subcultures define their taboo areas in order to identify and maintain the boundaries of the group. Furthermore, the breaching of taboos is a popular plot device in a variety of cultural texts, for example the treatment of cannibalism in Peter Greenaway's film *The Cook, the Thief, his Wife and Her Lover* (1989).

See also: **O**edipus complex; Psychoanalysis; Subculture

Further reading: Freud (2001 [1913]).

Transculturation, transculturality, transculturalism

The prefix 'trans' in these compound words is of Latin origin and means 'across, over or beyond'. The term 'transculturation' was introduced in the 1940s by Cuban cultural critic Fernando de Ortiz (1881–1969), to designate the complex processes of mutual cultural adjustment resulting from the colonial encounter between imperial and indigenous cultures in Cuba. Ortiz (1995 [1940]) coined this neologism in order to problematize and contest the then dominant term for cultural contact, 'acculturation', which implied a unidirectional adoption of the dominant culture by subordinate or marginal cultural groups. Culture in Cuba, Ortiz argued, is as much a product of acculturation as it is of deculturation, or cultural loss, and neoculturation, or the consequent creation of new cultural phenomena.

The concept was later applied to literary studies and extended to cover all of Latin America by Uruguayan literary critic Ángel Rama (1926–83). Focusing mainly on a selection of Latin American novels published from the 1960s to the 1980s, Rama (1982) emphasized the creative potential inherent in transculturation as a form of discursive cross-fertilization between cultures in contact.

Transculturation was introduced into the English-language scholarly discourse by the US literary and cultural critic Mary Louise Pratt (1992). For Pratt, the multifaceted processes of transculturation emerge from cultural encounters in what she calls 'contact zones', that is, spaces in which different cultures commingle and interreact. Pratt's contact zones are not necessarily confined to the colonial context, but rather, extend to cosmopolitan cities and other transcultural spaces created by globalization.

In the theory of transculturality elaborated by the German philosopher and cultural critic Wolfgang Welsch (1999), cultures are understood as changeable entities. Challenging the relevance of the notion of multiculturalism in contemporary societies, which posits the co-presence of separate cultures, Welsch argues that cultures cannot be bounded. They exist in complex networks that are at the same time global and local, universal and particular. According to Welsch, difference needs to be reconceptualized in terms of these transcultural networks, which underpin the fluidity and multidimensionality of people's identities and subjectivities in late modernity.

While transculturality represents an analytical model for understanding contemporary culture, transculturalism is understood as the ideology that upholds it, a particular sensibility that privileges fluidity and a perpetual renegotiation of identities.

See also: **Creolization; Hybridity;** *Mestizaje*; **Multicultural, multiculturalism**

Further reading: Pratt (1992).

Transnational, transnationalism

The notion of transnationalism came into prominence in cultural theory and critique in the 1990s, primarily through the work of US anthropologists Linda Basch, Nina Glick Schiller and Cristina Szanton Blanc. It designates the socio-cultural reality and lifestyle of a relatively new type of 'transmigrants', who maintain active and constantly evolving relationships in both the host and home countries, and at times in a number of other countries as well. The transnational interactions these migrants engage in may be social, cultural, economic or political. More often than not, they encompass different combinations of all these spheres of activity. Transnationalism is not synonymous with diaspora, which is usually understood as involving a more traumatic separation from the home country and a dispersal of the self-identified ethnic community across the globe.

Today's transnational migrants live across borders: their 'networks, activities and patterns of life encompass both their host and home societies' and their 'lives cut across national boundaries and bring two societies into a single social field' (Glick Schiller, Basch, and Blanc-Szanton 1992: 1). The reality of these migrants erodes the traditional identification of nation and state, community and territory. They occupy a deterritorialized space, which is best conceived in social terms.

While some critics dispute the novelty of transnationalism (Foner 2000), arguing that it in fact has a long history that pre-dates the emer-

T

gence of the nation-state, others emphasize the distinct character of the phenomenon in the contemporary globalized world, radically altered by the availability of inexpensive and fast travel and instantaneous communication technologies (Vertovec 1999).

See also: **Diaspora; Globalization**

Further reading: Vertovec and Cohen (eds) (1999).

Trope

A trope is a rhetorical figure of speech, which uses words in senses that transcend their literal meanings. Since the conventions in the use of tropes are largely culture-specific, they can serve to maintain the boundaries of a cultural or subcultural group. Tropes are pervasive in all forms of language use. They are often so domesticated in a particular cultural context that their figurative nature goes unnoticed and their 'reality' is taken for granted. Identifying and 'de-naturalizing' dominant tropes in texts and practices (for example, the trope of linear progress is often understood as dominant in Enlightenment discourse) may help us understand the underlying cultural and ideological assumptions of a given historical period.

The US rhetorician Kenneth Burke (1897–1993) referred to the four basic tropes – metaphor, metonymy, synecdoche and irony – as 'master tropes' (1969 [1945]: 503–17). Historian Hayden White (1973) argued that these master tropes are 'structurally homologous' to specific literary genres (romance, comedy, tragedy and satire, respectively), to world-views (formism, organicism, mechanism and contextualism) and to ideologies (anarchism, conservatism, radicalism and liberalism).

See also: **Irony; Metaphor, metonymy, synecdoche**

Further reading: White (1973).

Tropicalization/s, tropicopolitan

As a term that emerged in scholarly discourse in the 1990s, 'tropicalization' deftly combines the semantic fields of the words 'trope' (figure of speech) and, more loosely, 'the tropics' (geographical region). Related to the notion of Orientalism, 'tropicalization' designates those discursive strategies that represent the 'other' (an actual or symbolic inhabitant of the tropics) as primitive and exotic. Unlike Orientalism, tropicalization assumes the possibility of subversive redeployment of tropicalized discourse, foregrounding the 'transformative cultural agency of the subaltern subject' (Aparicio and Chávez-Silverman 1997: 2). US cultural critic Srinivas Aravamudan calls these subaltern subjects 'tropicopolitans', and argues that they 'function as residents of the tropics subjected to the politics of colonial tropology, who correspondingly seize agency through contesting language, space, and the language of space that typifies justifications of colonialism' (1999: 6). For Aravamudan, tropicalization 'enables postcolonial readers to re-appropriate colonialist metropolitan discourses and practices through a genealogy that attends to resistance as well as oppression' (1995: 70). Tropicalization may thus be understood as a form of transculturation, since both concepts designate multi-layered and multi-directional processes of cultural transformation in colonial contact zones.

See also: **Alterity; Discourse; Orientalism**

T

Uncanny

The Freudian notion of the uncanny (in German, *das Unheimliche*) describes something that is familiar, yet also disturbingly strange. The meaning of the adjective *heimlich* in German encompasses both what is agreeable and familiar, and what is hidden, secret or clandestine. *Heimlich*, Freud explained in a much quoted 1919 essay, is a 'word the meaning of which develops in the direction of ambivalence, until it finally coincides with its opposite, *unheimlich*. *Unheimlich* is in some way or other a sub-species of *Heimlich*' (1953–74, vol. 17: 226). The uncanny is occasioned by the 'return of the repressed', or, in Freud's terms, by the re-emergence of castration anxiety in adult life. Freud distinguished between two types of experiences that generate the effect of the uncanny: the first pertains to events in everyday life, the second to the sensations that arise from reading literary texts.

The concept of the uncanny has wide currency in contemporary literary theory and criticism, philosophy, art, architecture, film and media studies, and cultural studies. It is closely related to Kristeva's notion of the abject, which refers to something that has been cast out of the symbolic order, yet continues to repel us and attract us at the same time.

In his seminal structuralist study of the genre of the fantastic in literature, Tzvetan Todorov (1975 [1970]) defined the genre as the domain of ambiguity between 'reality' and 'illusion'. The fantastic, according to Todorov, occupies the duration of this uncertainty. Once the reader makes a decision to embrace one explanation or the other, the fantastic gives way to a different genre: the uncanny (French, *l'étrange*), if s/he decides that the narrated phenomenon is realistically possible or natural; and the marvellous (French, *le merveilleux*), if s/he interprets it as illusory or supernatural. The decision that defines a text as belonging to a specific genre thus emerges only after reading is completed, while the process of reading itself remains engulfed in ambiguity.

In poststructuralist and deconstructionist interpretations (most notably, Cixous 1976 [1972]), the uncanny came to represent a non-concept, which exemplifies the fundamental lack of stable meaning.

See also: **Abject; Deconstruction; Genre; Imaginary, symbolic, real; Oedipus complex; Poststructuralism**

Further reading: Royle (2003).

Unconscious, collective unconscious

The term 'unconscious' designates that part of the psyche that is not readily accessible to the conscious mind. In Freudian psychoanalysis, the unconscious represents a rich repository of repressed memories, which exert a strong influence on a person's behaviour. Conflicts between unconscious and conscious drives are said to generate anxiety. Analysts endeavour to reach parts of the unconscious by using techniques such as free association, hypnosis or dream interpretation. Freud distinguished between the conscious, the unconscious and the preconscious, suggesting that these three realms co-exist in a dynamic and fluid relationship. He understood the preconscious as constituted by those mental processes that 'press forward' to enter the conscious mind.

In cultural studies, the notion of the unconscious has been used to theorize the development of subjectivity as based on a socially imposed repression of unconscious impulses. It also figures prominently in critical readings of cultural texts and practices.

The collective unconscious is a concept that was originally developed by the Swiss psychiatrist Carl Gustav Jung (1875–1961). According to Jung, the collective unconscious is a reservoir of symbols, or 'archetypes', that are not individual in nature, but rather shared by all human beings. Jung believed that these archetypes, which he traced back to the earliest ages of humanity, continued to emerge in dreams, fairy tales, myths, religions and the arts.

Jungian theories have given rise to a type of literary criticism and cultural analysis more broadly, which is commonly referred to as archetypal criticism. Archetypal critics examine symbols and characters in cultural texts and practices to find archetypal motifs that are believed to be common to different languages, cultures and historical periods. These archetypes include animus (the male archetype in the female), anima (the female archetype in the male), shadow, mother, snake, fire, garden of paradise, and the like. The fundamental assumption of archetypal criticism, that archetypes represent primordial images common to all cultures and all epochs, is at odds with the emphasis on the contingency of cultural phenomena prevalent in poststructuralism.

U

See also: **Myth; Poststructuralism; Psychoanalysis**

V v

Value, value system

Value is a concept that provides a basis for determining whether some-thing is good, proper or desirable. Values generate hierarchies that position some objects, texts, behaviours, practices, experiences or personal traits above others. In structuralist and functionalist sociology, social integration is interpreted as depending on the existence of a shared value system which is both cohesive and normative. According to American sociologist Talcott Parsons (1902–79), value internalization generates social equilib-rium, toleration, mutual respect and cooperation, while a failure to inter-nalize shared values is likely to lead to conflict, coercion and violence.

In classical economics, use value is based on the practical utility of an item to a particular person or in a given context; exchange value is determined by what one can obtain in exchange for a commodity or service; and labour value reflects the amount of labour, especially in terms of time, required to produce the good. Karl Marx introduced the notion of surplus value, which refers to the difference between the price of a good and the cost of materials and labour. This value is retained by the capitalist and constitutes the prime mechanism for the reproduction and growth of capital.

In cultural studies, values are commonly regarded as relational, and a matter of continuous negotiation. The notion that a text, object or prac-tice has an intrinsic value regardless of its context is generally seen as problematic. There are at least two broad areas, in which issues of value are paramount: one is the domain of the aesthetic, and the other pertains to the ethical or the moral. In terms of aesthetics, there has been a backlash against the privileging of 'high' or 'elite' culture over what used to be considered 'low' and thus of lesser value. To quote the Australian cultural critic John Frow,

> in much recent writing in cultural studies the problem with the oppo-sition of high to low culture has been taken to be the fact that it expresses relations of cultural domination and subordination, and thereby marginalizes popular culture. This approach foregrounds the question of value, and it solves it by reversing the distribution of value between the two poles.   (1995: 27)

Frow has argued that the notion of 'mass culture' needs to be seen as a social construct contingent upon a 'complex interrelation of the machinery of aesthetic production and distribution; specific audience formations; the educational apparatus; and the conflicting formations of value that assign a place, or contradictory places, to the texts governed by the system' (1995: 19). Since the late twentieth century, the distinction between 'high' and 'low' cultural forms has become increasingly blurred, as high culture itself becomes fully incorporated into commodity production.

In the domain of ethics, critics have foregrounded a 'respect for individual difference along with forms of sharing and cooperation that are genuine and not enforced' as one of the key values promoted by cultural studies (Barker 2004: 206).

See also: **Mass culture, culture industry; Popular culture, folk culture; Taste**

Further reading: Connor (1992), Frow (1995).

Virtual, virtual community, virtual reality

The word 'virtual' derives from the Medieval Latin adjective *virtualis*, and ultimately from *virtus*, which means excellence, potency or efficacy, or literally manliness or manhood (from *vir*, man).

In the second half of the twentieth century, 'virtual' took on a new meaning in the language of telecommunications and digital technologies, where it designates something 'not physically existing as such but made by software to appear to do so' (*COED*). In the domain of technology, virtual is taken to be a near-synonym of simulated. Cyberspace, in particular, can be imagined as a virtual environment, which offers anonymity and the possibility of performing different identities. In this context, virtuality may be defined as the 'reinvention of familiar physical space in cyberspace' (Jordan 1999: 1). It needs to be noted, however, that virtual worlds, fictions and simulations, which can be experienced as manifestations of reality, pre-date the emergence of computer technology, the cinema being among the most conspicuous recent examples.

Drawing on a definition of the virtual offered by the French intellectual Marcel Proust (1871–1922), Gilles Deleuze argues that the virtual is 'real without being actual, ideal without being abstract' (1994: 208). Rather than implying an absence of the real (where this latter is understood as something concrete, materially embodied or physically present), the virtual may be seen as another register or manifestation of the real, which is in some cases 'better than the real' (Shields 2003: 46). In *Becoming Virtual*, the French network-culture theorist Pierre Lévy

V

describes the virtual as a powerful mode of engagement, which tends toward the creation of reality (2003: 27).

Virtual communities (often referred to as online communities) are groups of Internet users brought together by virtue of a shared interest, such as a hobby, lifestyle preference, or political agenda. Howard Rheingold has defined virtual communities as 'social aggregations that emerge from the Net when enough people carry on . . . public discussions long enough, with sufficient human feeling, to form webs of personal relationships in cyberspace' (1993: 5).

The term 'virtual reality' (VR) designates a computer-generated simulation of an environment that aims to reproduce the sensory information of the physical world as seamlessly as possible. The aim of virtual reality is to enable people to experience information in an immediate and dynamic way. In order to replicate sensory inputs, virtual reality systems may rely on devices such as data gloves or head-mounted displays. Virtual reality has found applications in a variety of fields, most notably military science, architecture, medicine and education. Creative virtual reality applications have also been developed for the visual arts, performance and music.

Virtuality is of interest to cultural studies, because it 'draws together the world of technology and its ability to represent nature, with the broad and overlapping spheres of social relations and meaning' (Hillis 1999: xv). Cultural studies focus primarily on the cultural environment emerging around the use of new technologies, taking the view that all technology is socially embedded and mediated by cultural relations.

See also: **Cyberspace; Network**

Further reading: Shields (2003).

V

Whiteness

In critical discourse, whiteness is understood as a malleable, relational, normative, historically specific and socially constructed category. A site of privilege in societies structured in racial terms, it typically remains invisible or unmarked, and underscores a range of cultural practices and identities.

Whiteness studies – a multidisciplinary strand of academic inquiry that seeks to deconstruct and contest the hegemonic constructions of racial identification – came to prominence in the US in the 1990s, to a large extent as a response to critiques of racism raised by scholars of colour. The underlying assumption of whiteness studies is that 'once the space of whiteness is exposed, culturally positioned, delimited, rendered visible, and deterritorialized, then, whiteness will lose its power to dominate' (Flores and Moon 2000: 99).

Whiteness studies, however, is not without its critics. It is particularly vulnerable to accusations of 'inverse narcissism', or a 'quest for academic visibility' undertaken by white academics (Wiegman 1999: 123). The most prominent among the detractors of whiteness studies are the 'race traitor' school, which 'advocates the abolition of whiteness through white disaffiliation from race privilege'; the 'white trash' school, which 'analyzes the "racialization" of the permanent poor in order to demonstrate the otherness of whiteness within', and the class solidarity school, which 'rethinks the history of working-class struggle as the preamble to forging new cross-racial alliances' (ibid.).

See also: **Race**

Further reading: Brander Rasmussen et al. (eds) (2001), Hill (1997 and 2004).

References

Adorno, Theodor Wiesengrund (1984 [1970]) *Aesthetic Theory*, trans. Christian Lenhardt (London: Routledge & Kegan Paul).
—— (1991) *The Culture Industry: Selected Essays on Mass Culture*, ed. and introduction by J. M. Bernstein (London and New York: Routledge).
Adorno, Theodor W. and Horkheimer, Max (2002 [1947]) *Dialectic of Enlightenment: Philosophical Fragments*, trans. Edmund Jephcott (Stanford, CA: Stanford University Press).
Aijaz, Ahmad (1992) *Theory: Classes, Nations, Literatures* (London: Verso).
Allatson, Paul (2007) *Key Terms in Latino/a Cultural and Literary Studies* (Malden, MA and Oxford: Blackwell Press).
Althusser, Louis (2001 [1970]) 'Ideology and Ideological State Apparatuses: Notes Toward an Investigation'. In *Lenin and Philosophy and Other Essays*, trans. Ben Brewster (New York: Monthly Review Press).
Althusser, Louis, and Etienne Balibar (1970) *Reading Capital*, trans. Ben Brewster (London: New Left).
Altman, Dennis (2000) 'Talking Sex'. *Postcolonial Studies*, 3.2: 171–8.
Amin, Samir (1989) *Eurocentrism*, trans. Russell Moore (New York: Zed Press).
Anderson, Benedict (1983) *Imagined Communities: Reflections on the Origins and Spread of Nationalism* (London: Verso).
Ang, Ien (1985) *Watching Dallas: Soap Opera and the Melodramatic Imagination* (London and New York: Methuen).
Anzaldúa, Gloria (1999 [1987]) *La Frontera/Borderlands*, 2nd edition (San Francisco, CA: Aunt Lute Books).
Aparicio, Frances and Chávez-Silverman, Susana (eds) (1997) *Tropicalizations: Transcultural Representations of Latinidad* (Hanover and London: University Press of New England).
Appadurai, Arjun (1986) 'Introduction: Commodities and the Politics of Value'. In Arjun Appadurai (ed.), *The Social Life of Things: Commodities in Cultural Perspective* (Cambridge: Cambridge University Press).
—— (1990) 'Disjuncture and Difference in the Global Cultural Economy'. *Theory, Culture and Society*, 7: 295–310.
Apter, Emily and Pietz, William (1993) *Fetishism and Cultural Discourse* (Ithaca, NY: Cornell University Press).
Aravamudan, Srinivas (1995) 'Lady Mary Wortley Montagu in the Hammam: Masquerade, Womanliness, and Levantinization'. *English Literary History*, 62.1: 69–104.
—— (1999) *Tropicopolitans: Colonialism and Agency, 1688–1804* (Durham, NC: Duke University Press).
Archer, Margaret (1996 [1988]) *Culture and Agency: The Place of Culture in Social Theory* (Cambridge: Cambridge University Press).
Arendt, Hannah (1970) *On Violence* (New York: Harcourt, Brace and World).

Ashcroft, Bill (2001) *Post-Colonial Transformation* (London and New York: Routledge).

Audinet, Jacques (2004) *The Human Face of Globalization: From Multicultural to Mestizaje*, trans. Frances Dal Chele (Lanham, MD: Rowman & Littlefield).

Austin, John L. (1962) *How to Do Things with Words* (Oxford: Clarendon Press).

Bakhtin, Mikhail (1968) *Rabelais and His World*, trans. H. Isowolsky (Cambridge Mass.: MIT Press).

——(1981) *The Dialogic Imagination*, ed. Michael Holquist, trans. Caryl Emerson and Michael Holquist (Austin, TX: University of Texas Press).

—— (1984 [1929]) *Problems of Dostoevsky's Poetics*, ed. and trans. Caryl Emerson, with an introduction by Wayne C. Booth (Minneapolis, MN and London: University of Minnesota Press).

Bal, Mieke (1996) *Double Exposures: The Subject of Cultural Analysis* (London and New York: Routledge).

—— (2000) 'Crossroad Theory and Travelling Concepts'. In Jan Baetens and Jose Lambert (eds), *The Future of Cultural Studies: Essays in Honour of Joris Vlasselaers* (Leuven, Belgium: Leuven University Press).

Bal, Mieke and Gonzales, Bryan (eds) (1999) *The Practice of Cultural Analysis: Exposing Interdisciplinary Interpretation* (Stanford, CA: Stanford University Press).

Balsamo, Anne (1996) *Technologies of the Gendered Body: Reading Cyborg Women* (Durham, NC: Duke University Press).

Barker, Chris (2000) *Cultural Studies: Theory and Practice* (London: Sage).

—— (2004) *The Sage Dictionary of Cultural Studies* (London: Sage).

Barker, Chris and Galasiński, Dariusz (2001) *Cultural Studies and Discourse Analysis* (London: Sage).

Barthes, Roland (1968 [1964]) *Elements of Semiology*, trans. Annette Lavers and Colin Smith (New York: Hill and Wang).

—— (1974 [1970]) *S/Z*, trans. Richard Miller (New York: Hill and Wang).

—— (1975 [1973]) *The Pleasure of the Text*, trans. Richard Miller (New York: Hill and Wang).

—— (1977 [1966]) 'Introduction to the Structural Analysis of Narratives'. In *Image-Music-Text*, trans. Stephen Heath (New York: Hill and Wang).

—— (1977 [1968]) 'The Death of the Author'. In *Image–Music–Text*, trans. Stephen Heath (New York: Hill and Wang).

—— (1984 [1957]) *Mythologies*, trans. Annette Lavers (New York: Hill and Wang).

Baudrillard, Jean (1981 [1972]) *For a Critique of the Political Economy of the Sign*, trans. Charles Levin (St Louis, MO: Telos Press).

—— (1983 [1981]) *Simulations*, trans. Paul Foss, Paul Patton and Philip Beitchman (New York: Semiotext(e)).

—— (1983) *In the Shadow of the Silent Majorities* (New York: Semiotexte).

—— (1995) 'Hyperreal America', trans. David Macey. *Economy and Society*, 22.2: 243–5.

—— (1998 [1970]) *The Consumer Society: Myths and Structures*, trans. Chris Turner (London: Sage).

Benda, Julien (1928 [1927]) *The Treason of the Intellectuals*, trans. Richard Aldington (New York: William Morrow).

Benhabib, Seyla (1992) *Situating the Self: Gender, Community and Postmodernism in Contemporary Ethics* (Oxford: Blackwell).

—— (1996) 'Toward a Deliberative Model of Democratic Legitimacy'. In Seyla Benhabib (ed.), *Democracy and Difference: Contesting the Boundaries of the Political* (Princeton, NJ: Princeton University Press).

Benjamin, Walter (1983 [1969]) *Charles Baudelaire: A Lyric Poet in the Era of High Capitalism*, trans. Harry Zohn (London: Verso).

—— (1985 [1936]) 'The Work of Art in the Age of Mechanical Reproduction', trans. Harry Zohn. In Hannah Arendt (ed.), *Illuminations: Essays and Reflections* (New York: Schocken Books).

—— (1988) *Jean Baudrillard: Selected Writings* (Cambridge: Polity Press).

Bennett, Tony (1986) 'The Politics of "the Popular" and Popular Culture'. In Tony Bennett, Colin Mercer and Janet Woollacott (eds), *Popular Culture and Social Relations* (Milton Keynes: Open University Press).

—— (1990) *Outside Literature* (London and New York: Routledge).

—— (1992a) 'Putting Policy into Cultural Studies'. In Lawrence Grossberg, Cary Nelson and Paula Treichler (eds), *Cultural Studies* (London and New York: Routledge).

—— (1992b) 'Useful Culture'. *Cultural Studies*, 6.3: 395–408.

—— (1995) *The Birth of the Museum: History, Theory, Politics* (London and New York: Routledge).

—— (2003) *Formalism and Marxism* (London and New York: Routledge).

Bennett, Tony, Grossberg, Lawrence and Morris, Meaghan (eds), (2005) *New Keywords: A Revised Vocabulary of Culture and Society* (Malden, MA: Blackwell).

Berman, Russell A. (1989) *Modern Culture and Critical Theory: Art, Politics and the Legacy of the Frankfurt School* (Madison, WI: University of Wisconsin Press).

Bérubé, Michael (ed.), (2004) *The Aesthetics of Cultural Studies* (Malden, MA: Blackwell).

Bhabha, Homi K. (1986) 'The Other Question: Difference, Discrimination, and the Discourse of Colonialism'. In Francis Barker, Peter Hulme and Margaret Iversen (eds), *Literature, Politics and Theory* (London: Methuen).

—— (1990) 'DissemiNation: Time, Narrative, and the Margins of the Modern Nation'. In Homi Bhabha (ed.), *Nation and Narration* (London and New York: Routledge).

—— (1994) *The Location of Culture* (London and New York: Routledge).

—— (1996) 'Unsatisfied: Notes on Vernacular Cosmopolitanism'. In Laura Garcia-Moreno and Peter Pfeiffer (eds), *Text and Nation* (Columbia, SC: Camden House).

Bleich, David (1975) *Readings and Feelings: An Introduction to Subjective Criticism* (Urbana, IL: National Council of Teachers of English).

Blumler, Jay and Katz, Elihu (1974) *The Uses of Mass Communications: Current Perspectives on Gratifications Research* (Beverly Hills, CA: Sage).

Blundell, Valda and Shepherd, John (eds), (1993) *Relocating Cultural Studies: Developments in Theory and Research* (London and New York: Routledge).

Boorstin, Daniel (1971 [1961]) *The Image: A Guide to Pseudo-Events in America* (New York: Atheneum).

Bourdieu, Pierre (1977 [1972]) *Outline of a Theory of Practice*, trans. Richard Nice (Cambridge: Cambridge University Press).

—— (1984) *Distinction: A Social Critique of the Judgement of Taste*, trans. Richard Nice (London: Routledge and Kegan Paul).

—— (1986) 'The Forms of Capital'. In John G. Richardson (ed.), *Handbook of Theory and Research for the Sociology of Education* (New York: Greenwood Press).

—— (1988 [1984]) *Homo Academicus*, trans. Peter Collier (Stanford, CA: Stanford University Press).

—— (1989) 'The Corporatism of the Universal: the Role of Intellectuals in the Modern World'. *Telos,* 81: 99–110.

—— (1990) *The Logic of Practice* (Stanford, CA: Stanford University Press).

—— (1993) *The Field of Cultural Production* (Cambridge: Polity Press).

Bourdieu, Pierre and Passeron, Jean-Claude (1977) 'Cultural Reproduction and Social Reproduction'. In Richard Brown (ed.), *Knowledge, Education, and Cultural Change* (London: Tavistock Publications).

Braidotti, Rosi (1991) *Patterns of Dissonance: A Study of Women in Contemporary Philosophy*, trans. Elizabeth Guild (Cambridge: Polity Press).

Brander Rasmussen, Birgit, Nexica, Irene J., Klinenberg, Eric and Wray, Matt (eds), (2001) *The Making and Unmaking of Whiteness* (Durham, NC: Duke University Press).

Branwyn, Gareth (1997) *Jamming the Media: A Citizen's Guide* (San Francisco, CA: Chronicle Books).

Braziel, Jana Evans and Mannur, Anita (eds), (2003) *Theorizing Diaspora: A Reader* (Oxford: Blackwell).

Breckenridge, Carol, Pollock, Sheldon, Bhabha, Homi and Chakrabarty, Dipesh (eds), (2002) *Cosmopolitanism* (London and Durham, NC: Duke University Press).

Brennan, Teresa (2004) *The Transmission of Affect* (Ithaca, NY: Cornell University Press).

Brennan, Timothy (1990) 'The National Longing for Form'. In Homi Bhabha (ed.), *Nation and Narration* (London and New York: Routledge).

—— (1997) *At Home in the World: Cosmopolitanism Now* (Cambridge, MA: Harvard University Press).

Brunsdon, Charlotte (1996) 'A Thief in the Night: Stories of Feminism in the 1970s at CCCS'. In David Morley and Kuan-Hsing Chen (eds), *Stuart Hall: Critical Dialogues in Cultural Studies* (London and New York: Routledge).

Buchli, Victor (ed.), (2002) *The Material Culture Reader* (New York: Berg).

Buckingham, David (1993) *Reading Audiences: Young People and the Media* (New York: Manchester University Press).

Buhle, Mary Jo (1998) *Feminism and Its Discontents: A Century of Struggle with Psychoanalysis* (Cambridge, MA and London: Harvard University Press).

Bürger, Peter (1984 [1974]) *Theory of the Avant-Garde*, trans. Michael Shaw (Minneapolis, MN: University of Minnesota Press).

Burke, Kenneth (1969 [1945]) *A Grammar of Motives* (Berkeley and Los Angeles, CA: University of California Press).

Burke, Sean (ed.), (1993) *The Death and Return of the Author* (Edinburgh: Edinburgh University Press).

—— (1995) *Authorship from Plato to the Postmodern: A Reader* (Edinburgh: Edinburgh University Press).

Butler, Judith (1990) *Gender Trouble: Feminism and the Subversion of Identity* (New York: Routledge).

—— (1993) *Bodies that Matter* (London and New York: Routledge).

—— (1998) 'Imitation and Gender Insubordination'. In Julie Rivkin and Michael Ryan (eds), *Literary Theory: An Anthology* (Malden, MA: Blackwell).

Calinescu, Matei (1987) *Five Faces of Modernity: Modernism, Avant-Garde, Decadence, Kitsch, Postmodernism* (Durham, NC: Duke University Press).

Callon, Michel and Latour, Bruno (1981) 'Unscrewing the Big Leviathan: How Actors Macro-Structure Reality and How Sociologists Help them to Do So'. In Karin Knorr-Cetina and Aaron Cicourel (eds), *Advances in Social Theory and Methodology: Toward an Integration of Micro- and Macro-Sociologies* (New York and London: Routledge).

Carey, James W. (1989) *Communication and Culture: Essays on Media and Society* (Boston, MA: Unwin Hyman).

Castells, Manuel (1996) *The Power of Identity*, vol. 2 of *The Information Age: Economy, Society and Culture* (Oxford: Blackwell).

—— (1997) *The Rise of the Network Society*, vol. 1 of *The Information Age: Economy, Society and Culture* (Oxford: Blackwell).

—— (1998) *End of Millennium*, vol. 3 of *The Information Age: Economy, Society and Culture* (Oxford: Blackwell).

Centre for Contemporary Cultural Studies (1982) *The Empire Strikes Back: Race and Racism in '70s Britain* (London: Hutchinson).

—— (2006 [1978]) *On Ideology* (London and New York: Routledge).

Chakrabarty, Dipesh (2000) *Provincializing Europe: Postcolonial Thought and Historical Difference* (Princeton, NJ: Princeton University Press).

Chandler, Daniel (2002) *Semiotics: The Basics* (London and New York: Routledge).

Cheng, Vincent J. (2004) *Inauthentic: The Anxiety over Culture and Identity* (New Brunswick, NJ: Rutgers University Press).

Chomsky, Noam (1965) *Aspects of the Theory of Syntax* (Cambridge, MA: MIT Press).

Cixous, Hélène (1976 [1972]) 'Fiction and its Fantoms: A Reading of Freud's *Das Unheimliche*', trans. Robert Dennomé. *New Literary History* 7.3: 525–48.

—— (1994) *The Hélène Cixous Reader*, ed. Susan Sellers, preface by Hélène Cixous, foreword by Jacques Derrida (London and New York: Routledge).

Classen, Constance (1993) *Worlds of Sense: Exploring the Senses in History and Across Cultures* (London and New York: Routledge).

—— (1998) *The Color of Angels: Cosmology, Gender, and the Aesthetic Imagination* (London and New York: Routledge).

Clifford, James (1988) *The Predicament of Culture: Twentieth-Century Ethnography, Literature, and Art* (Cambridge, MA: Harvard University Press).

—— (1997) *Routes: Travel and Translation in the Late Twentieth Century* (Cambridge, MA: Harvard University Press).

Clifford, James and Marcus, George (eds), (1986) *Writing Culture: The Poetics and Politics of Ethnography* (Berkeley and Los Angeles, CA: University of California Press).

Cohen, Robin (1987) *Global Diasporas: An Introduction* (London and New York: Routledge).

Colebrook, Claire (2003) *Irony* (London and New York: Routledge).

COED (*The Concise Oxford English Dictionary*) (2006), 11th edition, revised (Oxford Reference Online: Oxford University Press).

Connor, Steven (1992) *Theory and Cultural Value* (Oxford: Blackwell).

Cornwall, Andrea and Lindisfarne, Nancy (eds), (1994) *Dislocating Masculinity: Comparative Ethnographies* (London and New York: Routledge).

Couldry, Nick (2000) *Inside Culture: Re-Imagining the Method of Cultural Studies* (London: Sage).

Coupland, Douglas (1991) *Generation X: Tales for an Accelerated Culture* (New York: St Martin's Press).

Coupland, Justine (ed.), (2003) *Discourse, the Body, and Identity* (Basingstoke: Palgrave Macmillan).

Crowley, Tony (1996) *Language in History: Theories and Texts* (London and New York: Routledge).

Csordas, Thomas J. (1999) 'Embodiment and Cultural Phenomenology'. In Honi Fern Haber and Gail Weiss (eds), *Perspectives on Embodiment: The Intersections of Nature and Culture* (London and New York: Routledge).

Culler, Jonathan (1981) *The Pursuit of Signs: Semiotics, Literature, Deconstruction* (London and New York: Routledge).

—— (1982) *On Deconstruction: Theory and Criticism after Structuralism* (Ithaca, NY: Cornell University Press).

—— (1983) *Barthes* (Glasgow: William Collin).

Curry, Mark (2004) *Difference* (London: Routledge).

Davies, Ioan (1995) *Cultural Studies and Beyond: Fragments of Empire* (London and New York: Routledge).

Dean, Mitchell (1999) *Governmentality: Power and Rule in Modern Society* (London: Sage).

Debord, Guy (2005 [1967]) *The Society of the Spectacle*, trans. Ken Knabb (London: Rebel Press).

de Certeau, Michel (1984 [1980]) *The Practice of Everyday Life*, vol. 1, trans. Steven Rendall (Berkeley, CA: University of California Press).

de Certeau, Michel de, Giard, Luce and Mayol, Pierre (1998 [1980]) *The Practice of Everyday Life*, vol. 2, trans. Timothy J. Tomasik (Minneapolis, MN: University of Minnesota Press).

Deleuze, Gilles (1990 [1967]) 'The Simulacrum and Ancient Philosophy', trans. Mark Lester and Charles Stivale. In *The Logic of Sense* (New York: Columbia University Press).

—— (1994) *Difference and Repetition* (London: Athlone Press).

Deleuze, Gilles and Guattari, Félix (1977 [1971]) *Anti-Oedipus: Capitalism and Schizophrenia*, trans. Robert Hurley, Mark Seem and Helen R. Lane (New York: Viking).

—— (1987 [1980]) *A Thousand Plateaus*, trans. Brian Massumi (Minneapolis, MN: University of Minnesota Press).

de Man, Paul (1979) *Allegories of Reading: Figural Language in Rousseau, Nietzsche, Rilke, and Proust* (New Haven, CT: Yale University Press).

Dentith, Simon (2000) *Parody* (London and New York: Routledge).

Denzin, Norman and Lincoln, Yvonna S. (eds), (2000) *Handbook of Qualitative Research*, 2nd edition (London: Sage).

—— (2003) *Strategies of Qualitative Inquiry*, 2nd edition (London: Sage).

Depew, David and Hollinger, Robert (eds), (1999) *Pragmatism: From Progressivism to Postmodernism* (Westport, CT: Praeger).

Derrida, Jacques (1974 [1967]) *Of Grammatology*, trans. Gayatri Chakravorty Spivak (Baltimore, MD: Johns Hopkins University Press).

—— (1981) *A Derrida Reader* ed., Peggy Kamuf (New York: Columbia University Press).

—— (1982) *Margins of Philosophy*, trans. Alan Bass (Chicago: University of Chicago Press).

—— (1987 [1975]) *The Post Card: From Socrates to Freud and Beyond*, trans. Alan Bass (Chicago: Chicago University Press).

—— (1988 [1972]) 'Signature Event Context', trans. Samuel Weber and Jeffrey Mehlman. In *Limited Inc.* (Evanston, IL: Northwestern University Press).

—— (2001 [1967]) *Writing and Difference*, trans. Alan Bass (London and New York: Routledge).

Docherty, Thomas (1990) *After Theory: Postmodernism/Postmarxism* (London and New York: Routledge).

Donnan, Hastings and Wilson, Thomas (1999) *Borders: Frontiers of Identity, Nation and State* (Oxford: Berg).

Douglas, Mary and Isherwood, Baron (1996) *The World of Goods: Toward an Anthropology of Consumption*, 2nd edition (London and New York: Routledge).

Dowd, Garin et al. (eds), (2006) *Genre Matters: Essays in Theory and Criticism* (Bristol, UK and Portland, OR: Intellect).

Du Gayl, Paul and Hall, Stuart (eds), (1996) *Questions of Cultural Identity* (London: Sage).

Dunaway, David K. and Baum, Willa K. (eds), (1996) *Oral History: An Interdisciplinary Anthology*, 2nd edition (Walnut Creek, CA: AltaMira Press).

Dundes, Alan (ed.), (1984) *Sacred Narrative: Readings in the Theory of Myth* (Berkeley, CA: University of California Press).

Durkheim, Émile (1997 [1893]) *The Division of Labor in Society*, trans. George Simpson, introduction by Lewis A. Coser (New York: Free Press).

Eagleton, Terry (1991) *Ideology: An Introduction* (London: Verso).

Eco, Umberto (1976) *A Theory of Semiotics* (Bloomington, IN: Indiana University Press).

—— (1989 [1979]) *The Open Work*, trans. Anna Cancogni (Cambridge, MA: Harvard University Press).

—— (1997 [1975]) *Faith in Fakes: Travels in Hyperreality*, trans. William Weaver (London: Minerva).

Edgar, Andrew and Sedgwick, Peter (1999) *Cultural Theory: The Key Concepts* (London and New York: Routledge).

Fanon, Frantz (1963 [1961]) *The Wretched of the Earth*, preface by Jean-Paul Sartre, trans. Constance Farrington (New York: Grove Press).

Featherstone, Mike (1991) *Consumer Culture and Postmodernism* (London: Sage).

Felski, Rita (2004) 'The Role of Aesthetics in Cultural Studies'. In Michael Bérubé (ed.), *The Aesthetics of Cultural Studies* (Malden, MA: Blackwell).

Fish, Stanley (1980) *Is There a Text in This Class? The Authority of Interpretive Communities* (Cambridge, MA: Harvard University Press).

Fiske, John (1987) *Television Culture* (London and New York: Routledge).

—— (1990) *Introduction to Communication Studies* (London and New York: Routledge).

—— (1991 [1989]) *Understanding Popular Culture* (London and New York: Routledge).

Fiske, John and Hartley, John (2003 [1978]) *Reading Television* (New York: Routledge).

Flores, Lisa A. and Moon, Dreama (2000) 'Antiracism and the Abolition of Whiteness: Rhetorical Strategies of Domination among "Race Traitors"'. *Communication Studies*, 51.2: 97–115.

Flores, William V. (1997) 'Mujeres en Huelga: Cultural Citizenship and Gender Empowerment in a Cannery Strike'. In William V. Flores, and Rina Benmayor (eds), *Latino Cultural Citizenship: Claiming Identity, Space, and Rights* (Boston, MA: Beacon Press).

Foner, Nancy (2000) *From Ellis Island to JFK: New York's Two Great Waves of Immigration* (New Haven, CT: Yale University Press).

Foucault, Michel (1971 [1966]) *The Order of Things: An Archaeology of the Human Sciences* (New York: Pantheon).

—— (1972 [1969]) *The Archaeology of Knowledge and The Discourse on Language*, trans. Alan Sheridan (New York: Pantheon).

—— (1979 [1975]) *Discipline and Punish: The Birth of the Prison*, trans. Alan Sheridan (Harmondsworth: Penguin).

—— (1980 [1976]) *The History of Sexuality,* vol. 1: *An Introduction,* trans. Robert Hurley (New York: Vintage).

—— (1980) *Power/Knowledge: Selected Interviews and Other Writings, 1972–1977*, (ed.) Colin Gordon (New York: Pantheon).

—— (1984 [1969]) 'What is an Author?', trans. Josué V. Harari. In Paul Rabinow (ed.), *The Foucault Reader* (New York: Pantheon).

—— (1984 [1971]) 'Nietzsche, Genealogy, History', trans. Donald F. Bouchard and Sherry Simon. In Paul Rabinow (ed.), *The Foucault Reader* (New York: Pantheon).

—— (1986 [1967]) 'Of Other Spaces'. *Diacritics*, 16, Spring, 22–7.

Foucault, Michel and Deleuze, Gilles (1973) 'The Intellectuals and Power'. *Telos*, 16: 103–9.

Fraser, Nancy (1992) 'Rethinking the Public Sphere: a Contribution to the Critique of Actually Existing Democracy'. In Craig Calhoun (ed.), *Habermas and the Public Sphere* (Cambridge, MA: MIT Press).

French, Marilyn (1985) *Beyond Power* (New York: Summit Books).

Freud, Sigmund (1953–74) *The Standard Edition of the Complete Psychological Works of Sigmund Freud*, 24 vols (London: Hogarth Press).

—— (1960 [1923]) *The Ego and the Id*, trans. James Strachey (London and New York: W. W. Norton).

—— (1975 [1905]) *Three Essays on the Theory of Sexuality*, trans. James Strachey (New York: Basic Books).

—— (2001 [1913]) *Totem and Taboo: Some Points of Agreement between the Mental Lives of Savages and Neurotics*, trans. James Strachey (London and New York: Routledge).

Frisch, Michael (1990) *A Shared Authority: Essays on the Craft and Meaning of Oral and Public History* (Albany, NY: State University of New York Press).

Frow, John (1995) *Cultural Studies and Cultural Value* (Oxford: Clarendon Press).

—— (1997) *Time and Commodity Culture: Essays in Cultural Theory and Postmodernity* (Oxford: Clarendon Press).

Fukuyama, Francis (1992) *The End of History and the Last Man* (New York: Free Press).

Gabriel, Teshome H. (1990) 'Thoughts on Nomadic Aesthetics and the Black Independent Cinema: Traces of a Journey'. In Russell Ferguson et al. (eds), *Out There: Marginalization and Contemporary Cultures* (New York: The New Museum of Contemporary Art).

Gadamer, Hans-Georg (1975 [1962]) *Truth and Method*, trans. Garrett Barden and John Cumming (London: Sheed & Ward).

Gallagher, Catherine and Greenblatt, Stephen (2001) *Practising New Historicism* (Chicago and London: Chicago University Press).

Gamson, Joshua (1994) *Claims to Fame: Celebrity in Contemporary America* (Berkeley and Los Angeles, CA: University of California Press).

Gans, Herbert (1974) *Popular Culture and High Culture: An Analysis of Evaluation and Taste* (New York: Basic).

Gardiner, Judith Kegan (ed.), (2002) *Masculinity Studies and Feminist Theory: New Directions* (New York: Columbia University Press).

Gee, James Paul (1999) *An Introduction to Discourse Analysis* (London and New York: Routledge).

Geertz, Clifford (1972) 'Deep Play: Notes on the Balinese Cockfight'. *Daedalus*, 101: 1– 37, reprinted in Geertz (1973).

—— (1973) *The Interpretation of Cultures* (New York: Basic Books).

Gelder, Ken and Thornton, Sarah (eds), (1997) *The Subcultures Reader* (London and New York: Routledge).

Gellner, Ernest (1983) *Nations and Nationalism* (Oxford: Blackwell).

Genette, Gérard (1980) *Narrative Discourse: An Essay in Method* (Ithaca, NY: Cornell University Press).

Geyer, Felix and Heinz, Walter R. (eds), (1992) *Alienation, Society, and the Individual: Continuity and Change in Theory and Research* (New Brunswick, NJ: Transaction).

Giddens, Anthony (1984) *The Constitution of Society: Oultine of the Theory of Structuralism* (Cambridge: Polity Press).

—— (1990) *The Consequences of Modernity* (Stanford, CA: Stanford University Press).

Gillespie, Marie (1995) *Television, Ethnicity and Cultural Change* (London and New York: Routledge).

Gilroy, Paul (1993) *The Black Atlantic: Modernity and Double Consciousness* (London: Verso).

Giroux, Henry and Trend, David (1992) 'Cultural Workers, Pedagogy and the Politics of Difference: Beyond Cultural Conservatism'. *Cultural Studies*, 6.1: 51–72.

Glaser, Barney and Strauss, Anselm (1967) *The Discovery of Grounded Theory* (Chicago: Aldine).

Glick Schiller, Nina, Basch, Linda and Szanton Blanc, Cristina (1992) 'Transnationalism: a New Analytic Framework for Understanding Migration'. In Nina Glick Schiller, Linda Basch and Cristina Szanton Blanc (eds), *Towards a Transnational Perspective on Migration: Race, Class, Ethnicity and Nationalism Reconsidered. Annals of the New York Academy of Sciences* 645: 1–24.

Goldberg, David Theo (ed.), (1994) *Multiculturalism: A Critical Reader* (Malden, MA: Blackwell).

Gramsci, Antonio (1971 [1929–35]) *Selections from the Prison Notebooks*, trans. Quentin Hoare and Geoffrey Nowell-Smith (New York: International).

—— (1985 [1929–35]) *Selection from Cultural Writings* (London: Lawrence & Wishart).

Greenblatt, Stephen J. (2005) *The Greenblatt Reader*, ed. Michael Payne (Oxford: Blackwell).

Greimas, Algirdas Julien (1987 [1970]) *On Meaning: Selected Writings in Semiotic Theory*, trans. Paul J. Perron and Frank H. Collins (Minneapolis, MN: University of Minnesota Press).

Grossberg, Lawrence (1997a) *Bringing it All Back Home: Essays on Cultural Studies* (Durham, NC: Duke University Press).

—— (1997b) *Dancing in Spite of Myself: Essays on Popular Culture* (Durham, NC: Duke University Press).

Grossberg, Lawrence, Nelson, Cary and Treichler, Paula (1992) 'Cultural Studies: an Introduction'. In Lawrence Grossberg, Cary Nelson and Paula Treichler (eds), *Cultural Studies* (London and New York: Routledge), pp. 1–22.

Grosz, Elizabeth (1989) *Sexual Subversions: Three French Feminists* (Sydney: Allen & Unwin).

—— (1990) *Jacques Lacan: A Feminist Introduction* (London: Routledge).

Guha, Ranajit (1983) *Elementary Aspects of Peasant Insurgency in Colonial India* (Delhi: Oxford University Press).

Gurevitch, Michael et al. (eds), (1982) *Culture, Society and the Media* (London: Methuen).

Haber, Honi Fern and Weiss, Gail (eds), (1999) *Perspectives on Embodiment: The Intersections of Nature and Culture* (London and New York: Routledge).

Habermas, Jürgen (1975 [1973]) *Legitimation Crisis*, trans. Thomas McCarthy (Boston, MA: Beacon Press).

—— (1976 [1971]) *Theory and Practice* (Boston, MA: Beacon Press).

—— (1984 and 1987 [1981]) *The Theory of Communicative Action,* 2 vols, trans. Thomas McCarthy (Boston: Beacon Press).

—— (1987) *The Philosophical Discourse of Modernity: Twelve Lectures*, trans. Frederick Lawrence (Cambridge, MA: MIT Press).

—— (1991 [1962]) *The Structural Transformation of the Public Sphere: An Inquiry into a Category of Bourgeois Society*, trans. Thomas Burger (Cambridge, MA: MIT Press).

Haggerty, Kevin and Ericson, Richard (2000) 'The Surveillant Assemblage'. *British Journal of Sociology*, 51.4: 605–22.

Halberstam, Judith and Livingston, Ira (eds), (1995) *Posthuman Bodies* (Indianapolis, IN: Indiana University Press).

Halbwachs, Maurice (1992 [1941]) *On Collective Memory*, trans. Lewis A. Coser (Chicago, IL: University of Chicago Press).

Hall, Stuart (1977) 'Rethinking the "Base and Superstructure" Metaphor'. In Jon Bloomfield (ed.), *Papers on Class, Hegemony, and Party* (London: Lawrence and Wishart).

—— (1980a) 'Cultural Studies and the Centre: Some Problematics and Problems'. In Stuart Hall, Dorothy Hobson, Andrew Lowe and Paul Willis (eds), *Culture, Media, Language* (London: Hutchinson).

—— (1980b) 'Cultural Studies: Two Paradigms'. *Media, Culture and Society*, 2: 57–72.

—— (1980c) 'Encoding/decoding'. In Hall, Stuart, Hobson, Dorothy, Lowe, Andrew and Willis, Paul (eds), *Culture, Media, Language* (London: Hutchinson).

—— (1983) 'The Great Moving Right Show'. In Stuart Hall and Martin Jacques (eds), *The Politics of Thatcherism* (London: Lawrence and Wishart).

—— (1987) 'Minimal Selves'. In Houston Baker, Manthia Diawara and Ruth Lindeborg (eds), *Black British Cultural Studies: A Reader* (Chicago: University of Chicago Press).

—— (1988) *The Hard Road to Renewal* (London: Verso).

—— (1990a) 'Cultural Identity and Diaspora'. In Jonathan Rutherford (ed.), *Identity: Community, Culture, Difference* (London: Lawrence & Wishart).

—— (1990b) 'The Emergence of Cultural Studies and the Crisis of the Humanities'. *October*, 53: 11–90.

—— (1991) 'Old and New Identities, Old and New Ethnicities'. In Anthony King, (ed.), *Culture, Globalization and the World-System: Contemporary Conditions for the Representation of Identity* (London: Macmillan).

—— (1992) 'Cultural Studies and Its Theoretical Legacies'. In Lawrence Grossberg, Cary Nelson and Paula Treichler (eds), *Cultural Studies* (London and New York: Routledge).

—— (1995) 'New Cultures for Old'. In Doreen Massey and Pat Jess (eds), *A Place in the World* (Milton Keynes: Open University Press).

—— (1996a) 'On Postmodernism and Articulation: An Interview with Lawrence Grossberg'. In David Morley and Kuan-Hsing Chen (eds), *Critical Dialogues in Cultural Studies* (London and New York: Routledge).

—— (1996b) 'The West and the Rest: Discourse and Power'. In Stuart Hall, David Held, Don Hubert and Kenneth Thompson (eds), *Modernity: An Introduction to Modern Societies* (Oxford: Blackwell).

—— (1996c) 'Introduction: Who Needs Identity'. In Stuart Hall and Paul du Gay (eds), *Questions of Cultural Identity* (London: Sage).

—— (1997) 'The Work of Representation'. In Stuart Hall (ed.), *Representation: Cultural Representations and Signifying Practices* (London: Sage).

—— (2000) 'Conclusion: the Multi-cultural Question'. In Barnor Hesse (ed.), *Un/settled Multi-culturalisms: Diasporas, Entanglements, Transruptions* (London: Zed Books).

—— (2001) 'Foucault: Power, Knowledge and Discourse'. In Margaret Wetherell, Stephanie Taylor and Simeon J. Yates (eds), *Discourse Theory and Practice: A Reader* (London: Sage).

Hall, Stuart and Held, David (1989) 'Citizens and Citizenship'. In Stuart Hall and Martin Jacques (eds), *New Times: The Changing Face of Politics in the 1990s* (London: Lawrence & Wishart).

Hall, Stuart, Held, David, Hubert, Don and Thompson, Kenneth (eds), (1996) *Modernity: An Introduction to Modern Societies* (Oxford: Blackwell).

Hall, Stuart and Jacques, Martin (eds), (1989) *New Times: The Changing Face of Politics in the 1990s* (London: Lawrence & Wishart).

Hall, Stuart and Jefferson, Tony (eds), (1993 [1976]) *Resistance through Rituals: Youth Subcultures in Post-War Britain* (London and New York: Routledge).

Hannerz, Ulf (1991) 'Scenarios for Peripheral Cultures'. In Anthony King (ed.), *Culture, Globalization and the World-System* (London: Macmillan).

Hansen, Anders, Cottle, Simon, Negrine, Ralph and Newbold, Chris (1998) *Mass Communication Research Methods* (London: Macmillan).

Haraway, Donna (1990 [1984]) 'A Manifesto for Cyborgs: Science, Technology, and Socialist Feminism in the 1980s'. In Linda J. Nicholson (ed.), *Feminism/ Postmodernism* (London and New York: Routledge).

Hardt, Michael and Negri, Antonio (2000) *Empire* (Cambridge, MA: Harvard University Press).

—— (2004) *Multitude: War and Democracy in the Age of Empire* (New York: Penguin).

Hartley, John (1999) *Uses of Television* (London and New York: Routledge).

Haskell, Thomas L. (ed.), (1984) *The Authority of Experts: Studies in History and Theory* (Bloomington, IN: Indiana University Press).

Hawkes, Terence (2003) *Structuralism and Semiotics* (London and New York: Routledge).

Hayles, Katherine N. (1999) *How we Became Posthuman: Virtual Bodies in Cybernetics, Literature, and Informatics* (Chicago, IL: University of Chicago Press).

Hegel, Georg W. F. (1977 [1807]) *Phenomenology of Spirit*, trans. Arnold V. Miller, foreword by John N. Findlay (Oxford: Clarendon Press).

Heidegger, Martin (1962 [1927]) *Being and Time*, trans. John MacQuarrie and Edward Robinson (Oxford: Blackwell).

Held, David (1980) *Introduction to Critical Theory* (Berkeley, CA: University of California Press).

Hetherington, Kevin (1997) *The Badlands of Modernity: Heterotopia and Social Ordering* (London and New York: Routledge).

Hill, Mike (ed.), (1997) *Whiteness: A Critical Reader* (New York: New York University Press).

—— (2004) *After Whiteness: Unmaking an American Majority* (New York: New York University Press).

Hillis, Ken (1999) *Digital Sensations: Space, Identity, and Embodiment in Virtual Reality*, vol. 1 (Minneapolis, MN and London: University of Minnesota Press).

Hodgkin, Katharine and Radstone, Susannah (eds), (2003) *Regimes of Memory* (London and New York: Routledge).

Hoggart, Richard (1958) *The Uses of Literacy* (Harmondsworth: Penguin).

—— (1970*) Speaking to Each Other*, vol. 2: *About Literature* (Harmondsworth: Penguin).

Holland, Dorothy et al. (1998) *Identity and Agency in Cultural Worlds* (Cambridge, MA: Harvard University Press).

Holland, Norman (1975) *Readers Reading* (New Haven, CT: Yale University Press).

Holquist, Michael (1990) *Dialogism: Bakhtin and his World* (London and New York: Routledge).

Holub, Robert C. (1984) *Reception Theory: A Critical Introduction* (London and New York: Methuen).

Howes, David (ed.), (1991) *Varieties of Sensory Experience: A Sourcebook in the Anthropology of the Senses* (Toronto: University of Toronto Press).

Huchinson, John and Smith, Anthony (eds), (1994) *Nationalism* (Oxford: Oxford University Press).

Hunter, Ian (1992) 'Aesthetics and Cultural Studies'. In Lawrence Grossberg et al. (eds), *Cultural Studies* (London and New York: Routledge).

Hutchby, Ian and Wooffitt, Robin (1998) *Conversation Analysis: Principles, Practices, and Applications* (Cambridge: Polity Press).

Hutcheon, Linda (1988) *A Poetics of Postmodernism: History, Theory, Fiction* (London and New York: Routledge).

—— (1994) *Irony's Edge: The Theory and Politics of Irony* (London and New York: Routledge).

—— (2000 [1985]) *A Theory of Parody: The Teachings of Twentieth-Century Art Forms* (Urbana and Chicago: University of Illinois Press).

Huyssen, Andreas (1995) *Twilight Memories* (London and New York: Routledge).

Irigaray, Luce (1985 [1974]) *Speculum of the Other Woman*, trans. Gillian C. Gill (Ithaca, NY: Cornell University Press).

—— (1985 [1977]) *This Sex which is Not One*, trans. Catherine Porter (Ithaca, NY: Cornell University Press).

Iser, Wolfgang (1978) *The Act of Reading: A Theory of Aesthetic Response* (Baltimore, MD: Johns Hopkins University Press).

Jagose, Annamarie (1996) *Queer Theory: An Introduction* (New York: New York University Press).

Jakobson, Roman (1971 [1929]) *Selected Writings*, vol. 2: *Word and Language* (The Hague and Paris: Mouton).

Jameson, Fredric (1981) *The Political Unconscious: Narrative as a Socially Symbolic Act* (Ithaca, NY: Cornell University Press).

—— (1983) 'Postmodernism and Consumer Society'. In Hal Foster (ed.), *The Anti-Aesthetic: Essays on Postmodern Culture* (Port Townsend, WA: Bay Press).

—— (1991 [1984]) *Postmodernism, or, the Cultural Logic of Late Capitalism* (Durham, NC: Duke University Press).

Jauss, Hans Robert (1982) *Toward an Aesthetic of Reception*, trans. Timothy Bahti (Minneapolis, MN: University of Minnesota Press).

Jeffreys, Sheila (2003) *Unpacking Queer Politics* (Cambridge: Polity Press).

Johnson, Richard et al. (2004) *The Practice of Cultural Studies* (London: Sage).

Jordan, Tim (1999) *Cyberpower: The Culture and Politics of Cyberspace and the Internet* (London and New York: Routledge).

Kant, Immanuel (1963 [1784]) 'The Idea for a Universal History from a Cosmopolitan Point of View'. In Lewis White Beck (ed.), *Kant: On History* (Indianapolis, IN: BobbsMerrill, The Library of Liberal Arts).

—— (2000 [1790]) *The Critique of Judgment*, trans. John Henry Bernard (New York: Prometheus Books).

Kellner, Douglas (1995) *Media Culture: Cultural Studies, Identity and Politics Between the Modern and the Postmodern* (London and New York: Routledge).

—— (2003) *Media Spectacle* (London and New York: Routledge).

Kerr, Heather and Nettelbeck, Amanda (eds), (1998) *The Space Between: Australian Women Writing Fictocriticism* (Nedlands: University of Western Australia Press).

Kershner, Richard B. (1989) *Joyce, Bakhtin, and Popular Literature: Chronicles of Disorder* (Chapel Hill, NC: University of North Carolina Press).

Klein, Naomi (2000) *No Logo* (London: HarperCollins).

Korsmeyer, Carolyn (ed.), (2004) *Gender and Aesthetics: An Introduction* (London and New York: Routledge).

Kosofsky Sedgwick, Eve (1985) *Between Men: English Literature and Male Homosexual Desire* (New York: Columbia University Press).

Kristeva, Julia (1980 [1970]) *Desirc in Language: A Semiotic Approach to Literature and Art*, trans. Thomas Gora, Alice Jardine and Leon S. Roudiez (New York: Columbia University Press).

—— (1982) *Powers of Horror: An Essay on Abjection* (New York: Columbia University Press).

—— (2002) '"Nous Deux" or a (Hi)story of Intertextuality'. *Romanic Review*, 93.1–2: 7–14.

Kymlicka, Will (1990) *Contemporary Political Philosophy: An Introduction* (Oxford: Oxford University Press).

Lacan, Jacques (1977) *Écrits: A Selection*, trans. Alan Sheridan (New York: W. W. Norton).

—— (1996 [1958–59]) *Le Séminaire, Livre VI, Le Désir et son Interprétation: 1958–1959* (Paris: Association Freudienne Internationale).

Laclau, Ernesto (1993) 'Power and Representation'. In Mark Poster (ed.), *Politics, Theory, and Contemporary Culture* (New York: Columbia University Press).

—— (2005) *On Populist Reason* (London: Verso).

Laclau, Ernesto and Mouffe, Chantal (1985) *Hegemony and Socialist Strategy: Towards a Radical Democratic Politics* (London: Verso).

Lakoff, George and Johnson, Mark (2003 [1980]) *Metaphors we Live By* (Chicago and London: University of Chicago Press).

Landes, Joan B. (ed.), (1998) *Feminism, the Public and the Private* (Oxford: Oxford University Press).

Latour, Bruno (1987) *Science in Action: How to Follow Scientists and Engineers through Society* (Cambridge MA: Harvard University Press).

—— (2005) *Reassembling the Social: An Introduction to Actor-Network Theory* (Oxford: Oxford University Press).

Law, John and Hassard, John (eds), (1999) *Actor-Network Theory and After* (Oxford: Blackwell).

Leavis, F. R. (1933) *Mass Civilization and Minority Culture* (London: Minority Press).

226 References

Lefebvre, Henri (1991 [1947]) *Critique of Everyday Life*, vol. 1, trans. J. Moore (London: Verso).
—— (1991 [1974]) *The Production of Space*, trans. Donald Nicholson-Smith (Oxford: Blackwell).
Le Goff, Jacques (1992) *History and Memory*, trans. Steven Rendall and Elizabeth Claman (New York: Columbia University Press).
Lévi-Strauss, Claude (1977 [1958]) *Structural Anthropology*, trans. Monique Layton (London: Allen Lane).
—— (1966 [1962]) *The Savage Mind*, trans. John and Doreen Weightman (Chicago, IL: University of Chicago Press).
Lévy, Pierre (1998) *Becoming Virtual: Reality in the Digital Age*, trans. Robert Bononno (New York: Plenum Press).
Lewis, Reina (1995) *Gendering Orientalism: Race, Femininity, and Representation* (London and New York: Routledge).
Lievrouw, Leah and Livingstone, Sonia (eds), (2002) *Handbook of New Media: Social Shaping and Social Consequences* (London: Sage).
Lotman, Yuri (1990) *Universe of the Mind: A Semiotic Theory of Culture*, trans. Ann Shukman, introduction by Umberto Eco (Bloomington, IN: Indiana University Press).
Ludlow, Peter (ed.), (1996) *High Noon on the Electronic Frontier: Conceptual Issues in Cyberspace* (Cambridge, MA: MIT Press).
Lyotard, Jean-François (1984 [1979]) *The Postmodern Condition: A Report on Knowledge*, trans. Geoff Bennington and Brian Massumi (Manchester: Manchester University Press).
Macdonell, Diane (1986) *Theories of Discourse: An Introduction* (Oxford: Blackwell).
MacIntyre, Alasdair (1981) *After Virtue* (Notre Dame, IN: University of Notre Dame Press).
Mahon, Michael (1992) *Foucault's Nietzschean Genealogy: Truth, Power, and the Subject* (Albany, NY: State University of New York Press).
Malinowski, Bronisław (1987 [1929]) *The Sexual Life of Savages in North-Western Melanesia* (Boston, MA: Beacon Press).
Mansfield, Nick (2000) *Subjectivity: Theories of the Self from Freud to Haraway* (Sydney: Allen & Unwin).
Marshall, P. David (1997) *Celebrity and Power: Fame in Contemporary Culture* (Minneapolis, MN and London: University of Minnesota Press).
Marshall, Thomas H. (1950) *Citizenship, Social Class, and Other Essays* (Cambridge: Cambridge University Press).
Marx, Karl (1975 [1867]) *Capital: A Critique of Political Economy*, vol. 1, trans. Ben Fowkes (New York: International).
Mathiesen, Thomas (1997) 'The Viewer Society: Michel Foucault's "Panopticon" Revisited'. *Theoretical Criminology*, 1.2: 215–34.
Mauss, Marcel (1990 [1925]) *The Gift: The Form and Reason for Exchange in Archaic Societies*, trans. W. D. Halls (London and New York: Routledge).
McGuigan, Jim (1992) *Cultural Populism* (London and New York: Routledge).
—— (1996) *Culture and the Public Sphere* (London and New York: Routledge).
McLuhan, Marshall (1962) *The Gutenberg Galaxy: The Making of Typographic Man* (Toronto: University of Toronto Press).

McQuillan, Martin (ed.), (2000) *Narrative Reader* (London and New York: Routledge).

McRobbie, Angela (1993) 'Shut Up and Dance: Youth Culture and Changing Modes of Femininity'. *Cultural Studies*, 7.3: 406–26.

McRobbie, Angela, and Garber, Jenny (1993 [1975]) 'Girls and Subcultures'. In Stuart Hall and Tony Jefferson (eds), *Resistance through Rituals: Youth Subcultures in Post-War Britain* (London and New York: Routledge).

Meredyth, Denise (2001) *Citizenship and Cultural Policy* (London: Sage).

Merleau-Ponty, Maurice (1962 [1945]) *Phenomenology of Perception*, trans. Colin Smith (London: Routledge & Kegan Paul).

Miller, Daniel (ed.), (1987) *Material Culture and Mass Consumption* (Oxford: Blackwell).

—— (1995) *Acknowledging Consumption: A Review of New Studies* (London and New York: Routledge).

—— (1995) 'Consumption and Commodities', *Annual Review of Anthropology*, 24: 141–61.

—— (1998) *A Theory of Shopping* (Ithaca, NY: Cornell University Press).

Miller, Toby (1993) *The Well-Tempered Self: Citizenship, Culture and the Postmodern Subject* (Baltimore, MD: Johns Hopkins University Press).

—— (1998) *Technologies of Truth: Cultural Citizenship and the Popular Media* (Minneapolis, MN: University of Minnesota Press).

Mills, Sara (1997) *Discourse* (London and New York: Routledge).

Milner, Andrew (1994) *Contemporary Cultural Theory* (London: University College London Press).

Milner, Andrew and Browitt, Jeff (2002) *Contemporary Cultural Theory* (Sydney: Allen & Unwin).

Mitchell, Katharyne (1993) 'Multiculturalism, or the United Colors of Capitalism'. *Antipode*, 25: 263–94.

Modleski, Tania (1984) *Loving with a Vengeance* (London: Methuen).

Moores, Shaun (1994) *Interpreting Audiences: The Ethnography of Media Consumption* (London: Sage).

Morley, David (1980) *The Nationwide Audience: Structure and Decoding* (London: British Film Institute).

—— (1986) *Family Television: Cultural Power and Domestic Leisure* (London and New York: Routledge).

Morris, Meaghan (1992) 'A Gadfly Bites Back', *Meanjin*, 51.3: 545–51.

Moulthrop, Stuart (1994) 'Rhizome and Resistance: Hypertext and the Dreams of a New Culture'. In George Landow (ed.), *Hyper/Text/Theory* (Baltimore, MD: Johns Hopkins University Press).

Muecke, Stephen (1997) *No Road: Bitumen All the Way* (Fremantle: Fremantle Arts Center Press).

Mulhern, Francis (2000) *Culture/Metaculture* (London and New York: Routledge).

Murphy, Richard (1999) *Theorizing the Avant-Garde: Modernism, Expressionism, and the Problem of Postmodernity* (Cambridge: Cambridge University Press).

Murray, Mary (1995) *The Law of the Father? Patriarchy in the Transition from Feudalism to Capitalism* (London and New York: Routledge).

Nietzsche, Friedrich (1967 [1901]) *The Will to Power*, trans. Walter Kaufmann (New York: Random House).

Nora, Pierre (1996–8 [1984–92]) *Realms of Memory: Rethinking the French Past*, 3 vols, trans. Arthur Goldhammer (New York: Columbia University Press).

Nussbaum, Martha C. (1996) *For Love of Country: Debating the Limits of Patriotism* (Boston, MA: Beacon Press).

—— (1997) *Cultivating Humanity: A Classical Defense of Reform in Liberal Education* (Cambridge, MA: Harvard University Press).

Olalquiaga, Celeste (1996) *For Love of Country: Debating the Limits of Patriotism* (Boston, MA: Beacon Press).

—— (1998) *The Artificial Kingdom: A Treasury of the Kitsch Experience* (New York: Pantheon Books).

Ong, Aihwa (1996) 'Cultural Citizenship as Subject Making: Immigrants Negotiate Racial and Cultural Boundaries in the United States'. *Current Anthropology*, 35: 737–62.

Ong, Walter J. (1967) *The Presence of the Word* (New Haven, CT: Yale University Press).

—— (1982) *Orality and Literacy: The Technologizing of the Word* (London: Methuen).

O'Regan, Tom (1992) 'Some Reflections on the Policy Moment'. *Meanjin*, 51.3: 517–32.

Ortiz, Fernando (1995 [1940]) *Cuban Counterpoint: Tobacco and Sugar*, trans. Harriet de Onis (Durham, NC: Duke University Press).

O'Toole, Lawrence Michael and Shukman, Ann (1977) *Formalist Theory: Russian Poetics in Translation*, vol. 4 (Oxford: Holden Books).

Park, Robert Ezra, Burgess, Ernest Watson and McKenzie, Roderick Duncan (1967 [1925]) *The City* (Chicago and London: University of Chicago Press).

Parker, Ian (1992) *Discourse Dynamics: Critical Analysis for Social and Individual Psychology* (London and New York: Routledge).

Pateman, Carole (1988) *The Sexual Contract* (Stanford, CA: Stanford University Press).

Peirce, Charles Sanders (1931–58) *Collected Writings*, 8 vols (Cambridge, MA: Harvard University Press).

Perks, Robert and Thomson, Alistair (eds), (1997) *Oral History Reader* (London and New York: Routledge).

Pollock, John L. and Cruz, Joseph (1999 [1986]) *Contemporary Theories of Knowledge* (Lanham, MD: Rowman & Littlefield).

Popper, Karl (1960 [1945]) *The Poverty of Historicism* (New York: Harper and Row).

—— (1966 [1945]) *The Open Society and its Enemies* (London and New York: Routledge).

Poster, Mark (1989) *Critical Theory and Poststructuralism: In Search of a Context* (Ithaca, NY: Cornell University Press).

Poulantzas, Nicos (1973) *Political Power and Social Classes* (London: New Left Books).

Pratt, Marie Louise (1992) *Imperial Eyes: Travel Writing and Transculturation* (London and New York: Routledge).

Pratt, Murray (2002) 'Post-Queer and Beyond the PaCS: Contextualising French

Responses to the Civil Solidarity Pact'. In Kate Chedgzoy, Emma Francis and Murray Pratt (eds), *In a Queer Place: Sexuality and Belonging in British and European Contexts* (Aldershot, UK: Ashgate).

Prescott, John Robert Victor (1987) *Political Frontiers and Boundaries* (London: Unwin Hyman).

Radway, Janice (1987) *Reading the Romance: Women, Patriarchy and Popular Literature* (London: Verso).

Rama, Ángel (1982) *Transculturación Narrativa en América Latina* (Mexico City: SigloVeintiuno).

Rawls, John (1993) *Political Liberalism* (New York: Columbia University Press).

Renan, Ernest (1994 [1882]) 'Qu'est-ce qu'une nation?' In John Huchinson and Anthony Smith (eds), *Nationalism* (Oxford: Oxford University Press).

Rheingold, Howard (1993) *The Virtual Community: Homesteading on the Electronic Frontier* (Reading, MA: Addison-Wesley).

Ricœur, Paul (1984, 1985, 1988) *Time and Narrative*, 3 vols, trans. K. Kathleen McLaughlin and David Pellauer (Chicago and London: University of Chicago Press).

Rojek, Chris (2001) *Celebrity* (London: Reaktion).

Rorty, Richard (1983) 'Postmodernist Bourgeois Liberalism'. *Journal of Philosophy*, 80: 583–9.

—— (1989) *Contingency, Irony and Solidarity* (Cambridge and New York: Cambridge University Press).

—— (1991) *Objectivity, Relativism, and Truth: Philosophical Papers*, vol. I (Cambridge and New York: Cambridge University Press).

Rosaldo, Renato (1997) 'Cultural Citizenship, Inequality, and Multiculturalism'. In William V. Flores and Rina Benmayor (eds), *Latino Cultural Citizenship: Claiming Identity, Space, and Rights* (Boston, MA: Beacon Press).

Rosenberg, Harold (1959) *The Tradition of the New* (New York: Horizon Press).

Rosteck, Thomas (ed.), (1999) *At the Intersection: Cultural Studies and Rhetorical Studies* (New York: Guilford Press).

Royle, Nicholas (2003) *The Uncanny* (Manchester and New York: Manchester University Press).

Rubin, Gayle (1975) 'The Traffic in Women: Notes on the "Political Economy" of Sex'. In Rayna Reiter (ed.), *Toward an Anthropology of Women* (New York: Monthly Review Press).

Said, Edward (1983) *The World, the Text and the Critic* (Cambridge, MA: Harvard University Press).

—— (1994) *Representations of the Intellectual: The 1993 Reith Lectures* (New York: Pantheon).

—— (1995 [1978]) *Orientalism: Western Conceptions of the Orient* (Harmondsworth: Penguin).

Saussure, Ferdinand de (1983 [1915]) *The Course in General Linguistics*, trans. Roy Harris (London: Duckworth).

Schwartz, Bill (1996) 'Introduction: the Expanding Past'. *Qualitative Sociology*, 9.3: 275–82.

Schwarz, Henry and Ray, Sangeeta (eds), (2000) *A Companion to Postcolonial Studies* (Oxford: Blackwell).

Sedgwick, Eve Kosofsky (1985) *Between Men: English Literature and Male Homosocial Desire* (New York: Columbia University Press).

Shannon, Claude Elwood and Weaver, Warren (1949) *The Mathematical Theory of Communication* (Urbana, IL: University of Illinois Press).

Shiach, Morag (ed.), (1999) *Feminism and Cultural Studies* (New York: Oxford University Press).

Shields, Rob (2003) *The Virtual* (London and New York: Routledge).

Shilling, Chris (2004) *Body in Culture, Technology and Society* (London: Sage).

Simmel, Georg (1991 [1908]) 'The Problem of Style'. *Theory, Culture and Society*, 8.3: 63–71.

Slater, Don (1998) 'Analysing Cultural Objects: Content Analysis and Semiotics'. In Clive Seale (ed.), *Researching Society and Culture* (London: Sage).

Smedley, Audrey (1993) *Race in North America: Origin and Evolution of a Worldview* (Boulder, CO: Westview Press).

Smith, Anthony D. (1986) *The Ethnic Origins of Nations* (Oxford: Blackwell).

—— (1991) *National Identity* (Harmondsworth: Penguin).

Solomos, John (ed.), (1999) *Theories of Race and Racism: Reader* (London and New York: Routledge).

Spivak, Gayatri Chakravorty (1984–5) 'Criticism, Feminism and the Institution'. *Thesis Eleven*, 10.11: 175–89.

—— (1988a [1985]) 'Can the Subaltern Speak?'. In Cary Nelson and Lawrence Grossberg (eds), *Marxism and the Interpretation of Culture* (Urbana, IL: University of Illinois Press).

—— (1988b) *In Other Worlds: Essays in Cultural Politics* (London and New York: Routledge).

—— (2005) 'Scattered Speculations on the Subaltern and the Popular'. *Postcolonial Studies*, 8.4: 475–86.

Stallybrass, Peter, and White, Allon (1986) *The Politics and Poetics of Transgression* (Ithaca, NY: Cornell University Press).

Stokes, Jane (2003) *How to do Media and Cultural Studies* (London: Sage).

Strinati, Dominic (2004) *An Introduction to Theories of Popular Culture* (London and New York: Routledge).

Thompson, Edward P. (1966 [1963]) *The Making of the English Working Class* (New York: Vintage).

Todorov, Tzvetan (1975 [1970]) *The Fantastic: A Structural Approach to a Literary Genre*, trans. Richard Howard (Ithaca, NY: Cornell University Press).

—— (1977 [1971]) *The Poetics of Prose*, trans. Richard Howard (Ithaca, NY: Cornell University Press).

Tomkins, Silvan (1995) *Shame and its Sisters: A Silvan Tomkins Reader*, ed. Eve Kosofsky Sedgwick and Adam Frank (Durham and London: Duke University Press).

Tramacchi, Des (2004) 'Entheogenic Dance Extasis: Cross-Cultural Contexts'. In Graham St John (ed.), *Rave Culture and Religion* (London and New York: Routledge).

Turkle, Sherry (1995) *Life on the Screen: Identity in the Age of the Internet* (New York: Simon & Schuster).

Turner, Graeme (2002) *British Cultural Studies: An Introduction* (London and New York: Routledge).

—— (2004) *Understanding Celebrity* (London: Sage).

Urban, Greg (2001) *Metaculture: How Culture Moves through the World* (Minneapolis, MN: University of Minnesota Press).

Vattimo, Gianni (1988) *The End of Modernity: Nihilism and Hermeneutics in Postmodern Culture*, trans. Jon R. Snyder (Baltimore: Johns Hopkins University · Press).

Vertovec, Steven (1999) 'Conceiving and Researching Transnationalism'. *Ethnic and Racial Studies*, 22.2: 447–63.

Vertovec, Steven and Cohen, Robin (eds), (1999) *Migration, Diasporas and Transnationalism* (Cheltenham: Edward Elgar).

Viroli, Maurizio (1995) *For Love of Country: An Essay on Patriotism and Nationalism* (Oxford: Clarendon Press).

Voigt, David Q. (1980) 'American Sporting Rituals'. In Ray B. Browne (ed.), *Rituals and Ceremonies in Popular Culture* (Bowling Green, OH: Bowling Green State University Popular Press).

Wartenberg, Thomas E. (1990) *The Forms of Power: From Domination to Transformation* (Philadelphia: Temple University Press).

Weber, Max (1947) *Essays in Sociology*, trans. and ed. Hans Heinrich Gerth and C. Wright Mills (London: Routledge & Kegan Paul).

—— (1968 [1925]) *Economy and Society: An Outline of Interpretive Sociology*. 3 vols (New York: Bedminster).

—— (1992 [1905]) *The Protestant Ethic and the Spirit of Capitalism*, trans. Talcott Parsons, introduction by Anthony Giddens (London and New York: Routledge).

Weedon, Chris (2004) *Identity and Culture: Narratives of Difference and Belonging* (Milton Keynes: Open University Press).

Weeks, Jeffrey (2003) *Sexuality*, 2nd edition (London and New York: Routledge).

Welsch, Wolfgang (1999) 'Transculturality: The Puzzling Form of Cultures Today'. In Mike Featherstone and Scott Lash (eds), *Spaces of Culture: City, Nation, World* (London: Sage).

Wetherell, Margaret, Taylor, Stephanie and Yates, Simeon, J. (eds), *Discourse Theory and Practice: A Reader* (London: Sage).

White, Hayden (1973) *Metahistory: The Historical Imagination in Nineteenth-Century Europe* (Baltimore, MD: Johns Hopkins University Press).

Wiegman, Robyn (1999) 'Whiteness Studies and the Paradox of Particularity'. *Boundary 2*, 26.3: 115–50.

Williams, Patrick and Chrisman, Laura (eds) (1994) *Colonial Discourse and Post-Colonial Theory* (New York: Columbia University Press).

Williams, Raymond (1958) *Culture and Society, 1780–1950* (London: Chatto & Windus).

—— (1962) *Communications* (Harmondsworth: Penguin).

—— (1965 [1961]) *The Long Revolution* (Harmondsworth: Penguin).

—— (1970) *The English Novel from Dickens to Lawrence* (New York: Oxford University Press).

—— (1973) 'Base and Superstructure'. *New Left Review* 82: 3–16.

—— (1976) *Keywords: A Vocabulary of Culture and Society* (New York: Oxford University Press).

—— (1977) *Marxism and Literature* (London and New York: Oxford University Press).

—— (1980) *Culture and Materialism* (London and New York: Verso).

—— (1989) *Resources of Hope: Culture, Democracy, Socialism*, ed. Robin Gable, introduction by Robin Blackburn (London and New York: Verso).

Willis, Paul (1990) *Common Culture: Symbolic Work at Play in the Everyday Cultures of the Young* (Milton Keynes: Open University Press).

Wilson, Tony (1993) *Watching Television: Hermeneutics, Reception, and Popular Culture* (Cambridge: Polity).

Witte, Stephen P. (1992) 'Context, Text, Intertext: Toward a Constructivist Semiotic of Writing'. *Written Communication*, 9.2: 237–308.

Wolff, Janet (1990 [1985]) *Feminine Sentences: Essays on Women and Culture* (Berkeley and Los Angeles, CA: University of California Press).

Yarbrough, Stephen R. (1999) *After Rhetoric: The Study of Discourse Beyond Language and Culture* (Carbondale, IL: Southern Illinois University Press).

Young, Iris Marion (1990) *Justice and the Politics of Difference* (Princeton, NJ: Princeton University Press).

Young, Robert J. C. (1995) *Colonial Desire: Hybridity in Theory, Culture and Race* (London and New York: Routledge).

Yuval-Davis, Nira (1997) *Gender and Nation* (London: Sage).

Žižek, Slavoj (1989) *The Sublime Object of Ideology* (London and New York: Verso).

—— (1991) *Looking Awry: An Introduction to Jacques Lacan through Popular Culture* (Cambridge, MA: MIT Press).

Index